Play It Again, Schroeder!

Charles M. Schulz

Ballantine Books

New York

D0121330

A Ballantine Books Trade Paperback Original

Copyright © 2007 United Feature Syndicate, Inc.

All rights reserved.

Published in the United States by Ballantine Books, an
imprint of The Random House Publishing Group, a division
of Random House, Inc., New York.

BALLANTINE and colophon are registered trademarks of
Random House, Inc.

The comic strips in this book were originally published in
newspapers worldwide.

ISBN 978-0-345-47985-3

Printed in the United States of America

www.ballantinebooks.com

2 4 6 8 9 7 5 3 1

Book design by Diane Hobbing of Snap-Haus Graphics

Play it Again, Schroeder!

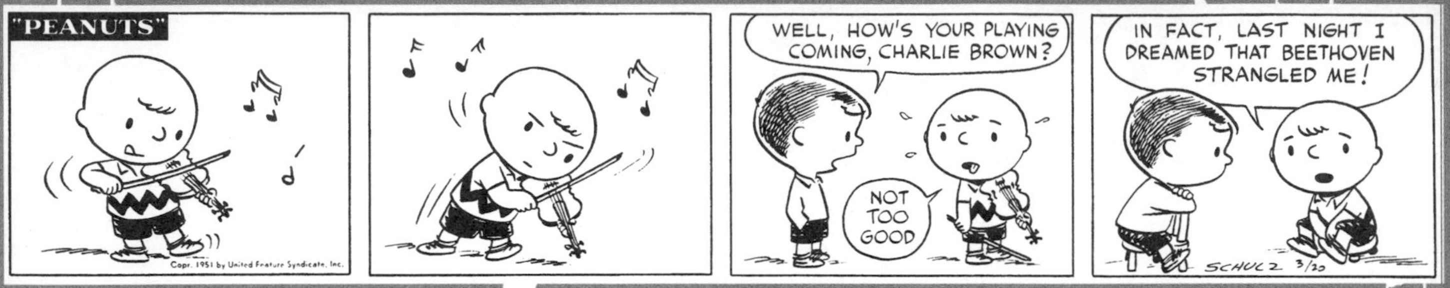
"PEANUTS"
Copr. 1951 by United Feature Syndicate, Inc.
WELL, HOW'S YOUR PLAYING COMING, CHARLIE BROWN?
NOT TOO GOOD
IN FACT, LAST NIGHT I DREAMED THAT BEETHOVEN STRANGLED ME!
SCHULZ 3/20

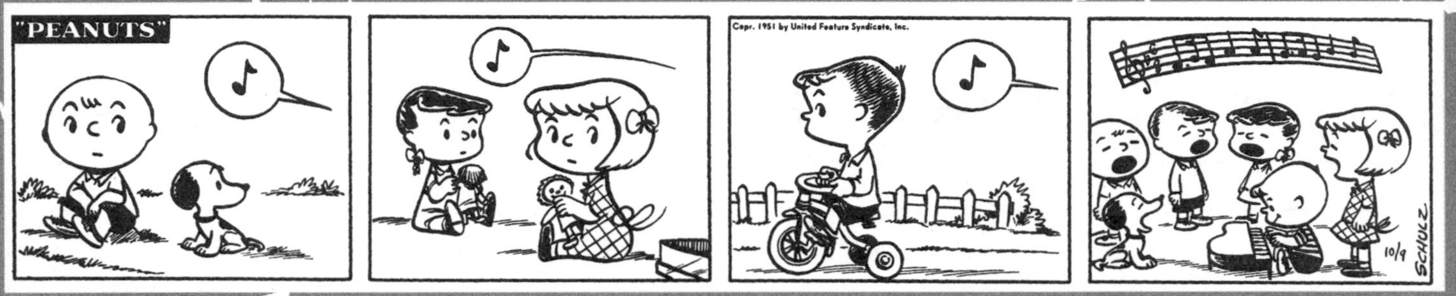
"PEANUTS"
Copr. 1951 by United Feature Syndicate, Inc.
10/9
SCHULZ

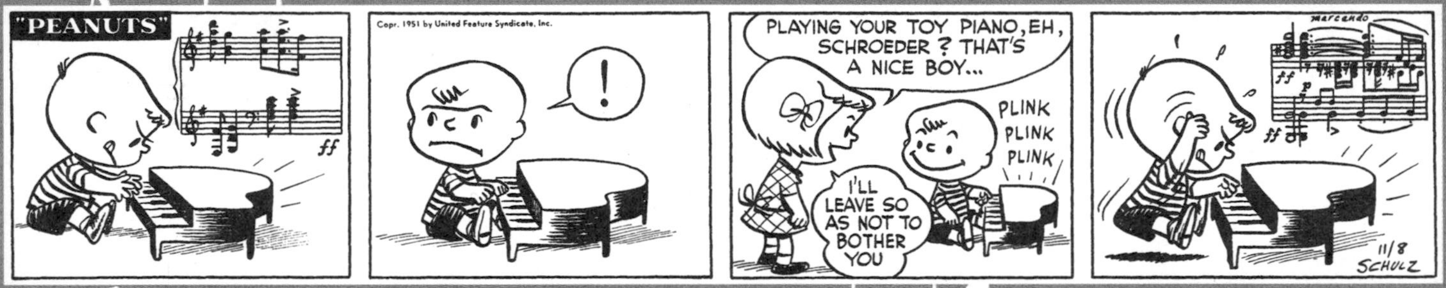
"PEANUTS"
Copr. 1951 by United Feature Syndicate, Inc.
PLAYING YOUR TOY PIANO, EH, SCHROEDER? THAT'S A NICE BOY...
PLINK PLINK PLINK
I'LL LEAVE SO AS NOT TO BOTHER YOU
marcando
11/8
SCHULZ

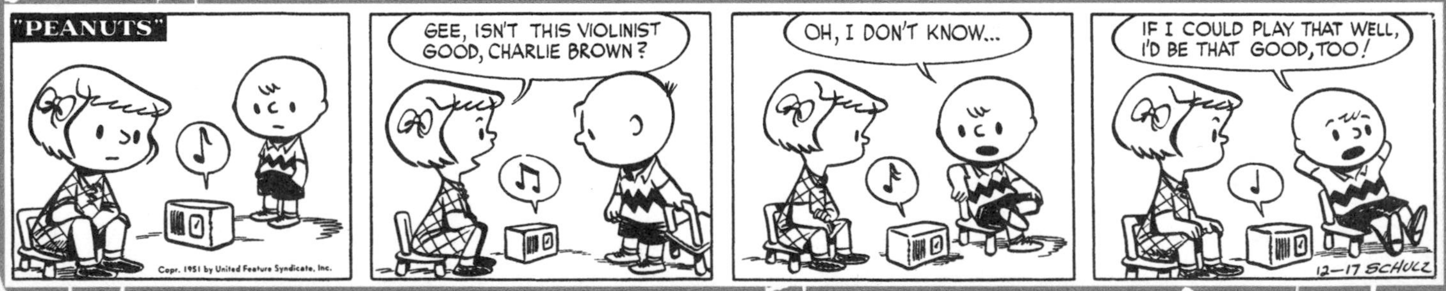
"PEANUTS"
Copr. 1951 by United Feature Syndicate, Inc.
GEE, ISN'T THIS VIOLINIST GOOD, CHARLIE BROWN?
OH, I DON'T KNOW...
IF I COULD PLAY THAT WELL, I'D BE THAT GOOD, TOO!
12-17 SCHULZ

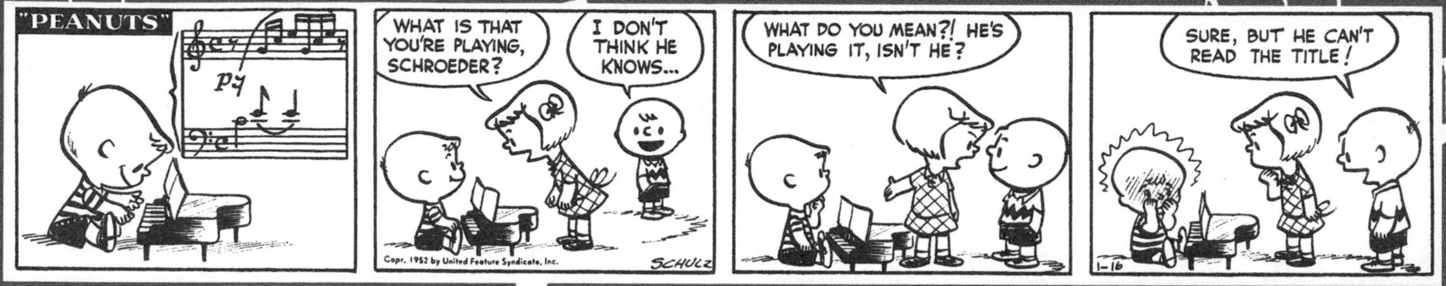
"PEANUTS"
WHAT IS THAT YOU'RE PLAYING, SCHROEDER?
I DON'T THINK HE KNOWS...
WHAT DO YOU MEAN?! HE'S PLAYING IT, ISN'T HE?
SURE, BUT HE CAN'T READ THE TITLE!
Copr. 1952 by United Feature Syndicate, Inc.
SCHULZ
1-16

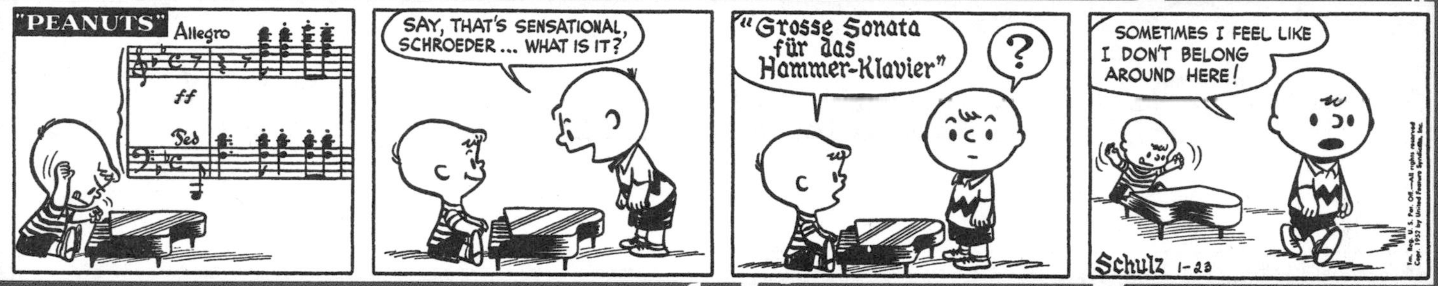
"PEANUTS"
Allegro
ff
SAY, THAT'S SENSATIONAL, SCHROEDER ... WHAT IS IT?
"Grosse Sonata für das Hammer-Klavier"
?
SOMETIMES I FEEL LIKE I DON'T BELONG AROUND HERE!
Schulz 1-23

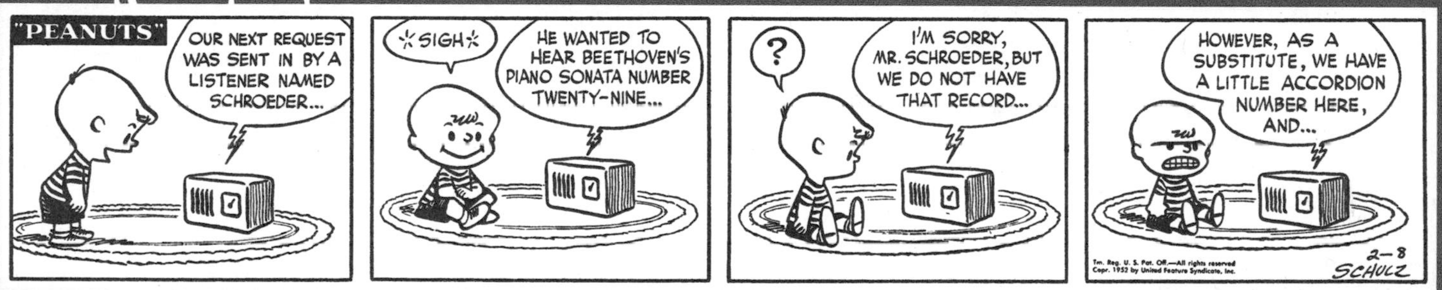
"PEANUTS"
OUR NEXT REQUEST WAS SENT IN BY A LISTENER NAMED SCHROEDER...
SIGH
HE WANTED TO HEAR BEETHOVEN'S PIANO SONATA NUMBER TWENTY-NINE...
?
I'M SORRY, MR. SCHROEDER, BUT WE DO NOT HAVE THAT RECORD...
HOWEVER, AS A SUBSTITUTE, WE HAVE A LITTLE ACCORDION NUMBER HERE, AND...
Tm. Reg. U. S. Pat. Off.—All rights reserved
Copr. 1952 by United Feature Syndicate, Inc.
2-8
SCHULZ

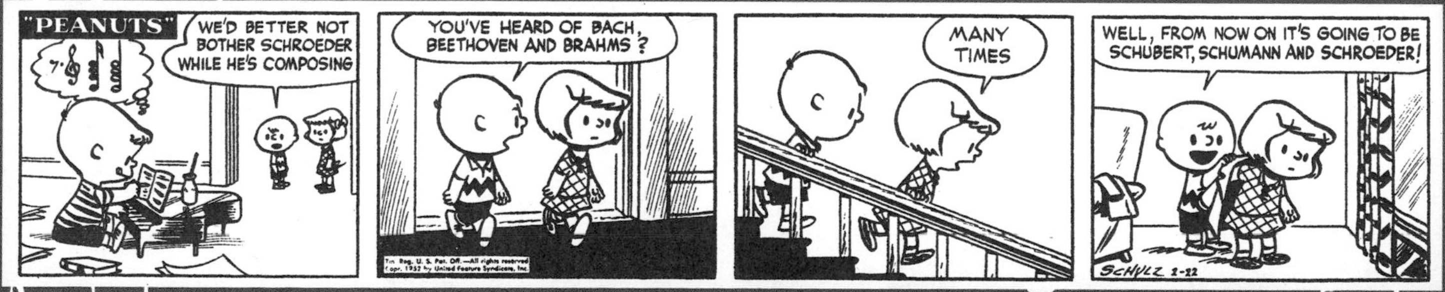
"PEANUTS"
WE'D BETTER NOT BOTHER SCHROEDER WHILE HE'S COMPOSING
YOU'VE HEARD OF BACH, BEETHOVEN AND BRAHMS?
MANY TIMES
WELL, FROM NOW ON IT'S GOING TO BE SCHUBERT, SCHUMANN AND SCHROEDER!
SCHULZ 2-22

"PEANUTS"
I GUESS THERE'S NO DOUBT ABOUT IT...
MUSIC IS REALLY SCHROEDER'S FORTE
I GET IT.... PIANOFORTE!! OH, HO, HO, HO! YAK! YAK! HO! HO!
BONK!
?
WHEW ??? HAVE YOU EVER BEEN HIT WITH A PIANOFORTE?
Tm. Reg. U. S. Pat. Off.—All rights reserved
Copr 1952 by United Feature Syndicate, Inc.
3-15 SCHULZ

"PEANUTS"
Allegro
ff
Ped
AN EXTREMELY POWERFUL WORK!
Tm. Reg. U. S. Pat. Off.—All rights reserved
Copr. 1952 by United Feature Syndicate, Inc.
3-25
SCHULZ

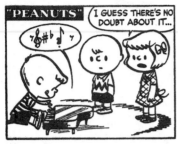

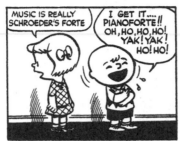

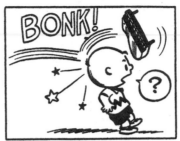

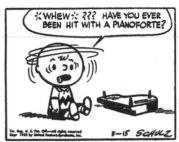

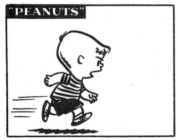

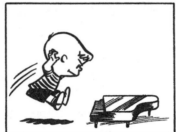

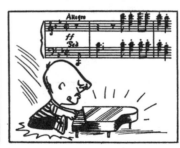

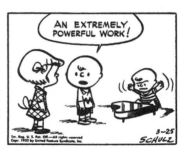

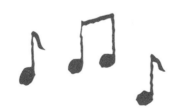

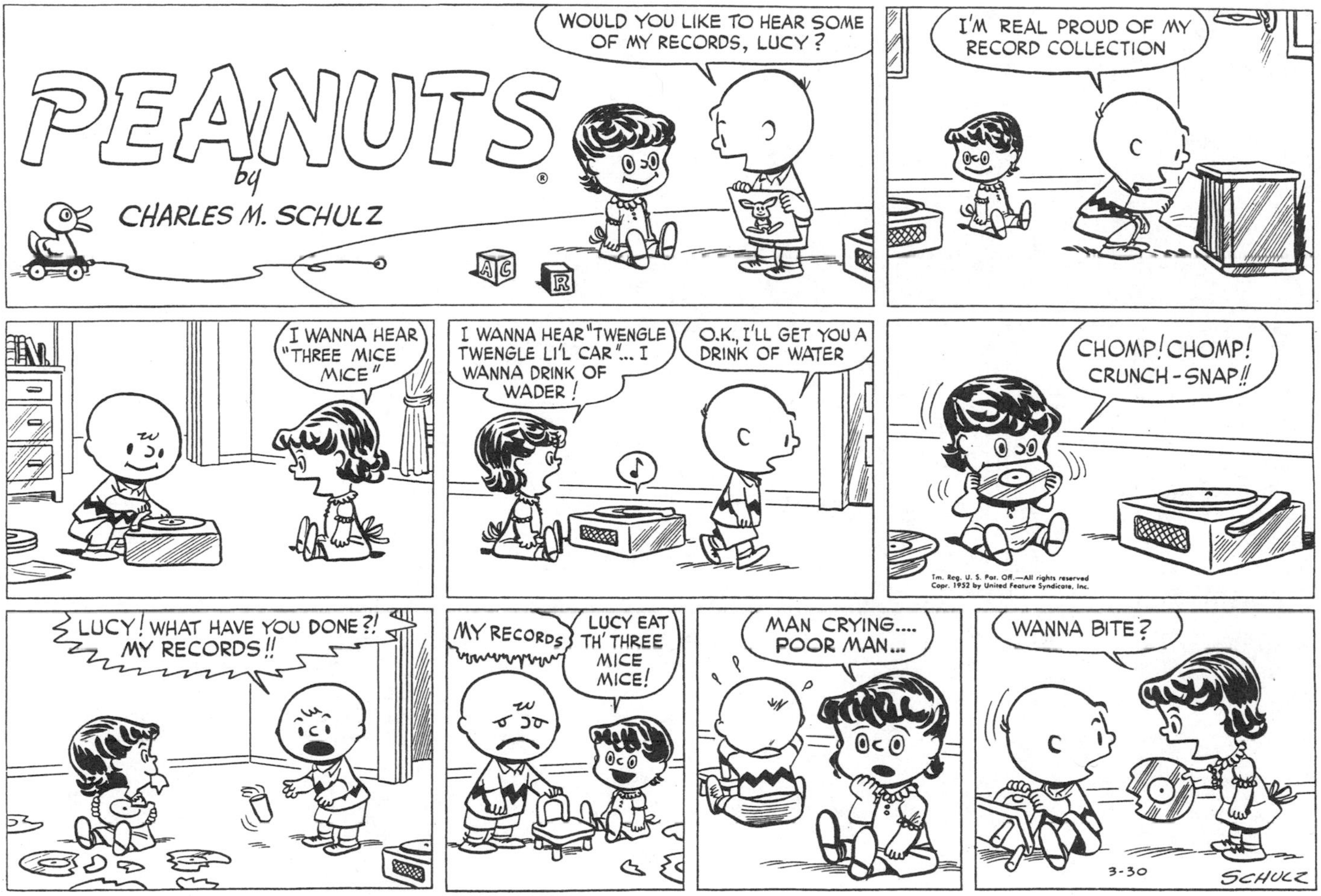
PEANUTS
by
CHARLES M. SCHULZ
WOULD YOU LIKE TO HEAR SOME OF MY RECORDS, LUCY?
I'M REAL PROUD OF MY RECORD COLLECTION
I WANNA HEAR "THREE MICE MICE"
I WANNA HEAR "TWENGLE TWENGLE LI'L CAR"... I WANNA DRINK OF WADER!
O.K., I'LL GET YOU A DRINK OF WATER
CHOMP! CHOMP! CRUNCH-SNAP!!
Tm. Reg. U. S. Pat. Off.—All rights reserved
Copr. 1952 by United Feature Syndicate, Inc.
LUCY! WHAT HAVE YOU DONE?! MY RECORDS!!
MY RECORDS
LUCY EAT TH' THREE MICE MICE!
MAN CRYING.... POOR MAN...
WANNA BITE?
3-30
SCHULZ

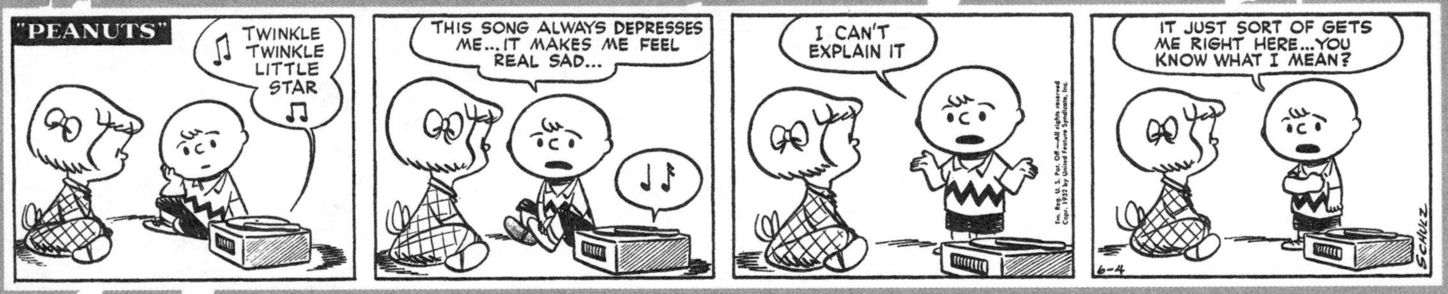
"PEANUTS"
TWINKLE TWINKLE LITTLE STAR
THIS SONG ALWAYS DEPRESSES ME...IT MAKES ME FEEL REAL SAD...
I CAN'T EXPLAIN IT
Tm. Reg. U. S. Pat. Off.—All rights reserved
Copr. 1952 by United Feature Syndicate, Inc.
IT JUST SORT OF GETS ME RIGHT HERE...YOU KNOW WHAT I MEAN?
6-4
SCHULZ

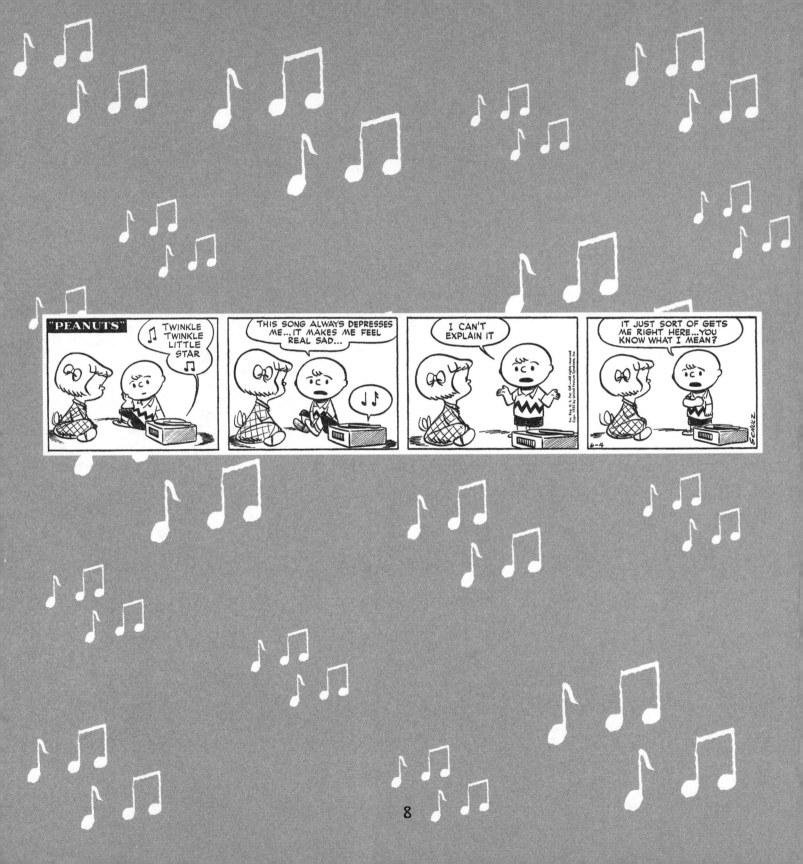

WHY, CERTAINLY, SCHROEDER... I'LL BE RIGHT OVER...
PEANUTS
BY SCHULZ
ABSOLUTELY, SCHROEDER... I'M ON MY WAY!
KNOCK KNOCK
IT'S NICE OF YOU TO INVITE US OVER TO LISTEN TO YOUR RECORDS, SCHROEDER
I'VE ALWAYS LIKED GOOD MUSIC
ME, TOO...EVER SINCE I WAS A KID...
I GUESS A LOVE FOR MUSIC JUST RUNS IN MY FAMILY
MINE, TOO...WE ALWAYS HAVE OUR RADIO ON
TALK TALK TALK
THEY SAY THAT MUSIC SOOTHES THE SAVAGE BEAST
I BELIEVE THAT BECAUSE I REMEMBER READING ONCE WHERE...
!
?
OUT! OUT! OUT!!
Tm. Reg. U. S. Pat. Off.—All rights reserved
Copr. 1952 by United Feature Syndicate, Inc.
6-15
I WONDER WHAT MADE HIM GET SO MAD.?.
WHO KNOWS? SOME PEOPLE ARE IMPOSSIBLE TO UNDERSTAND!
SCHULZ

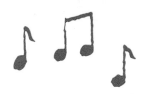

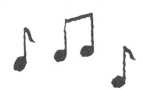

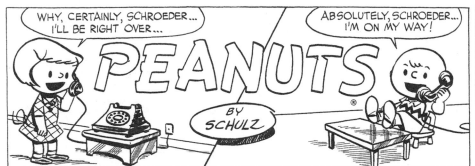

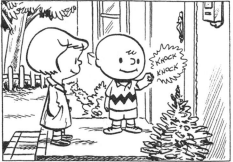

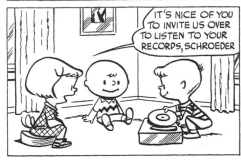

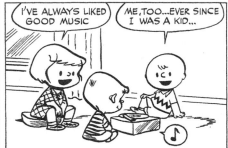

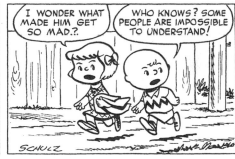

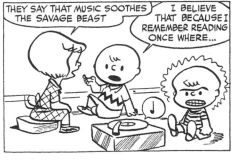

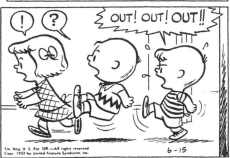

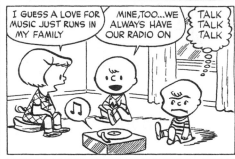

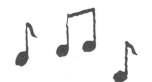

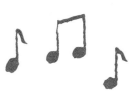

"PEANUTS"
SCHROEDER! GET OUT OF THE STREET!
NO!
WHAT DO YOU WANT TO DO... DEPRIVE THE WORLD OF ALL THAT GREAT MUSIC ?
Tm Reg U S Pat Off—All rights reserved Copr 1952 by United Feature Syndicate, Inc.
ALL IS VANITY!
6-28
SCHULZ

"PEANUTS"
GUESS WHAT I'M WHISTLING, CHARLIE BROWN...
"OLD BLACK JOE"? "TAKE ME OUT TO THE BALL GAME"? "HOME ON THE RANGE"?
Copr. 1952 by United Feature Syndicate, Inc.
NOPE...IT WAS THE LAST HALF OF THE TENTH MEASURE OF SINDING'S OP.32, NO.3
7-8
Y'KNOW, I ALMOST SAID THAT...I DON'T KNOW WHY I DIDN'T!
SCHULZ

"PEANUTS"
TURN THIS RADIO OFF! I'M GOING TO WATCH TELEVISION!
?
CLICK!
!
Tm Reg U S Pat Off—All rights reserved Copr 1952 by United Feature Syndicate Inc
9-18
SCHULZ

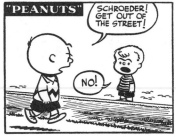

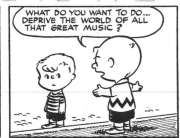

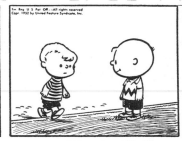

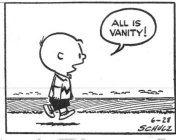

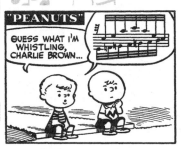

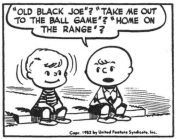

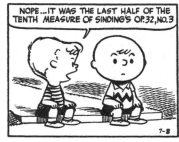

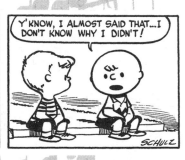

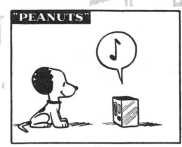

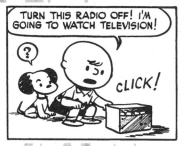

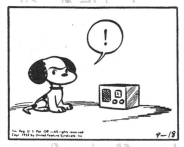

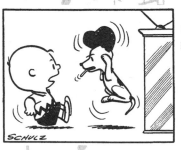

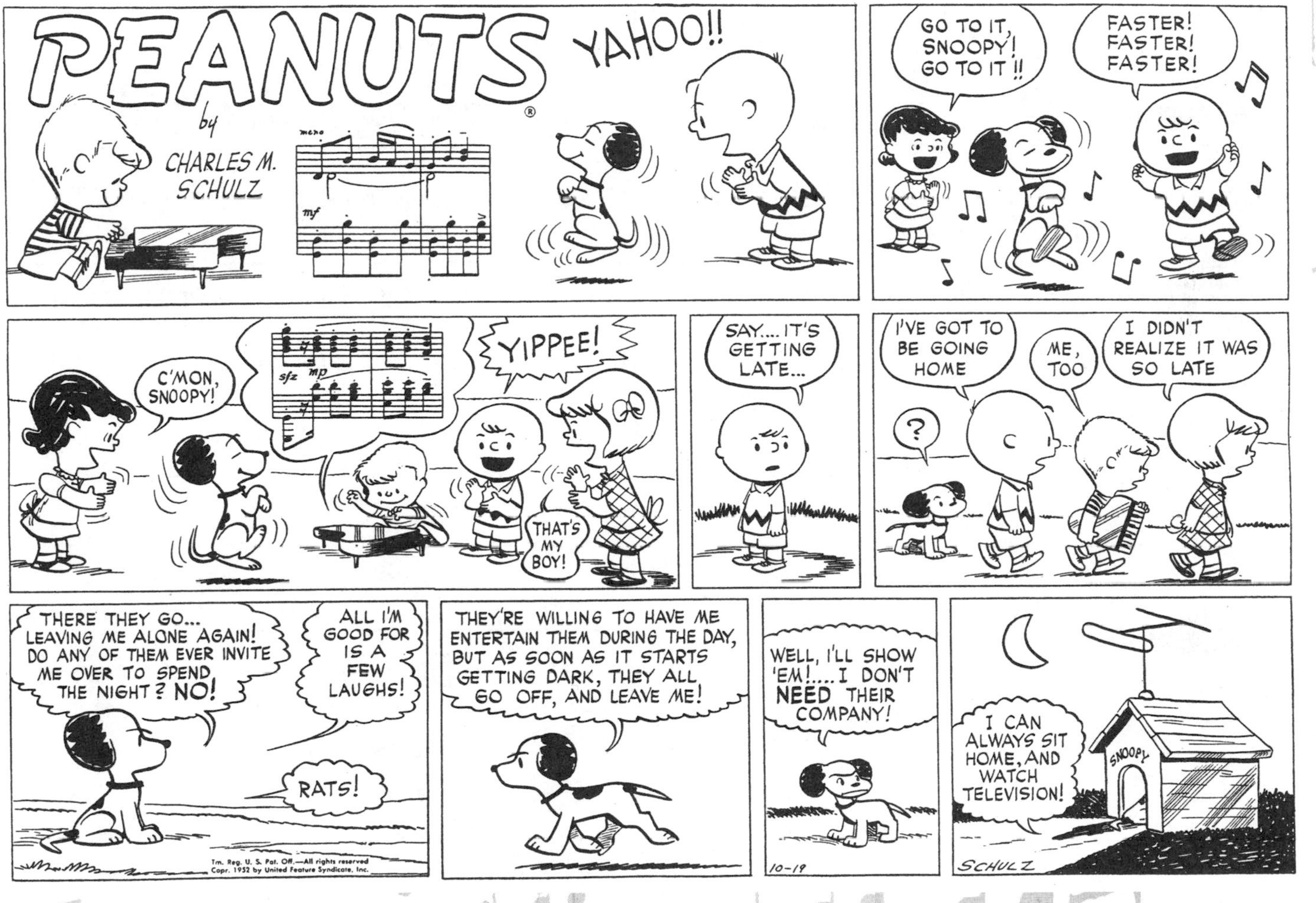
PEANUTS
by CHARLES M. SCHULZ
YAHOO!!
GO TO IT, SNOOPY! GO TO IT!!
FASTER! FASTER! FASTER!
C'MON, SNOOPY!
YIPPEE!
THAT'S MY BOY!
SAY.... IT'S GETTING LATE...
I'VE GOT TO BE GOING HOME
ME, TOO
I DIDN'T REALIZE IT WAS SO LATE
?
THERE THEY GO... LEAVING ME ALONE AGAIN! DO ANY OF THEM EVER INVITE ME OVER TO SPEND THE NIGHT? NO!
ALL I'M GOOD FOR IS A FEW LAUGHS!
RATS!
Tm. Reg. U. S. Pat. Off.—All rights reserved
Copr. 1952 by United Feature Syndicate, Inc.
THEY'RE WILLING TO HAVE ME ENTERTAIN THEM DURING THE DAY, BUT AS SOON AS IT STARTS GETTING DARK, THEY ALL GO OFF, AND LEAVE ME!
10-19
WELL, I'LL SHOW 'EM!.... I DON'T NEED THEIR COMPANY!
I CAN ALWAYS SIT HOME, AND WATCH TELEVISION!
SNOOPY
SCHULZ

"PEANUTS"
THAT WAS AWFUL!
THAT WAS THE WORST PIANO PLAYING I'VE EVER HEARD!!
YOU HAVE ABSOLUTELY NO TALENT WHATSOEVER!
I'M HELPING SCHROEDER TO GET USED TO INSULTS FROM THE MUSIC CRITICS...
12-19
SCHULZ

"PEANUTS"
Charlie Brown
Charlie Brown
lie
wn
SCHULZ
Schroeder
1-22
Tm. Reg. U. S. Pat. Off.—All rights reserved Copr. 1953 by United Feature Syndicate, Inc.

"PEANUTS"
AH! THIS IS JUST THE SONG I'VE BEEN WAITING TO HEAR..
Tm. Reg. U S Pat. Off.—All rights reserved Copr. 1953 by United Feature Syndicate, Inc.
HMM...THAT IS NICE...TA DE DA DE DUM TE TA DE DUM... DA DE DUM TE DA DE DUM
DA DE DA DE DA DE DUM DE DA DE DAAA DEE DA DA DE DA
?
SCHULZ
2-13

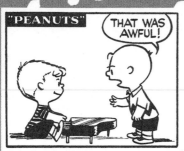

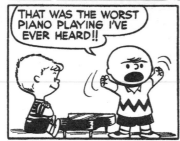

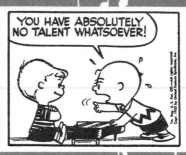

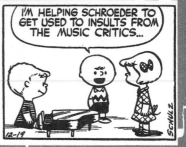

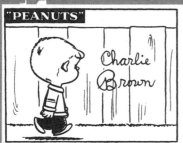

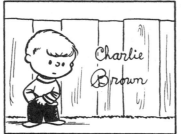

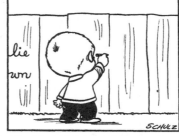

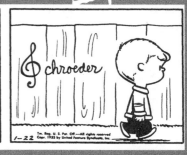

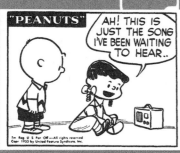

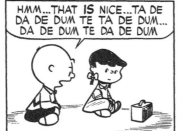

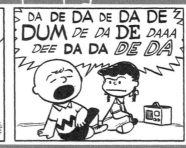

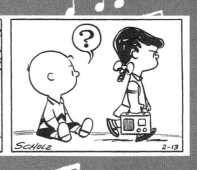

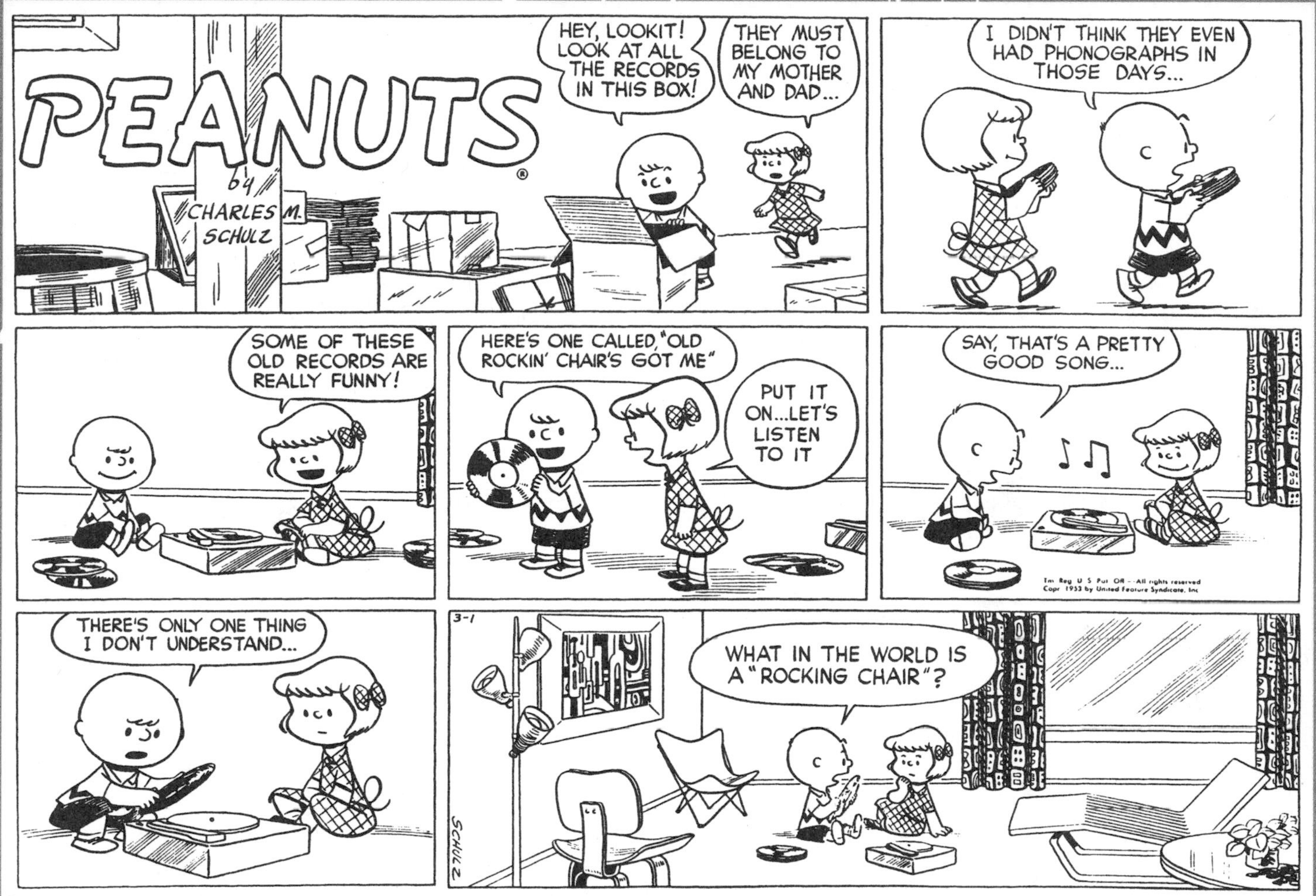
PEANUTS
by CHARLES M. SCHULZ
HEY, LOOKIT! LOOK AT ALL THE RECORDS IN THIS BOX!
THEY MUST BELONG TO MY MOTHER AND DAD...
I DIDN'T THINK THEY EVEN HAD PHONOGRAPHS IN THOSE DAYS...
SOME OF THESE OLD RECORDS ARE REALLY FUNNY!
HERE'S ONE CALLED, "OLD ROCKIN' CHAIR'S GOT ME"
PUT IT ON...LET'S LISTEN TO IT
SAY, THAT'S A PRETTY GOOD SONG...
Tm Reg U S Pat Off—All rights reserved
Copr 1953 by United Feature Syndicate, Inc
THERE'S ONLY ONE THING I DON'T UNDERSTAND...
3-1
WHAT IN THE WORLD IS A "ROCKING CHAIR"?
SCHULZ

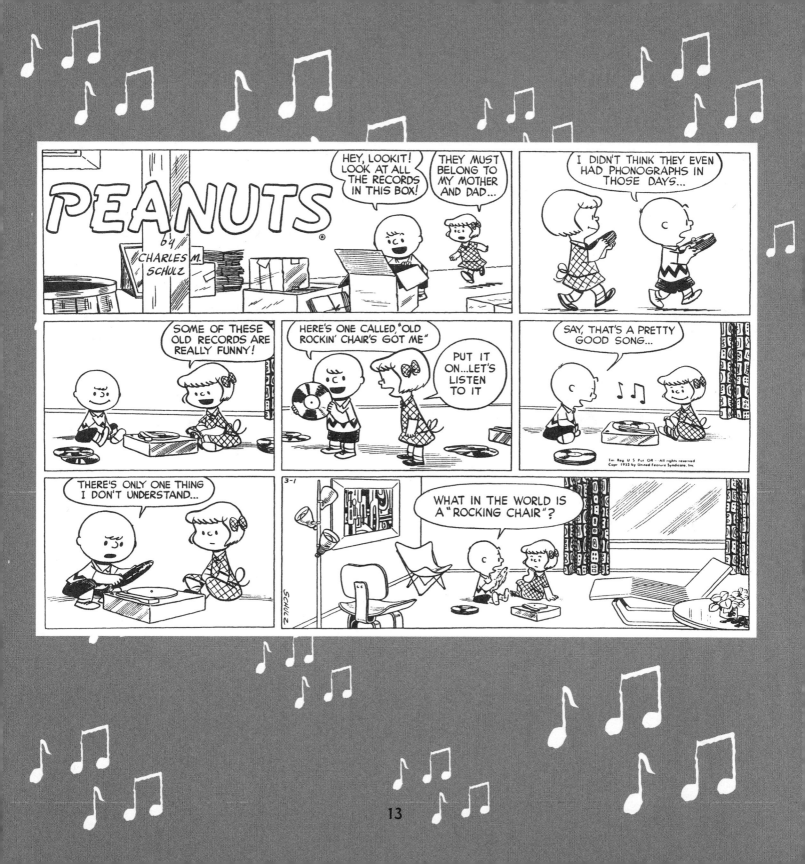

"PEANUTS"
WHAT'S THAT YOU'RE PLAYING, SCHROEDER?
"Shafe Können Sicher Weiden"
!
NO WONDER I DIDN'T RECOGNIZE IT...
YOU WERE PLAYING IN GERMAN
3/14
SCHULZ

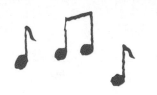

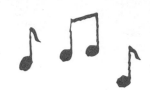

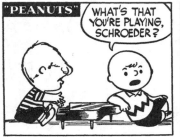

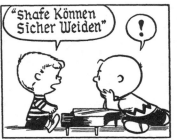

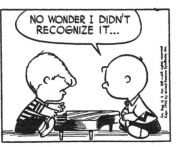

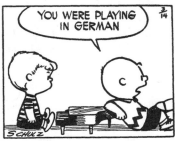

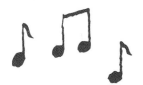

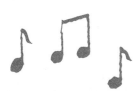

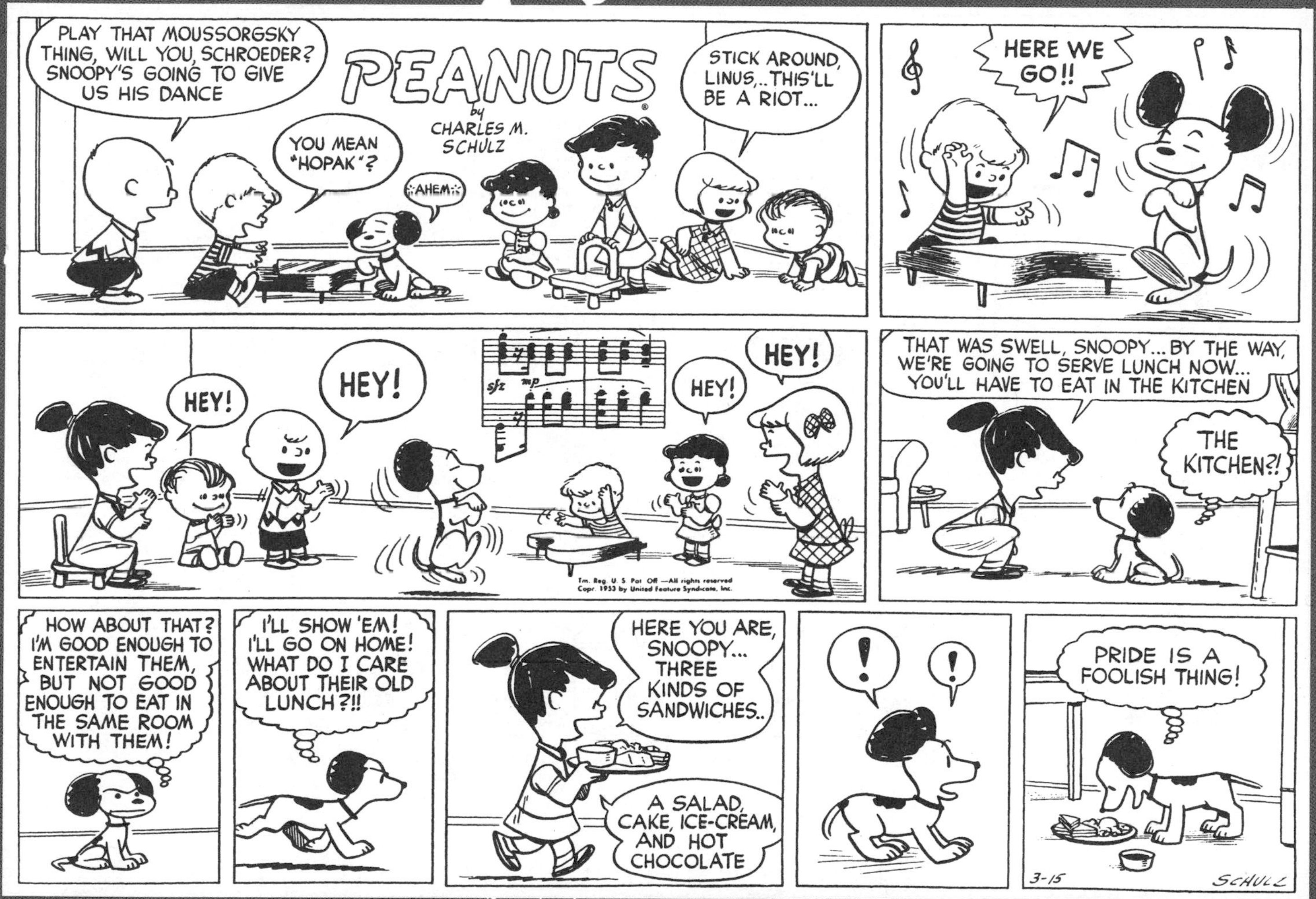

PLAY THAT MOUSSORGSKY THING, WILL YOU, SCHROEDER? SNOOPY'S GOING TO GIVE US HIS DANCE
PEANUTS
by CHARLES M. SCHULZ
YOU MEAN "HOPAK"?
AHEM
STICK AROUND, LINUS,..THIS'LL BE A RIOT...
HERE WE GO!!
HEY!
HEY!
HEY!
HEY!
sfz
mp
Tm. Reg. U. S. Pat. Off.—All rights reserved
Copr. 1953 by United Feature Syndicate, Inc.
THAT WAS SWELL, SNOOPY...BY THE WAY, WE'RE GOING TO SERVE LUNCH NOW... YOU'LL HAVE TO EAT IN THE KITCHEN
THE KITCHEN?!
HOW ABOUT THAT? I'M GOOD ENOUGH TO ENTERTAIN THEM, BUT NOT GOOD ENOUGH TO EAT IN THE SAME ROOM WITH THEM!
I'LL SHOW 'EM! I'LL GO ON HOME! WHAT DO I CARE ABOUT THEIR OLD LUNCH?!!
HERE YOU ARE, SNOOPY... THREE KINDS OF SANDWICHES..
A SALAD, CAKE, ICE-CREAM, AND HOT CHOCOLATE
!
!
PRIDE IS A FOOLISH THING!
3-15
SCHULZ

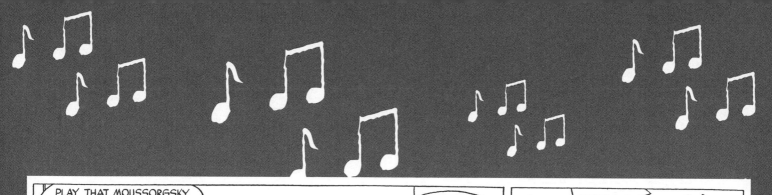

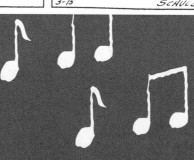

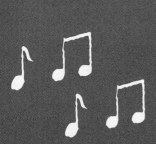

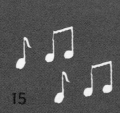

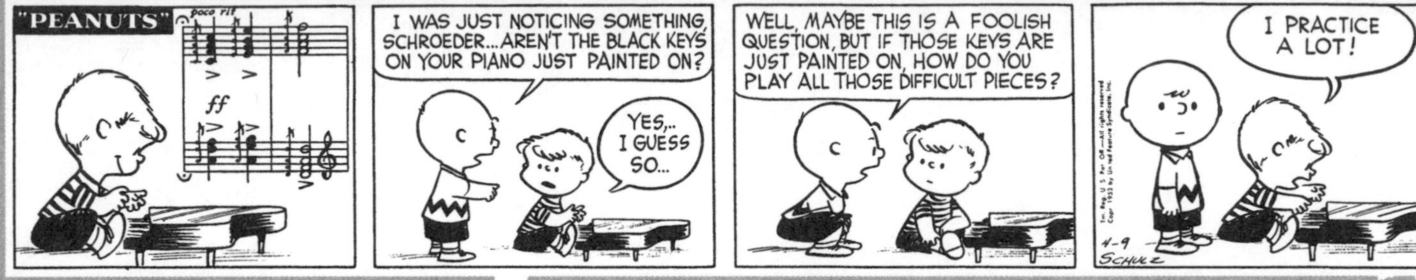
"PEANUTS"
poco rit
ff
I WAS JUST NOTICING SOMETHING, SCHROEDER...AREN'T THE BLACK KEYS ON YOUR PIANO JUST PAINTED ON?
YES,.. I GUESS SO...
WELL, MAYBE THIS IS A FOOLISH QUESTION, BUT IF THOSE KEYS ARE JUST PAINTED ON, HOW DO YOU PLAY ALL THOSE DIFFICULT PIECES?
I PRACTICE A LOT!
4-9
SCHULZ

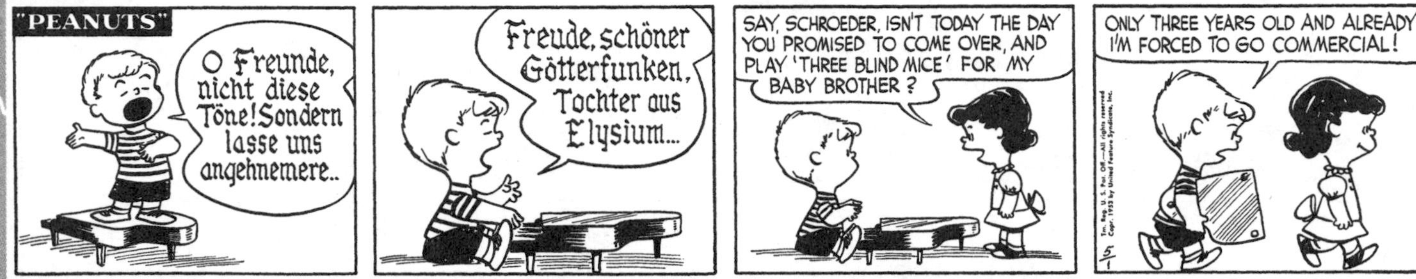
"PEANUTS"
O Freunde, nicht diese Töne! Sondern lasse uns angehnemere..
Freude, schöner Götterfunken, Tochter aus Elysium...
SAY, SCHROEDER, ISN'T TODAY THE DAY YOU PROMISED TO COME OVER, AND PLAY 'THREE BLIND MICE' FOR MY BABY BROTHER?
ONLY THREE YEARS OLD AND ALREADY I'M FORCED TO GO COMMERCIAL!
5/1
SCHULZ

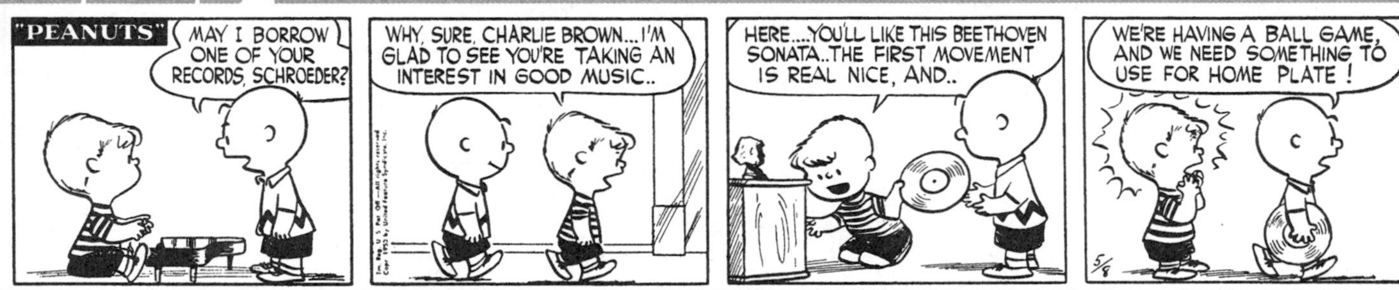
"PEANUTS"
MAY I BORROW ONE OF YOUR RECORDS, SCHROEDER?
WHY, SURE, CHARLIE BROWN...I'M GLAD TO SEE YOU'RE TAKING AN INTEREST IN GOOD MUSIC..
HERE....YOU'LL LIKE THIS BEETHOVEN SONATA..THE FIRST MOVEMENT IS REAL NICE, AND..
WE'RE HAVING A BALL GAME, AND WE NEED SOMETHING TO USE FOR HOME PLATE!
5/8
SCHULZ

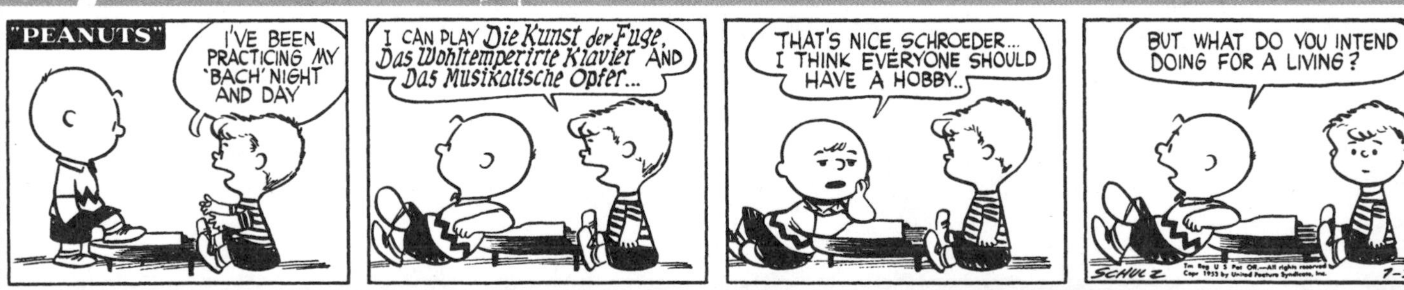
"PEANUTS"
I'VE BEEN PRACTICING MY 'BACH' NIGHT AND DAY
I CAN PLAY Die Kunst der Fuge, Das Wohltemperirte Klavier AND Das Musikalische Opfer...
THAT'S NICE, SCHROEDER... I THINK EVERYONE SHOULD HAVE A HOBBY..
BUT WHAT DO YOU INTEND DOING FOR A LIVING?
SCHULZ
7-20

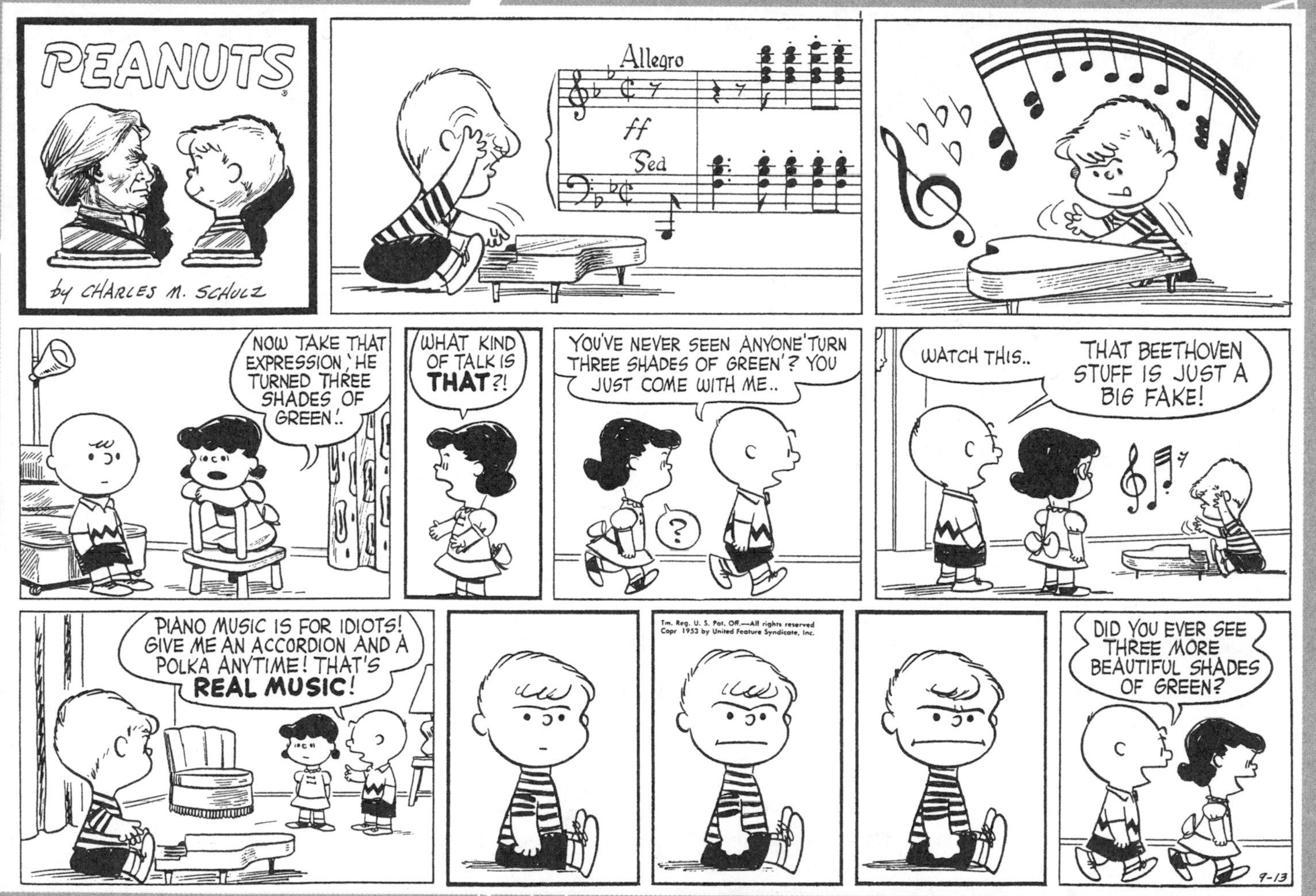

PEANUTS
by CHARLES M. SCHULZ
Allegro
ff
Ped
NOW TAKE THAT EXPRESSION, HE TURNED THREE SHADES OF GREEN!..
WHAT KIND OF TALK IS **THAT**?!
YOU'VE NEVER SEEN ANYONE 'TURN THREE SHADES OF GREEN'? YOU JUST COME WITH ME..
?
WATCH THIS..
THAT BEETHOVEN STUFF IS JUST A BIG FAKE!
PIANO MUSIC IS FOR IDIOTS! GIVE ME AN ACCORDION AND A POLKA ANYTIME! THAT'S **REAL MUSIC**!
Tm. Reg. U. S. Pat. Off.—All rights reserved Copr 1953 by United Feature Syndicate, Inc.
DID YOU EVER SEE THREE MORE BEAUTIFUL SHADES OF GREEN?
9-13

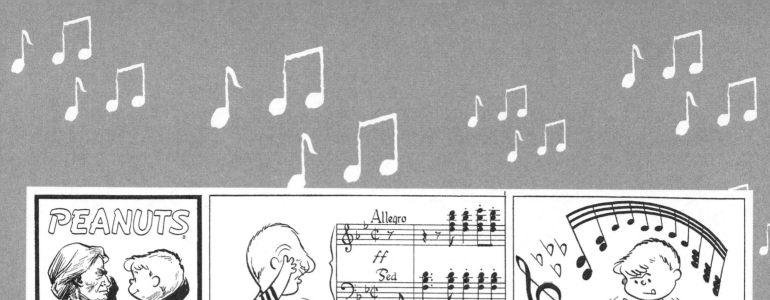

"PEANUTS"
LET'S SEE, NOW...HMM..
Tm Reg U S Pat Off—All rights reserved Copr 1953 by United Feature Syndicate Inc
NOTHING HERE..NOPE.. NOTHING HERE EITHER
I'M SORRY, CHARLIE BROWN..
I GUESS NOTHING HAS BEEN WRITTEN FOR PIANO AND CIGAR-BOX BANJO..
10-1
SCHULZ

"PEANUTS"
DO YOU KNOW WHAT DAY THIS IS, SCHROEDER?
THIS IS 'COLUMBUS DAY'!
Tm Reg U S Pat Off—All rights reserved Copr 1953 by United Feature Syndicate, Inc.
OH?
SCHULZ
10-12
WHAT DID HE COMPOSE?

"PEANUTS"
?
Tm Reg U S Pat Off—All rights reserved Copr 1953 by United Feature Syndicate, Inc.
!
SCHULZ
11-11

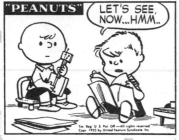

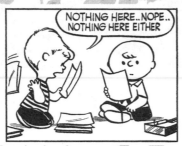

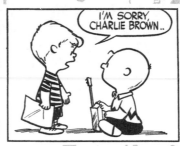

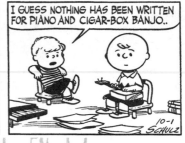

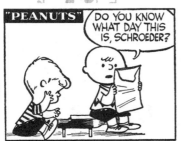

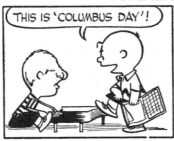

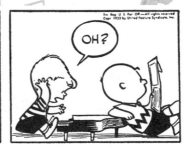

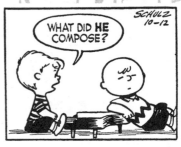

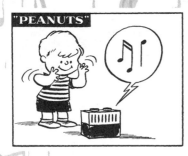

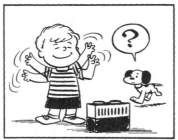

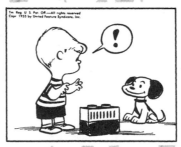

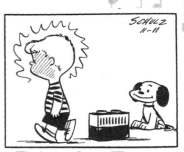

"PEANUTS"
OUR TELEVISION SET IS BROKEN SO WE'LL HAVE TO LISTEN TO THE RADIO INSTEAD..
?
!
12-30
GOOD GRIEF! I MUST BE GOING BLIND!
SCHULZ

"PEANUTS"
1-21
SCHULZ

"PEANUTS"
I LIKE THAT RECORD SCHROEDER, WHAT IS IT?
HAYDN'S 'TOY SYMPHONY'
OH? HAYDN WROTE SOME NICE THINGS, DIDN'T HE?
WELL, HAYDN REALLY DIDN'T WRITE THIS.. MOZART DID...
I'VE ALWAYS LIKED MOZART..
WHAT I MEAN TO SAY IS.. MOZART'S FATHER WROTE IT
2-9
SCHULZ

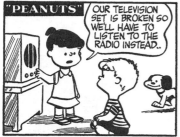

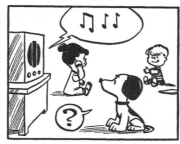

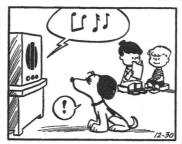

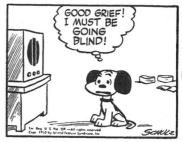

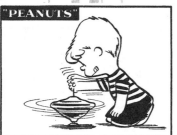

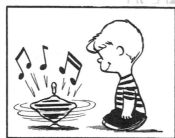

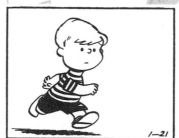

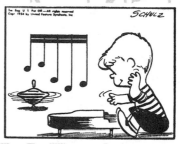

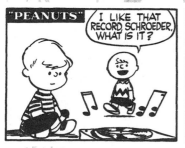

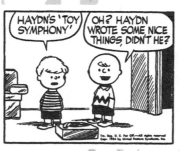

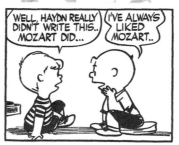

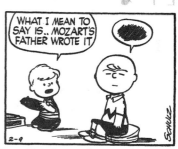

"PEANUTS"
HERE, SCHROEDER.. A JACK-IN-THE-BOX DESIGNED ESPECIALLY FOR YOU..
?
GO AHEAD...TURN THE HANDLE..
BEETHOVEN!
3-26
SCHULZ

"PEANUTS"
"MARY WORE HER RED DRESS, RED DRESS, RED DRESS...MARY WORE HER RED DRESS ALL DAY LONG..
"MARY WORE A RED HAT, RED HAT, RED HAT... MARY WORE A RED HAT ALL DAY LONG...
"MARY WORE HER RED SHOES, RED SHOES, RED SHOES.... MARY WORE HER RED SHOES ALL DAY LONG..."
SCHULZ
4-24
THAT POOR GIRL WAS OUT OF HER MIND!

"PEANUTS"
I JUST BOUGHT A NEW CHOPIN RECORD
IT HAS A DIRGE IN IT
OH?
MAYBE YOU COULD RETURN IT, AND GET YOUR MONEY BACK...
5-20
SCHULZ

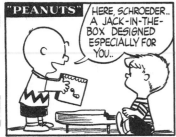

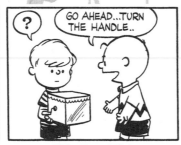

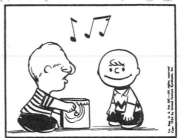

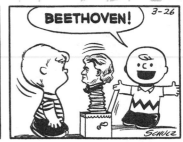

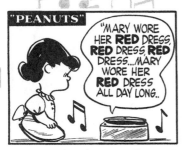

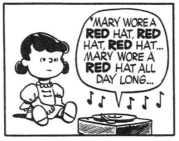

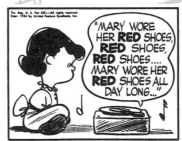

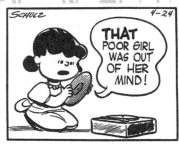

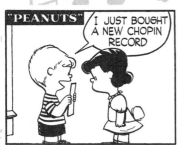

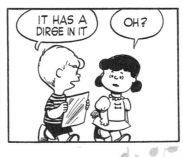

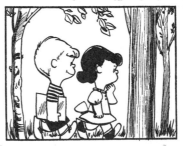

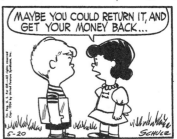

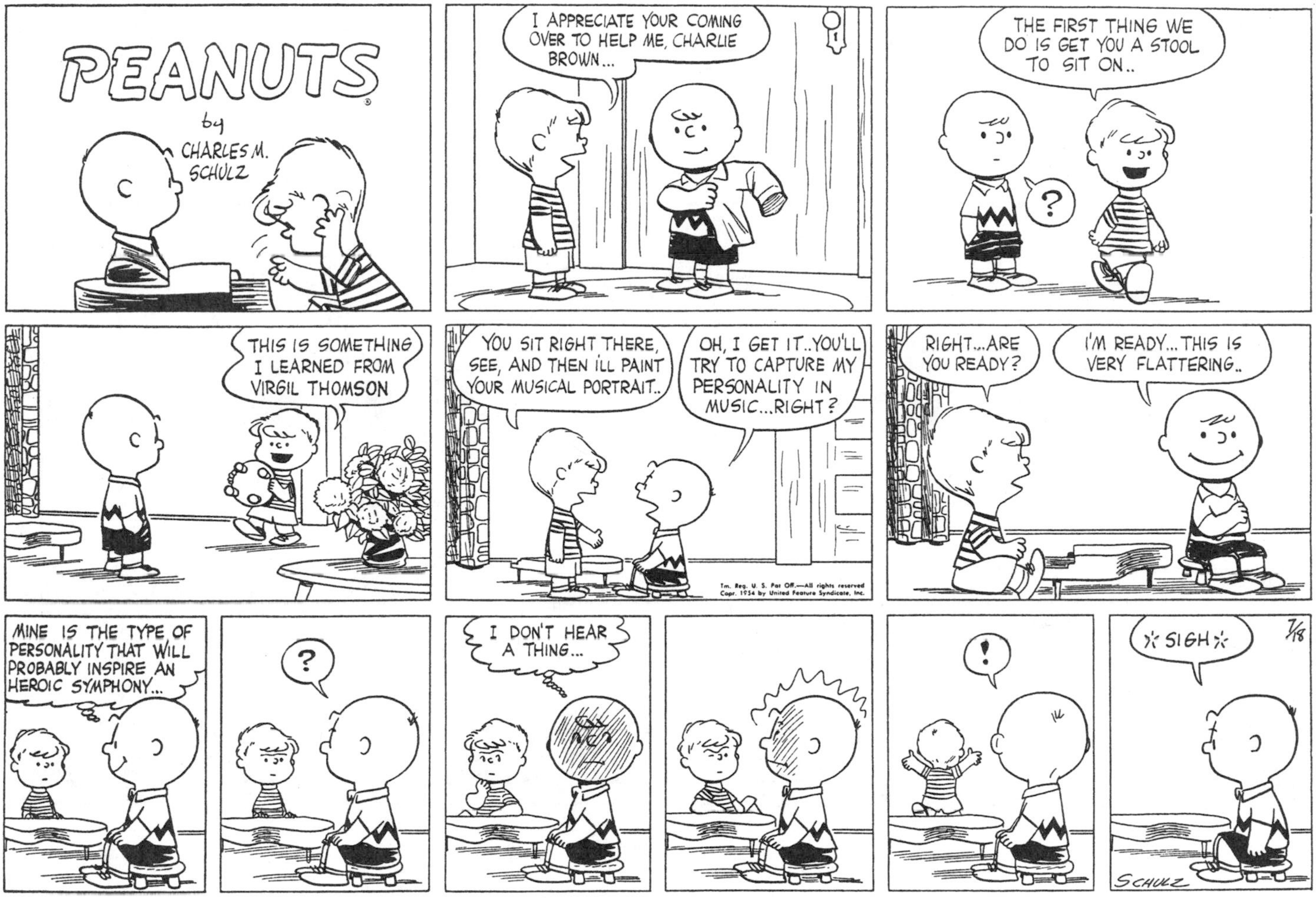
PEANUTS
by CHARLES M. SCHULZ
I APPRECIATE YOUR COMING OVER TO HELP ME, CHARLIE BROWN...
THE FIRST THING WE DO IS GET YOU A STOOL TO SIT ON..
?
THIS IS SOMETHING I LEARNED FROM VIRGIL THOMSON
YOU SIT RIGHT THERE, SEE, AND THEN I'LL PAINT YOUR MUSICAL PORTRAIT..
OH, I GET IT..YOU'LL TRY TO CAPTURE MY PERSONALITY IN MUSIC...RIGHT?
Tm. Reg. U. S. Pat. Off.—All rights reserved Copr. 1954 by United Feature Syndicate, Inc.
RIGHT...ARE YOU READY?
I'M READY...THIS IS VERY FLATTERING..
MINE IS THE TYPE OF PERSONALITY THAT WILL PROBABLY INSPIRE AN HEROIC SYMPHONY...
?
I DON'T HEAR A THING...
!
SIGH
7/18
SCHULZ

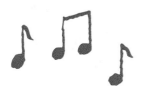

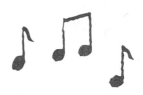

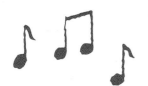

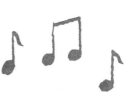

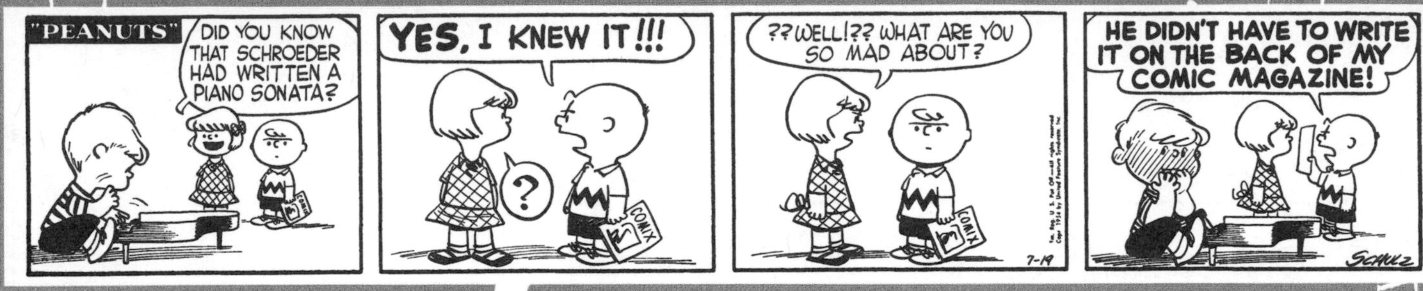
"PEANUTS"
DID YOU KNOW THAT SCHROEDER HAD WRITTEN A PIANO SONATA?
YES, I KNEW IT!!!
?
??WELL!?? WHAT ARE YOU SO MAD ABOUT?
COMIX
7-19
HE DIDN'T HAVE TO WRITE IT ON THE BACK OF MY COMIC MAGAZINE!
SCHULZ

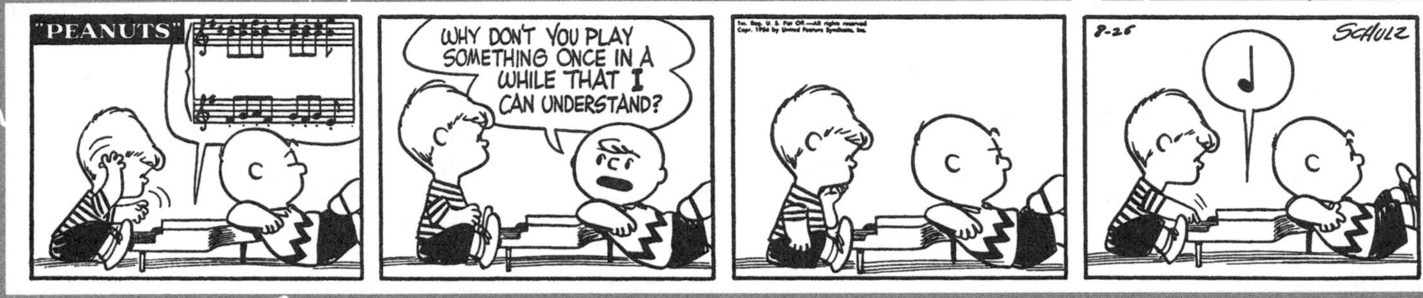
"PEANUTS"
WHY DON'T YOU PLAY SOMETHING ONCE IN A WHILE THAT I CAN UNDERSTAND?
8-26
SCHULZ

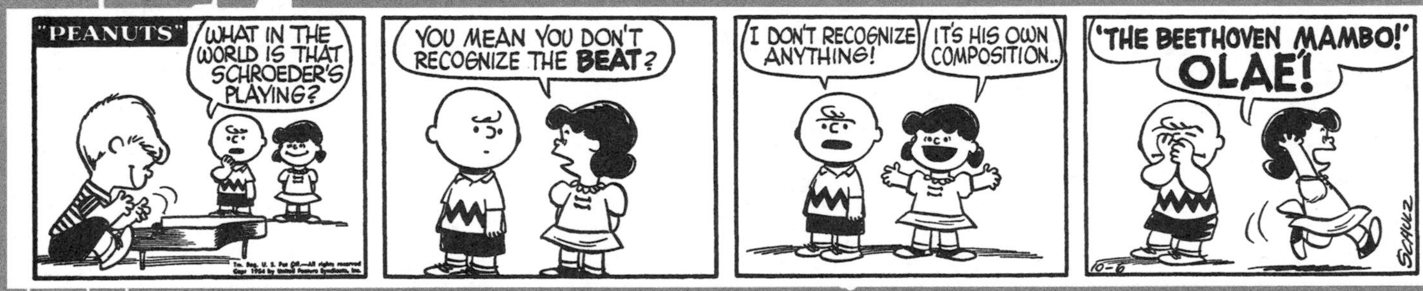
"PEANUTS"
WHAT IN THE WORLD IS THAT SCHROEDER'S PLAYING?
YOU MEAN YOU DON'T RECOGNIZE THE BEAT?
I DON'T RECOGNIZE ANYTHING!
IT'S HIS OWN COMPOSITION..
'THE BEETHOVEN MAMBO!' OLAE!
10-6
SCHULZ

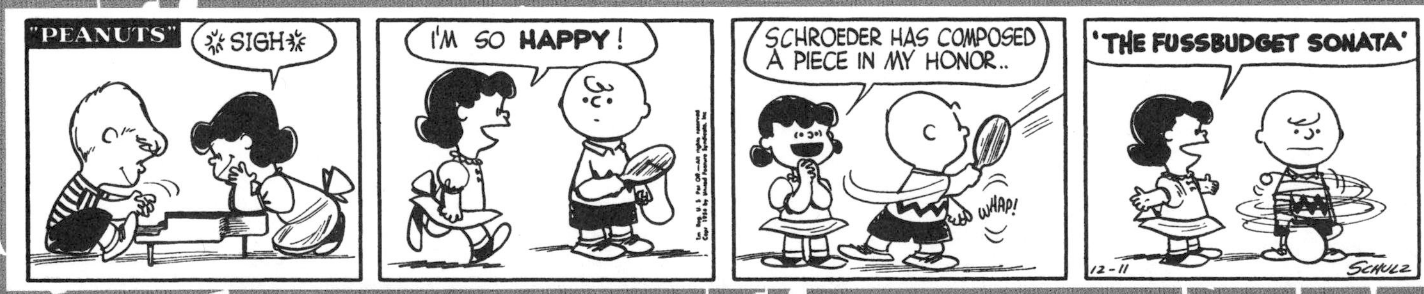
"PEANUTS"
SIGH
I'M SO HAPPY!
SCHROEDER HAS COMPOSED A PIECE IN MY HONOR..
WHAP!
'THE FUSSBUDGET SONATA'
12-11
SCHULZ

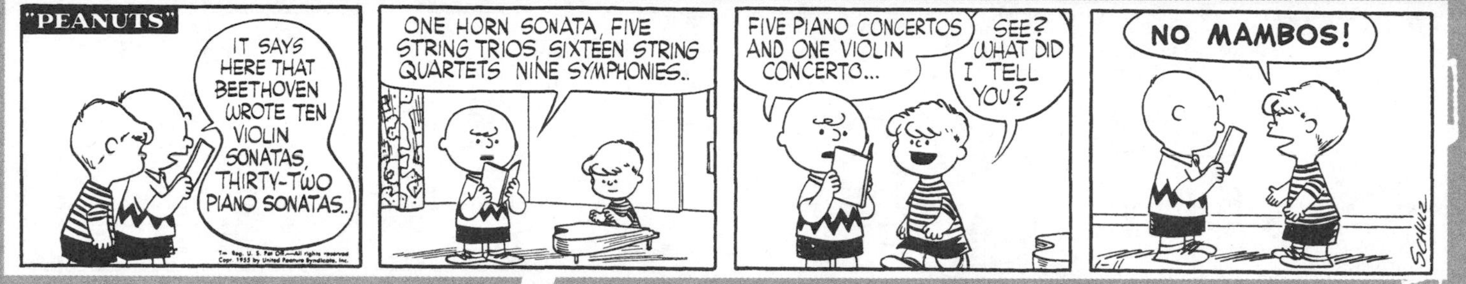
"PEANUTS"
IT SAYS HERE THAT BEETHOVEN WROTE TEN VIOLIN SONATAS, THIRTY-TWO PIANO SONATAS..
ONE HORN SONATA, FIVE STRING TRIOS, SIXTEEN STRING QUARTETS NINE SYMPHONIES..
FIVE PIANO CONCERTOS AND ONE VIOLIN CONCERTO...
SEE? WHAT DID I TELL YOU?
NO MAMBOS!
1-11
SCHULZ

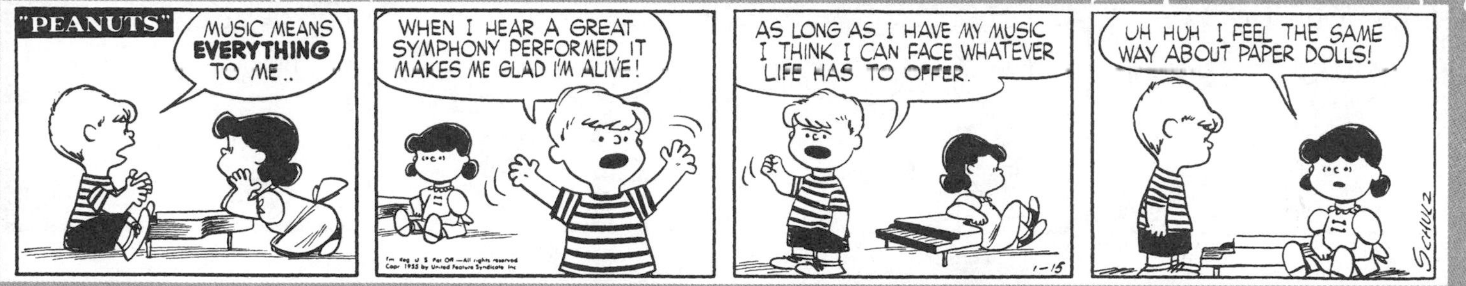
"PEANUTS"
MUSIC MEANS **EVERYTHING** TO ME..
WHEN I HEAR A GREAT SYMPHONY PERFORMED IT MAKES ME GLAD I'M ALIVE!
AS LONG AS I HAVE MY MUSIC I THINK I CAN FACE WHATEVER LIFE HAS TO OFFER.
1-15
UH HUH I FEEL THE SAME WAY ABOUT PAPER DOLLS!
SCHULZ

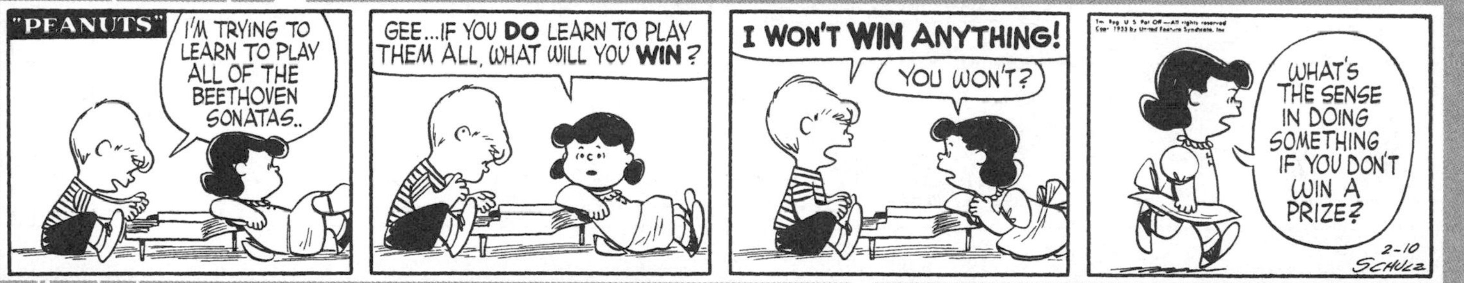
"PEANUTS"
I'M TRYING TO LEARN TO PLAY ALL OF THE BEETHOVEN SONATAS..
GEE...IF YOU **DO** LEARN TO PLAY THEM ALL, WHAT WILL YOU **WIN**?
I WON'T **WIN** ANYTHING!
YOU WON'T?
WHAT'S THE SENSE IN DOING SOMETHING IF YOU DON'T WIN A PRIZE?
2-10
SCHULZ

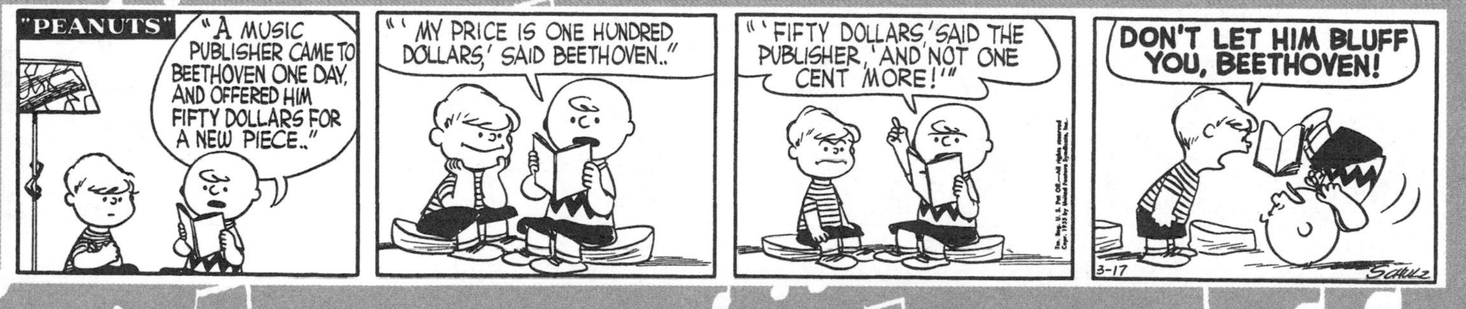
"PEANUTS"
"A MUSIC PUBLISHER CAME TO BEETHOVEN ONE DAY, AND OFFERED HIM FIFTY DOLLARS FOR A NEW PIECE.."
"'MY PRICE IS ONE HUNDRED DOLLARS,' SAID BEETHOVEN.."
"'FIFTY DOLLARS,' SAID THE PUBLISHER, 'AND NOT ONE CENT MORE!'"
3-17
DON'T LET HIM BLUFF YOU, BEETHOVEN!
SCHULZ

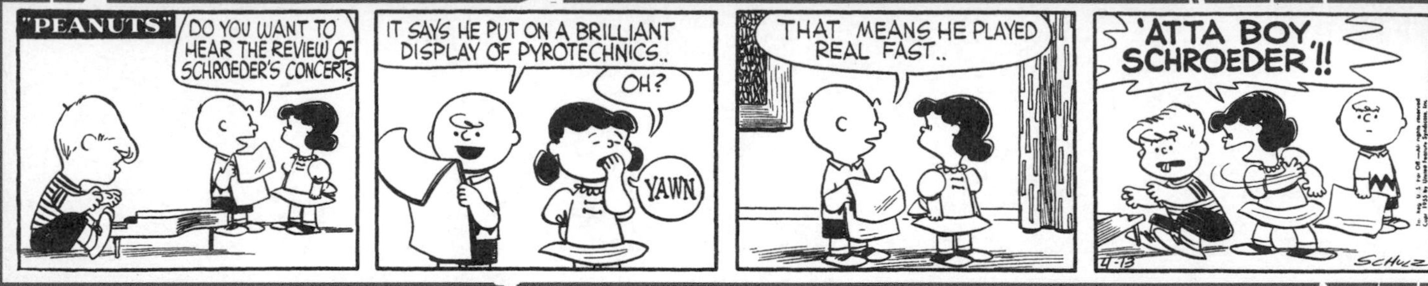
"PEANUTS"
DO YOU WANT TO HEAR THE REVIEW OF SCHROEDER'S CONCERT?
IT SAYS HE PUT ON A BRILLIANT DISPLAY OF PYROTECHNICS..
OH?
YAWN
THAT MEANS HE PLAYED REAL FAST..
'ATTA BOY SCHROEDER'!!
4-13
SCHULZ

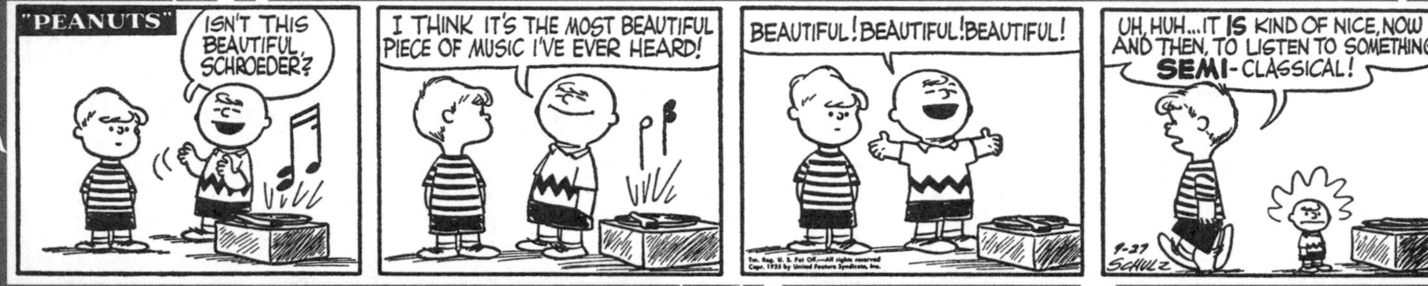
"PEANUTS"
ISN'T THIS BEAUTIFUL, SCHROEDER?
I THINK IT'S THE MOST BEAUTIFUL PIECE OF MUSIC I'VE EVER HEARD!
BEAUTIFUL! BEAUTIFUL! BEAUTIFUL!
UH, HUH...IT IS KIND OF NICE, NOW AND THEN, TO LISTEN TO SOMETHING SEMI-CLASSICAL!
9-27
SCHULZ

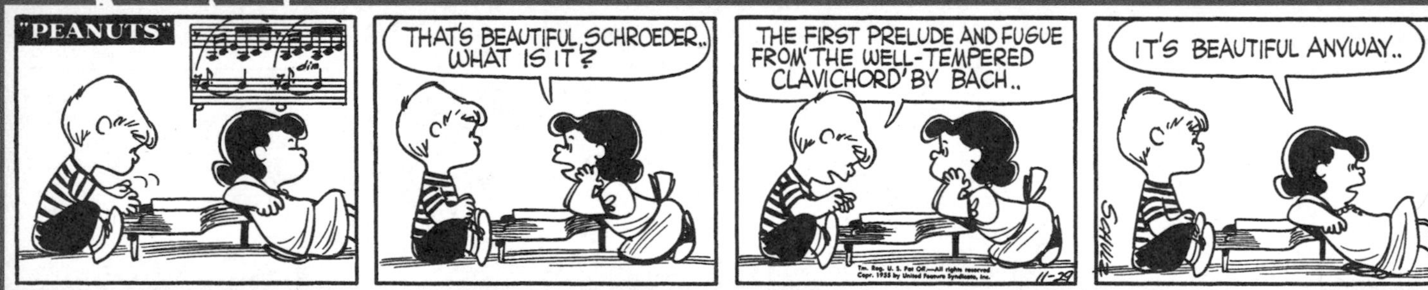
"PEANUTS"
THAT'S BEAUTIFUL, SCHROEDER.. WHAT IS IT?
THE FIRST PRELUDE AND FUGUE FROM 'THE WELL-TEMPERED CLAVICHORD' BY BACH..
IT'S BEAUTIFUL ANYWAY..
11-29
SCHULZ

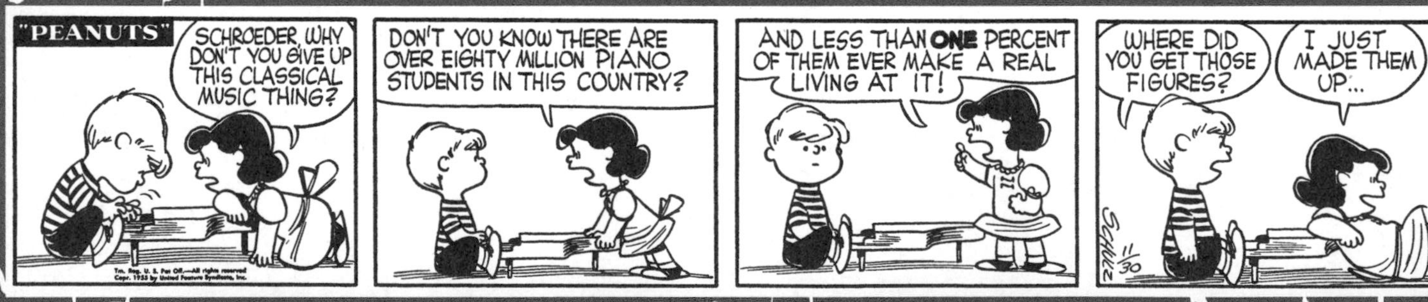
"PEANUTS"
SCHROEDER, WHY DON'T YOU GIVE UP THIS CLASSICAL MUSIC THING?
DON'T YOU KNOW THERE ARE OVER EIGHTY MILLION PIANO STUDENTS IN THIS COUNTRY?
AND LESS THAN ONE PERCENT OF THEM EVER MAKE A REAL LIVING AT IT!
WHERE DID YOU GET THOSE FIGURES?
I JUST MADE THEM UP...
SCHULZ
11/30

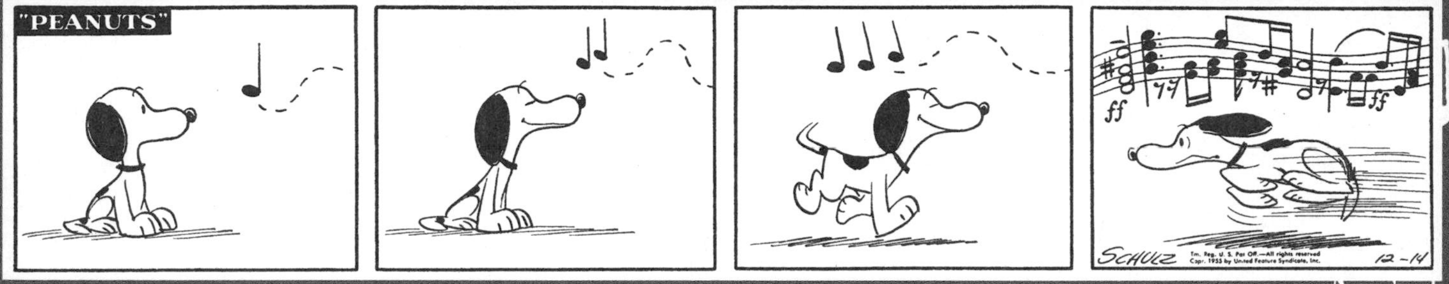
"PEANUTS"
ff
ff
SCHULZ
12-14

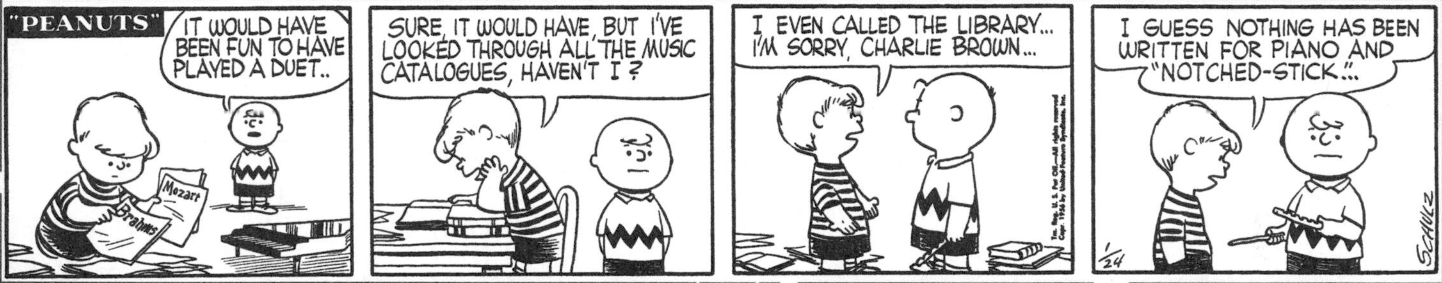
"PEANUTS"
IT WOULD HAVE BEEN FUN TO HAVE PLAYED A DUET..
Mozart
Brahms
SURE, IT WOULD HAVE, BUT I'VE LOOKED THROUGH ALL THE MUSIC CATALOGUES, HAVEN'T I?
I EVEN CALLED THE LIBRARY... I'M SORRY, CHARLIE BROWN...
I GUESS NOTHING HAS BEEN WRITTEN FOR PIANO AND "NOTCHED-STICK"!..
1/24
SCHULZ

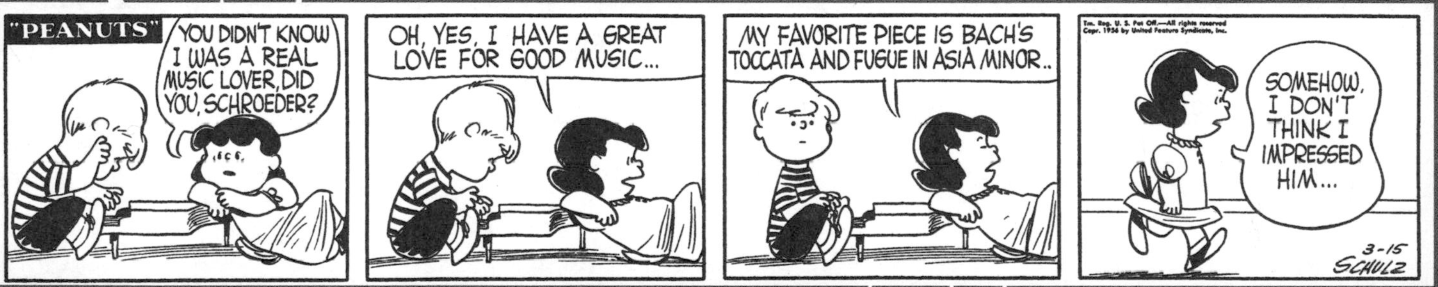
"PEANUTS"
YOU DIDN'T KNOW I WAS A REAL MUSIC LOVER, DID YOU, SCHROEDER?
OH, YES, I HAVE A GREAT LOVE FOR GOOD MUSIC...
MY FAVORITE PIECE IS BACH'S TOCCATA AND FUGUE IN ASIA MINOR..
SOMEHOW, I DON'T THINK I IMPRESSED HIM...
3-15
SCHULZ

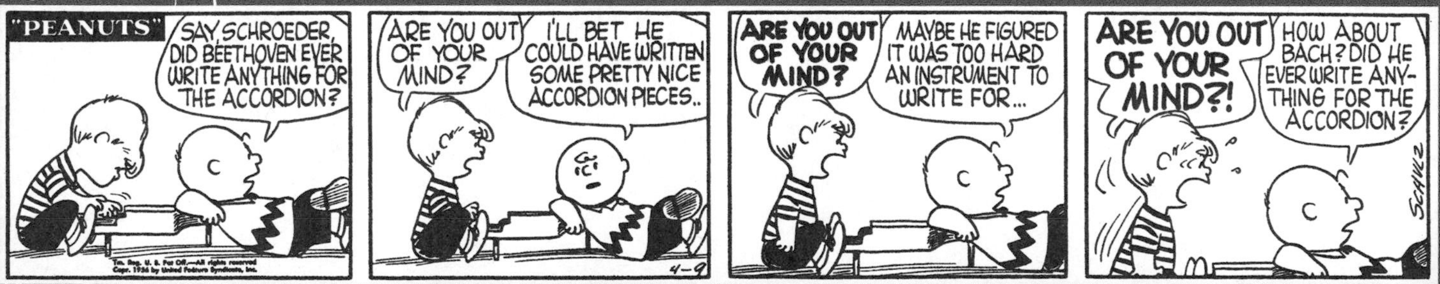
"PEANUTS"
SAY, SCHROEDER, DID BEETHOVEN EVER WRITE ANYTHING FOR THE ACCORDION?
ARE YOU OUT OF YOUR MIND?
I'LL BET HE COULD HAVE WRITTEN SOME PRETTY NICE ACCORDION PIECES..
4-9
ARE YOU OUT OF YOUR MIND?
MAYBE HE FIGURED IT WAS TOO HARD AN INSTRUMENT TO WRITE FOR...
ARE YOU OUT OF YOUR MIND?!
HOW ABOUT BACH? DID HE EVER WRITE ANYTHING FOR THE ACCORDION?
SCHULZ

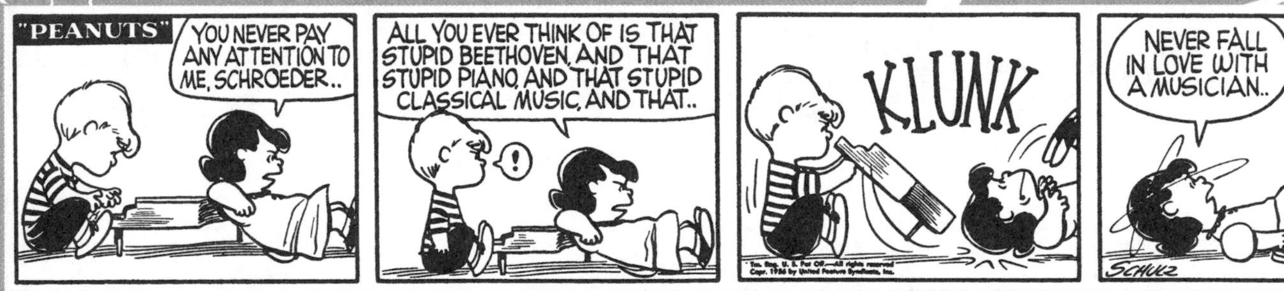
"PEANUTS"
YOU NEVER PAY ANY ATTENTION TO ME, SCHROEDER..
ALL YOU EVER THINK OF IS THAT STUPID BEETHOVEN, AND THAT STUPID PIANO, AND THAT STUPID CLASSICAL MUSIC, AND THAT..
!
KLUNK
NEVER FALL IN LOVE WITH A MUSICIAN..
SCHULZ
5-1

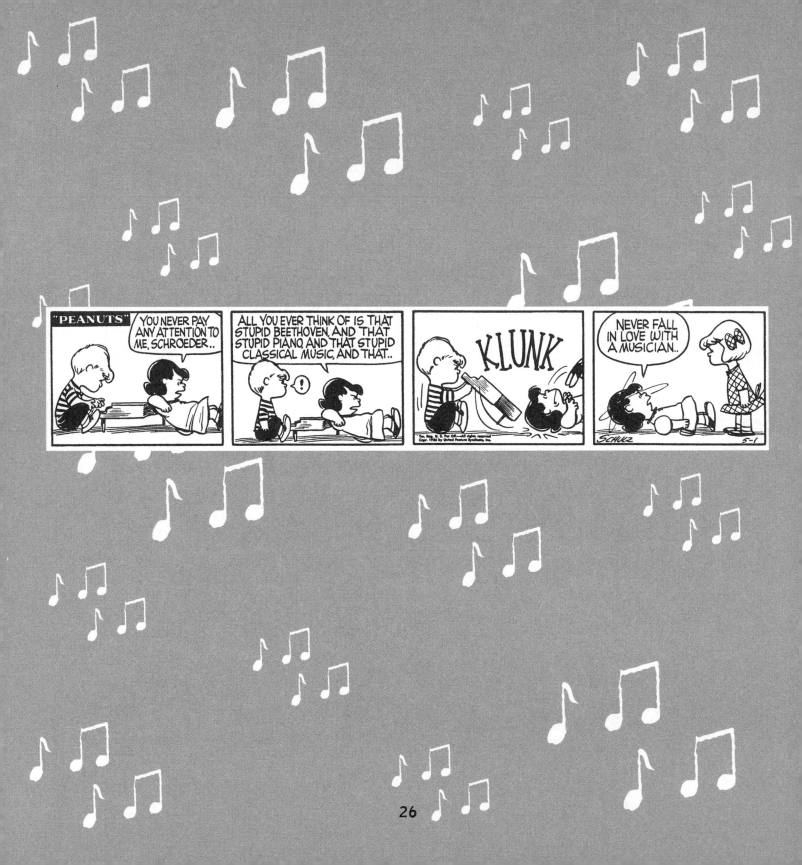

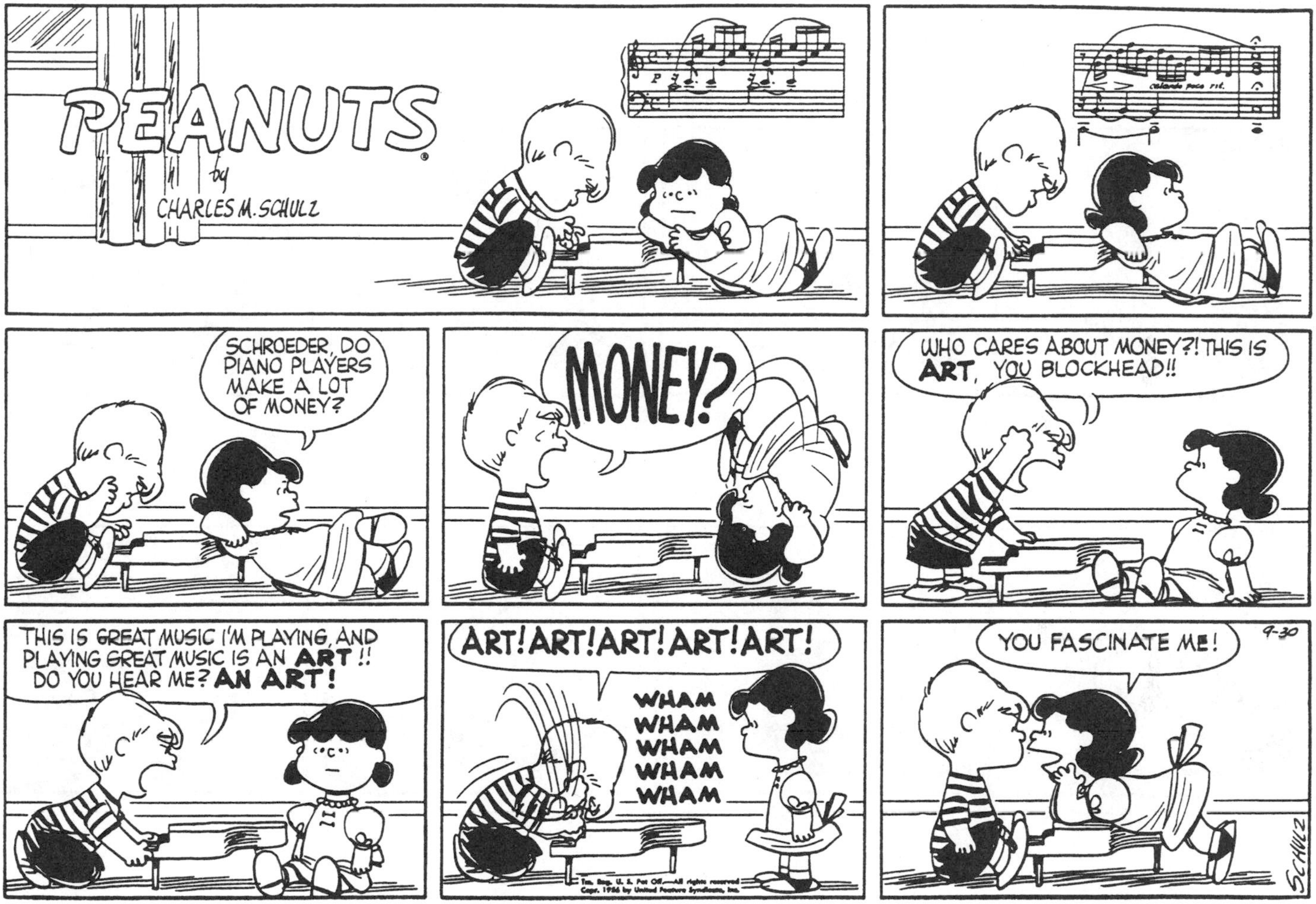
PEANUTS
by
CHARLES M. SCHULZ
SCHROEDER, DO PIANO PLAYERS MAKE A LOT OF MONEY?
MONEY?
WHO CARES ABOUT MONEY?! THIS IS ART, YOU BLOCKHEAD!!
THIS IS GREAT MUSIC I'M PLAYING, AND PLAYING GREAT MUSIC IS AN ART!! DO YOU HEAR ME? AN ART!
ART! ART! ART! ART! ART!
WHAM
WHAM
WHAM
WHAM
WHAM
9-30
YOU FASCINATE ME!
SCHULZ

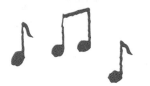

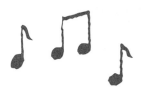

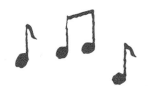

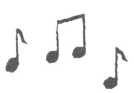

PEANUTS
SMACK!
Tm. Reg. U. S. Pat Off.—All rights reserved
Copr. 1956 by United Feature Syndicate, Inc.
YOU NEVER KNOW HOW CHOPIN IS GOING TO AFFECT SOMEONE..
10-12
SCHULZ

PEANUTS
11-2
NOTHING AFFECTS AN OLD GRAD LIKE THE PLAYING OF "POMP AND CIRCUMSTANCE"!
SCHULZ

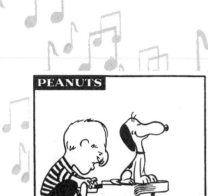

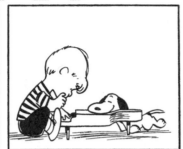

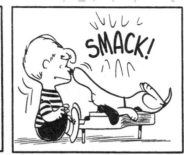

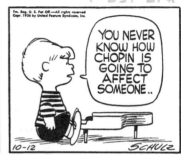

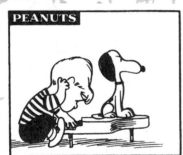

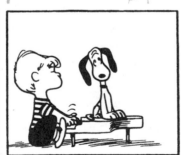

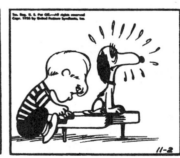

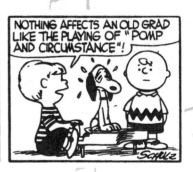

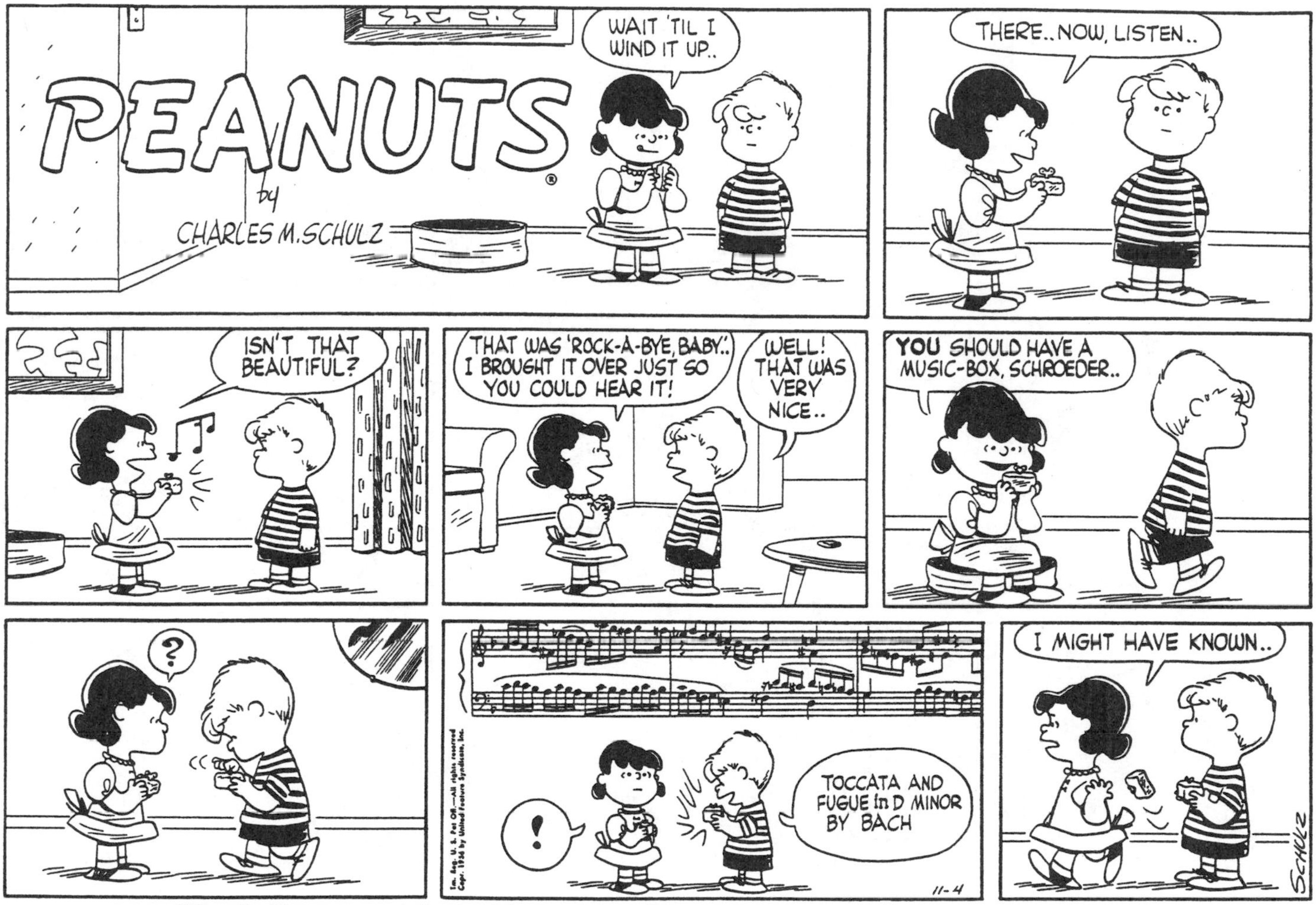
PEANUTS
by
CHARLES M. SCHULZ
WAIT 'TIL I WIND IT UP..
THERE..NOW, LISTEN..
ISN'T THAT BEAUTIFUL?
THAT WAS 'ROCK-A-BYE, BABY.' I BROUGHT IT OVER JUST SO YOU COULD HEAR IT!
WELL! THAT WAS VERY NICE..
YOU SHOULD HAVE A MUSIC-BOX, SCHROEDER..
?
!
TOCCATA AND FUGUE in D MINOR BY BACH
Tm. Reg. U. S. Pat. Off.—All rights reserved
Copr. 1956 by United Feature Syndicate, Inc.
11-4
I MIGHT HAVE KNOWN..
SCHULZ

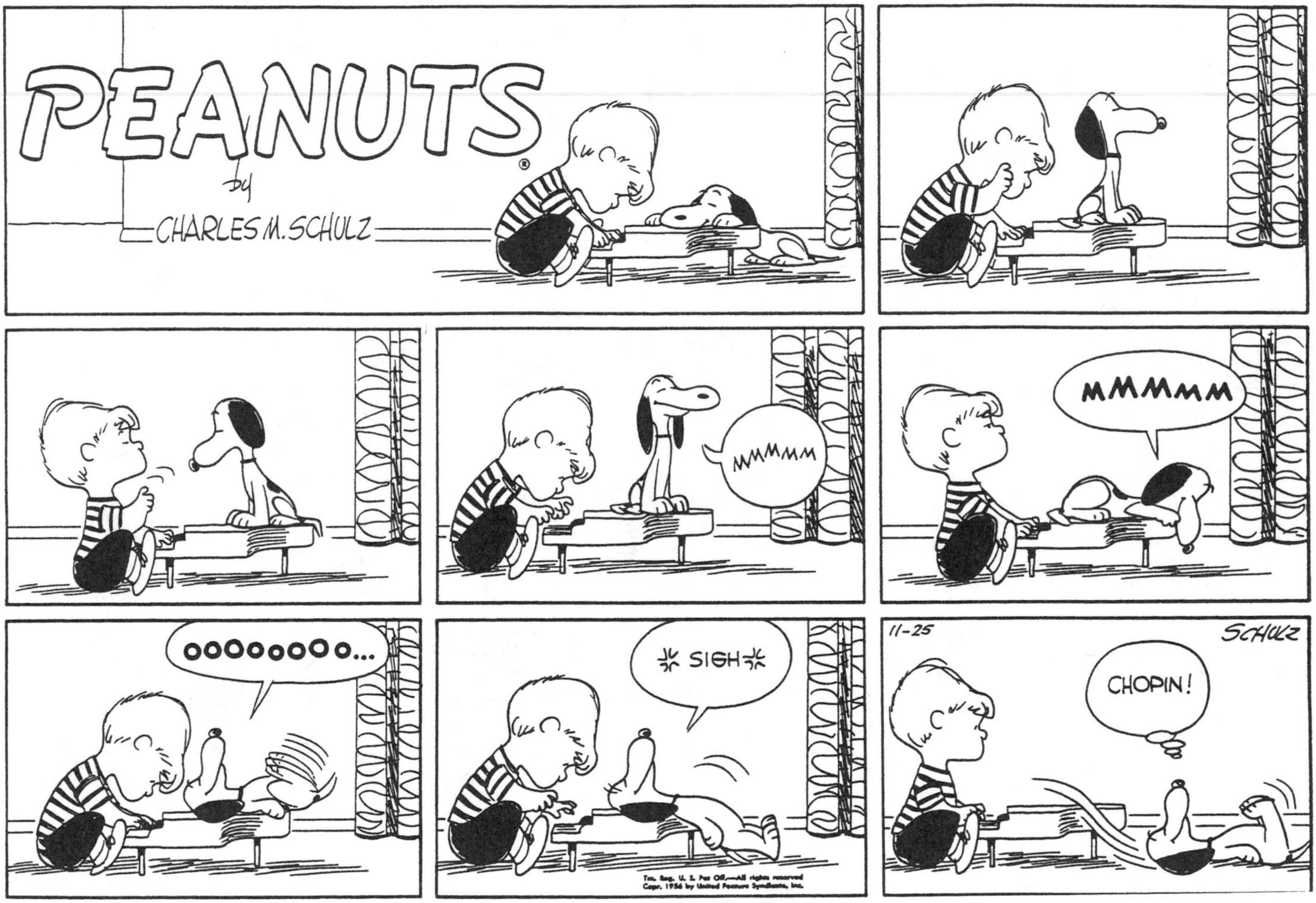
PEANUTS
by
CHARLES M. SCHULZ
MMMMM
MMMMM
OOOOoooOo...
SIGH
Tm. Reg. U. S. Pat. Off.—All rights reserved
Copr. 1956 by United Feature Syndicate, Inc.
11-25
SCHULZ
CHOPIN!

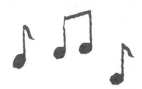

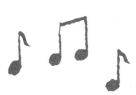

PEANUTS
by
CHARLES M. SCHULZ
BEAUTIFUL! BEAUTIFUL!
MMMMMMMMM
MMMMM
♪
?
Tm. Reg. U. S. Pat. Off.—All rights reserved
Copr. 1956 by United Feature Syndicate, Inc.
!
12-30
SCHULZ
SIGH

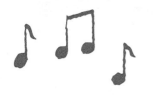

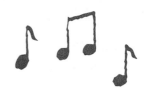

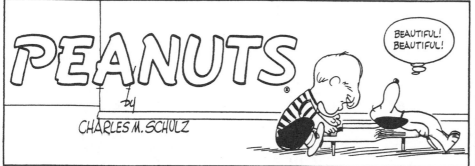

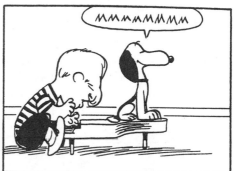

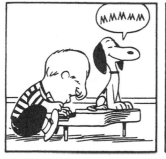

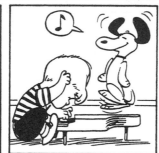

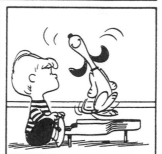

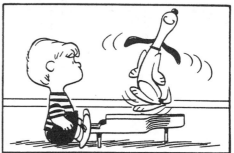

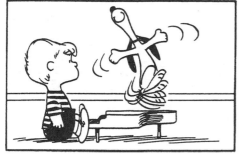

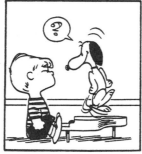

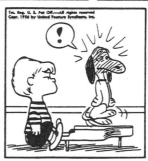

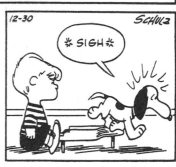

PEANUTS
BEAUTIFUL! BEAUTIFUL!
MMM..
Tm. Reg. U. S. Pat Off.—All rights reserved
Copr. 1957 by United Feature Syndicate, Inc.
MMMMMMMM
AH, MENDELSSOHN!
1-30
SCHULZ

PEANUTS
BEAUTIFUL! JUST BEAUTIFUL!
Tm. Reg. U. S. Pat Off.—All rights reserved
Copr. 1957 by United Feature Syndicate, Inc.
PAPA HAYDN!
2-2
SCHULZ

PEANUTS
"BEETHOVEN TOOK THIS REBUFF VERY HARD."
"FOR WEEKS AFTERWARD HE WAS EXTREMELY UNHAPPY...."
2-20
HOW COULD ANYONE BE BEETHOVEN AND NOT BE HAPPY?
SCHULZ

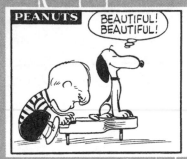

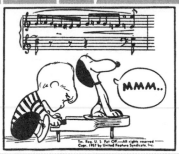

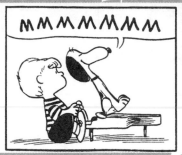

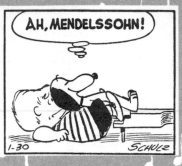

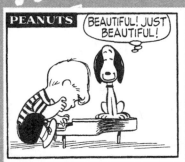

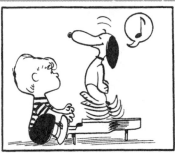

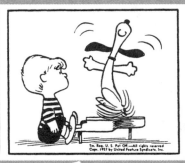

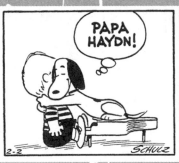

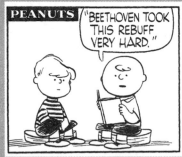

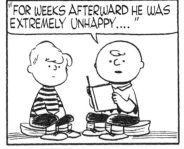

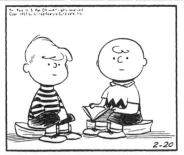

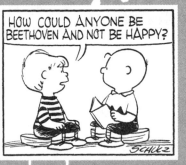

PEANUTS
THIS IS MENDELSSOHN'S 'SONGS WITHOUT WORDS'..
Tm. Reg. U. S. Pat. Off.—All rights reserved Copr. 1957 by United Feature Syndicate, Inc.
3-8
COULDN'T HE THINK OF ANY?
SCHULZ

PEANUTS
LOOK, SCHROEDER.. THE CATCHER IS SUPPOSED TO BE THE BACKBONE OF THE TEAM..
HOW ABOUT SHOWING A LITTLE **SPIRIT**? CAN'T YOU YELL A LITTLE OR **WHISTLE**?!
4-15
Tm. Reg. U. S. Pat. Off.—All rights reserved Copr. 1957 by United Feature Syndicate, Inc.
"NOCTURNE IN E FLAT MAJOR" BY CHOPIN
GOOD GRIEF!
SCHULZ

PEANUTS
SNOOPY LIKES CHOPIN...
HE ALSO SEEMS TO LIKE BRAHMS AND BARTOK...
BUT **BEETHOVEN** REALLY MAKES HIM STAND UP, AND TAKE NOTICE!
SCHULZ 4-29
Tm. Reg. U. S. Pat. Off.—All rights reserved Copr. 1957 by United Feature Syndicate, Inc.

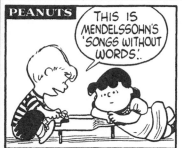

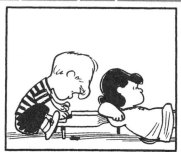

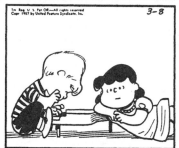

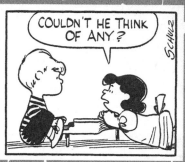

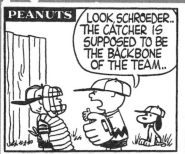

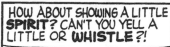

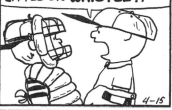

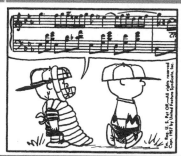

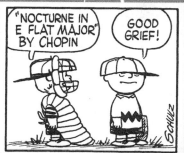

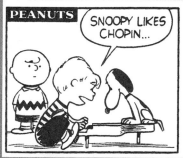

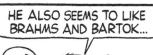

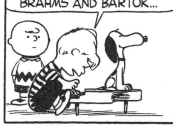

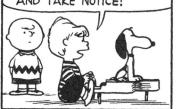

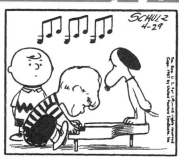

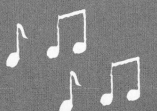

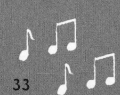

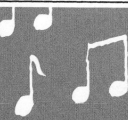

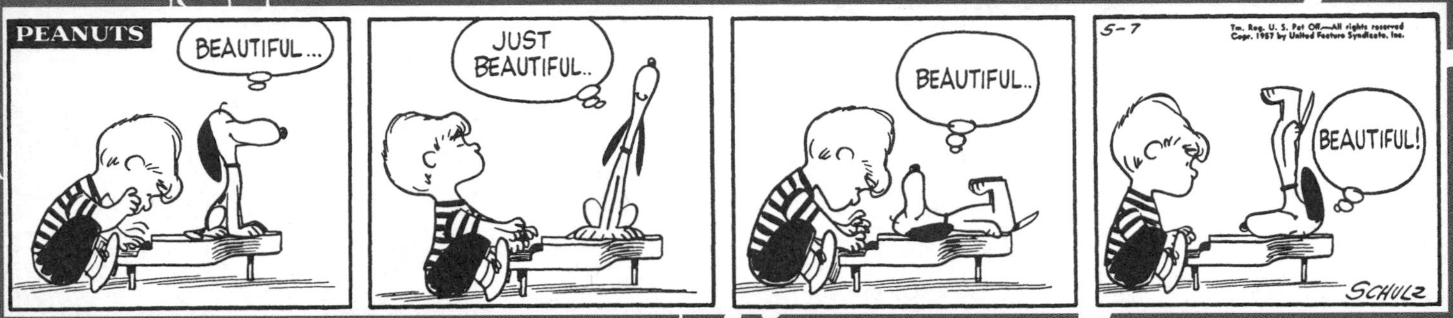
PEANUTS
BEAUTIFUL...
JUST BEAUTIFUL..
BEAUTIFUL..
5-7
Tm. Reg. U. S. Pat. Off.—All rights reserved Copr. 1957 by United Feature Syndicate, Inc.
BEAUTIFUL!
SCHULZ

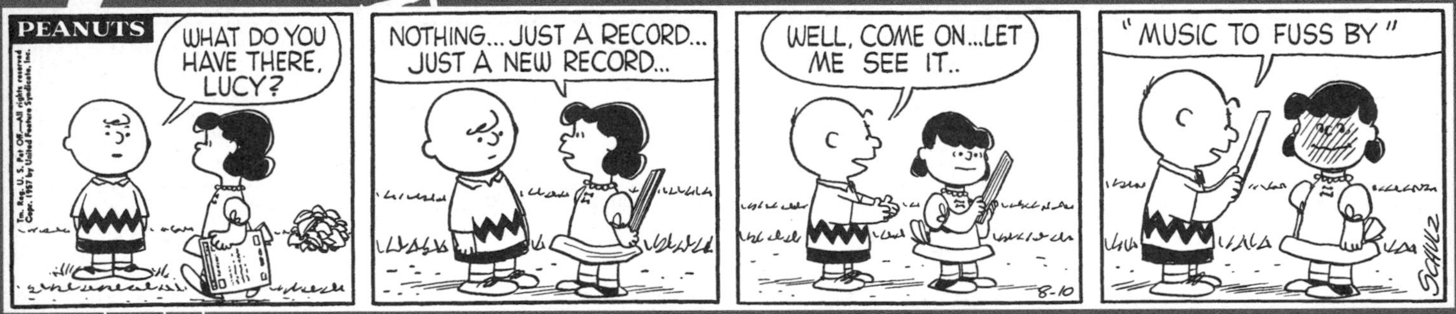
PEANUTS
Tm. Reg. U. S. Pat. Off.—All rights reserved Copr. 1957 by United Feature Syndicate, Inc.
WHAT DO YOU HAVE THERE, LUCY?
NOTHING... JUST A RECORD... JUST A NEW RECORD...
WELL, COME ON...LET ME SEE IT..
8-10
"MUSIC TO FUSS BY"
SCHULZ

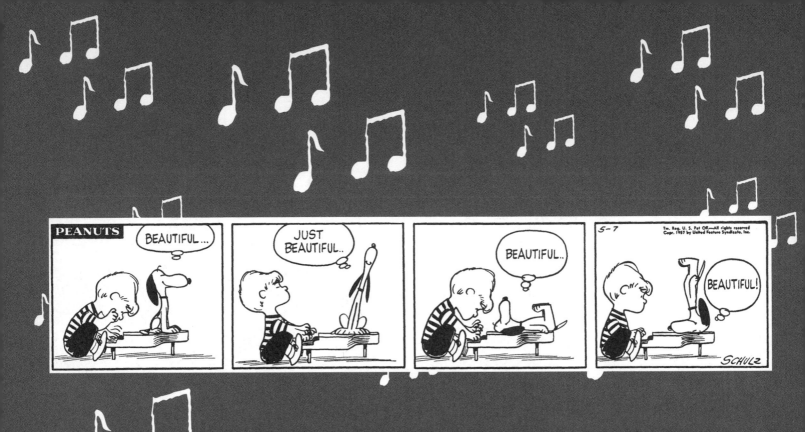

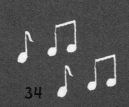

PEANUTS
Tm. Reg. U. S. Pat Off.—All rights reserved
Copr. 1957 by United Feature Syndicate, Inc.
12-30
SCHULZ

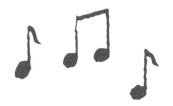

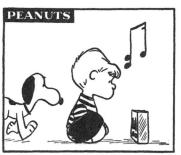

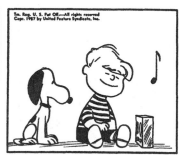

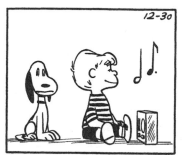

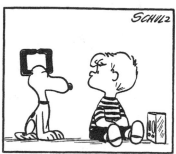

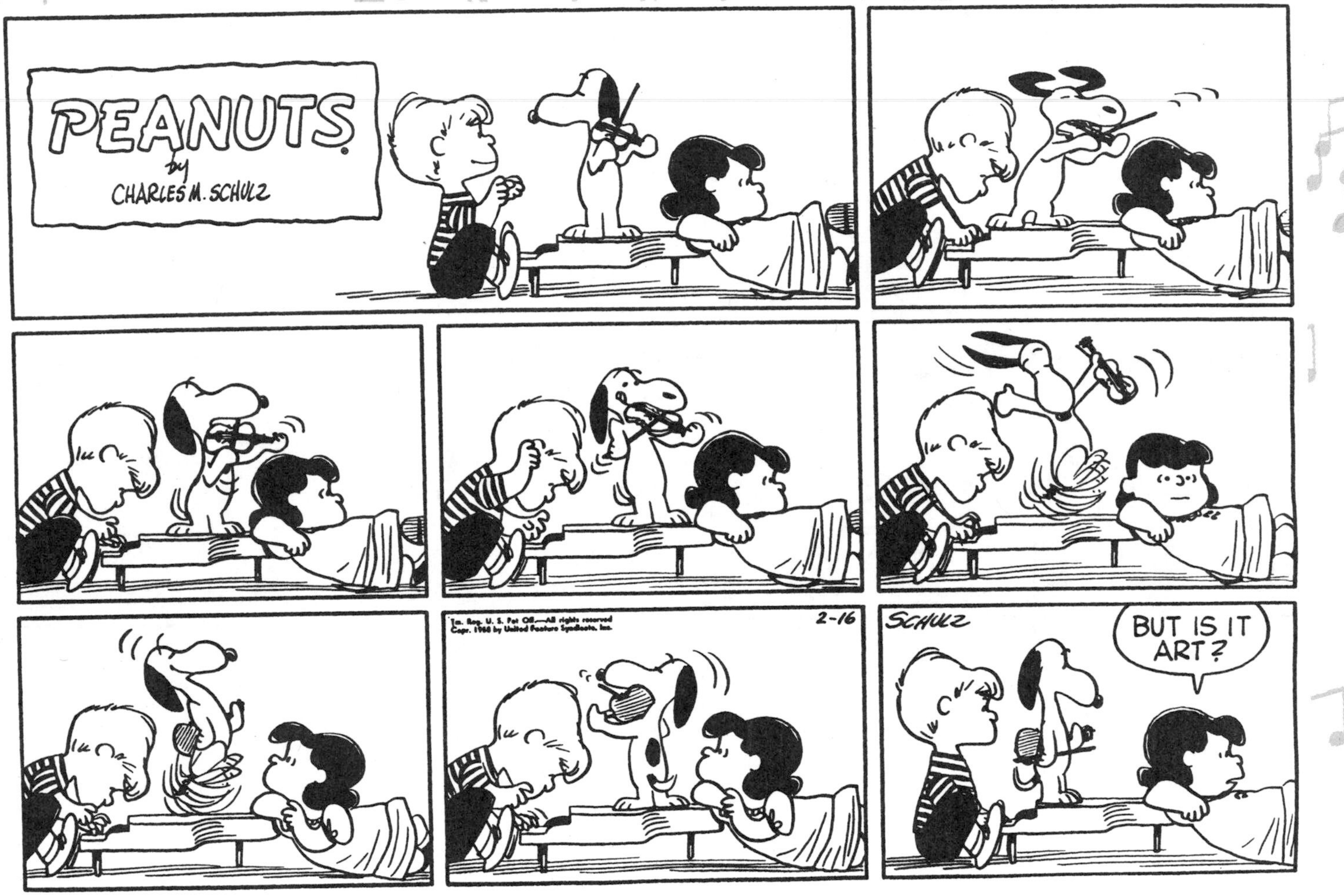
PEANUTS
by
CHARLES M. SCHULZ
Tm. Reg. U. S. Pat. Off.—All rights reserved
Copr. 1958 by United Feature Syndicate, Inc.
2-16
SCHULZ
BUT IS IT ART?

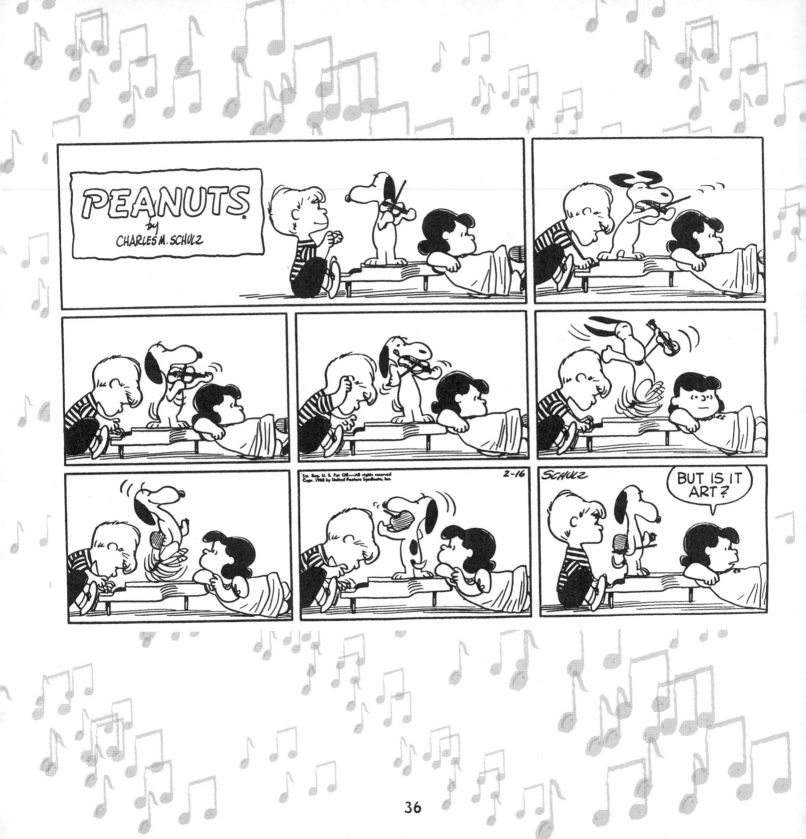

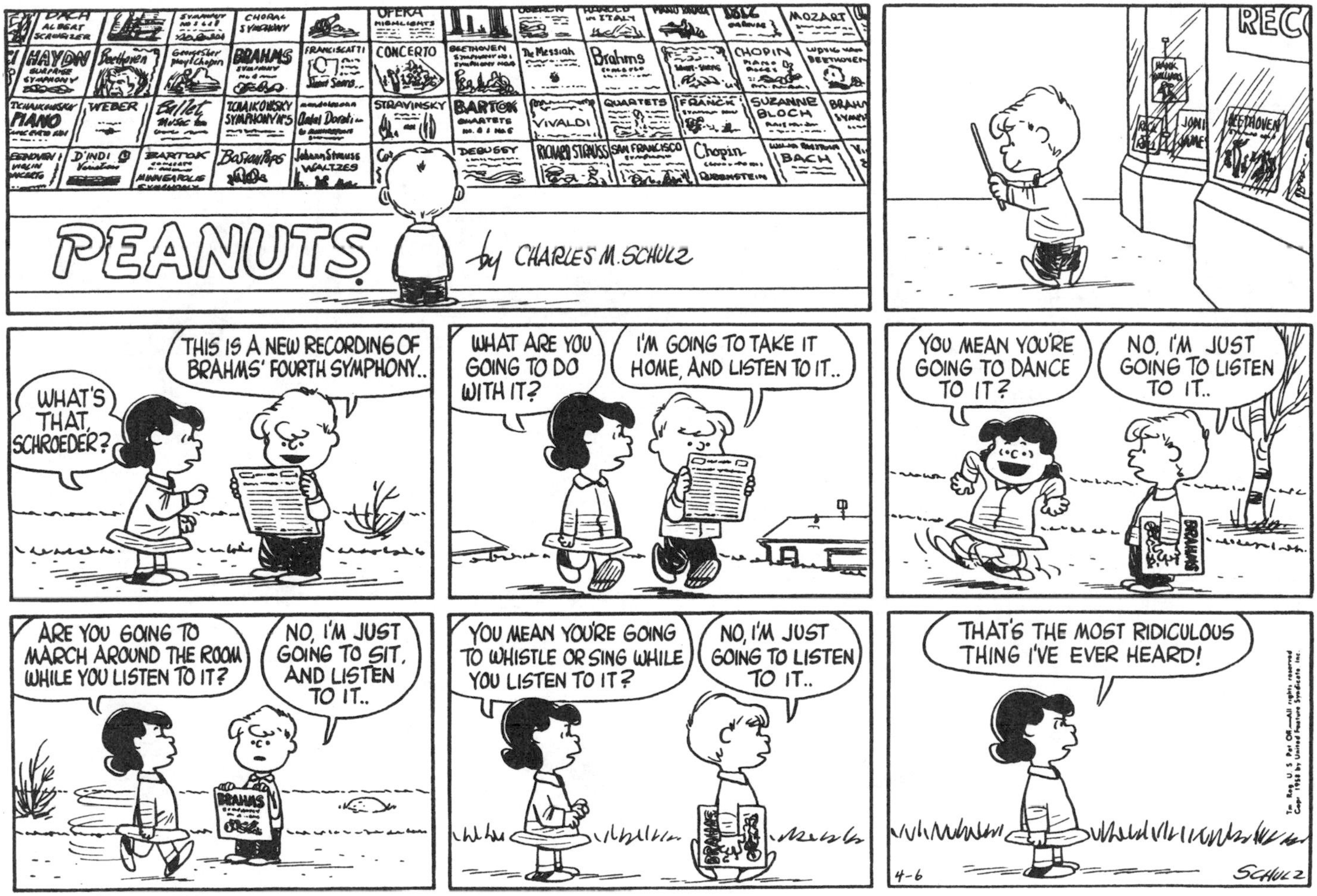
PEANUTS
by CHARLES M. SCHULZ
WHAT'S THAT, SCHROEDER?
THIS IS A NEW RECORDING OF BRAHMS' FOURTH SYMPHONY..
WHAT ARE YOU GOING TO DO WITH IT?
I'M GOING TO TAKE IT HOME, AND LISTEN TO IT..
YOU MEAN YOU'RE GOING TO DANCE TO IT?
NO, I'M JUST GOING TO LISTEN TO IT..
ARE YOU GOING TO MARCH AROUND THE ROOM WHILE YOU LISTEN TO IT?
NO, I'M JUST GOING TO SIT, AND LISTEN TO IT..
YOU MEAN YOU'RE GOING TO WHISTLE OR SING WHILE YOU LISTEN TO IT?
NO, I'M JUST GOING TO LISTEN TO IT..
THAT'S THE MOST RIDICULOUS THING I'VE EVER HEARD!
4-6
SCHULZ

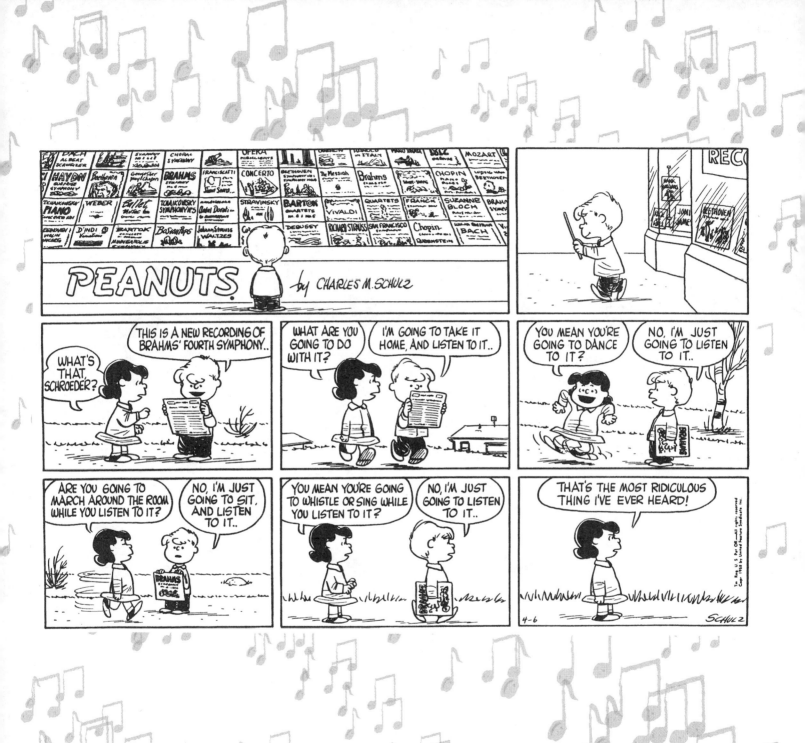

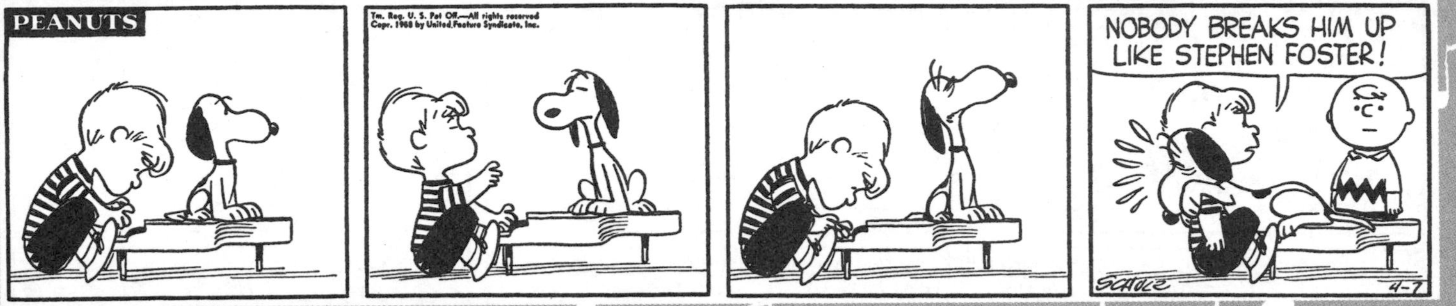
PEANUTS
Tm. Reg. U. S. Pat Off.—All rights reserved
Copr. 1958 by United Feature Syndicate, Inc.
NOBODY BREAKS HIM UP LIKE STEPHEN FOSTER!
SCHULZ
4-7

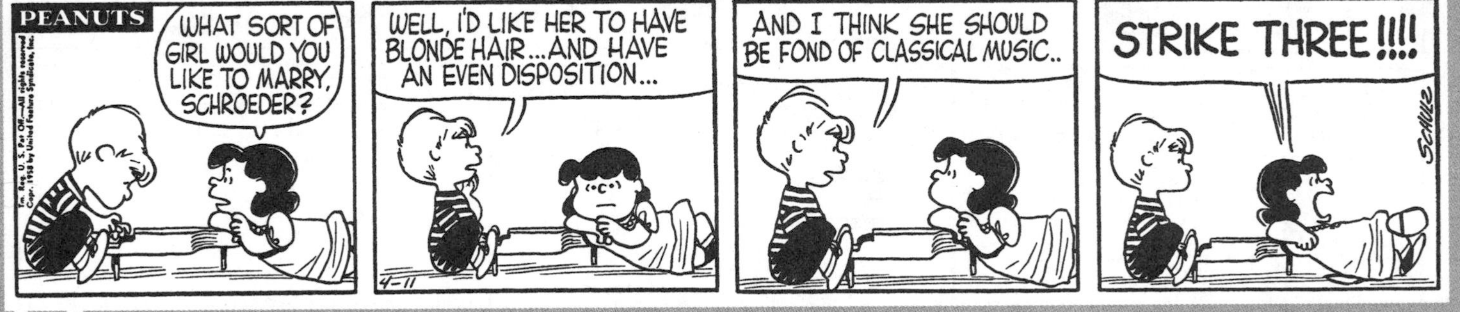
PEANUTS
Tm. Reg. U. S. Pat Off.—All rights reserved
Copr. 1958 by United Feature Syndicate, Inc.
WHAT SORT OF GIRL WOULD YOU LIKE TO MARRY, SCHROEDER?
WELL, I'D LIKE HER TO HAVE BLONDE HAIR...AND HAVE AN EVEN DISPOSITION...
4-11
AND I THINK SHE SHOULD BE FOND OF CLASSICAL MUSIC..
STRIKE THREE!!!!
SCHULZ

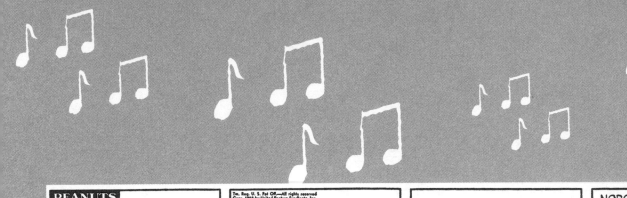

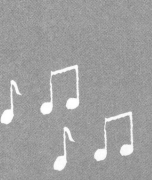

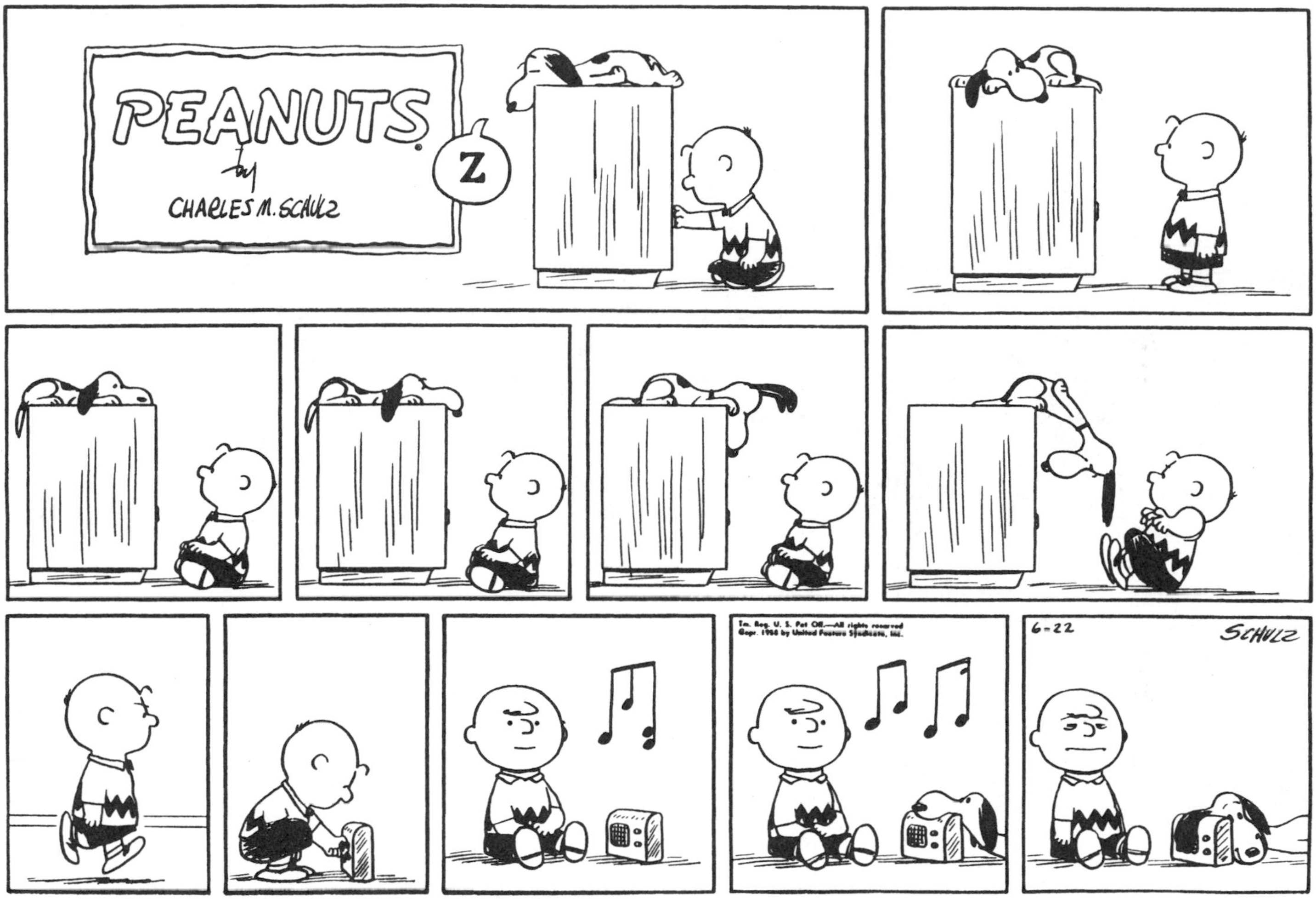
PEANUTS
by
CHARLES M. SCHULZ
Z
Tm. Reg. U. S. Pat. Off.—All rights reserved
Copr. 1958 by United Feature Syndicate, Inc.
6-22
SCHULZ

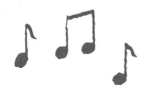

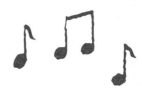

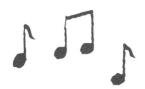

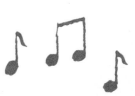

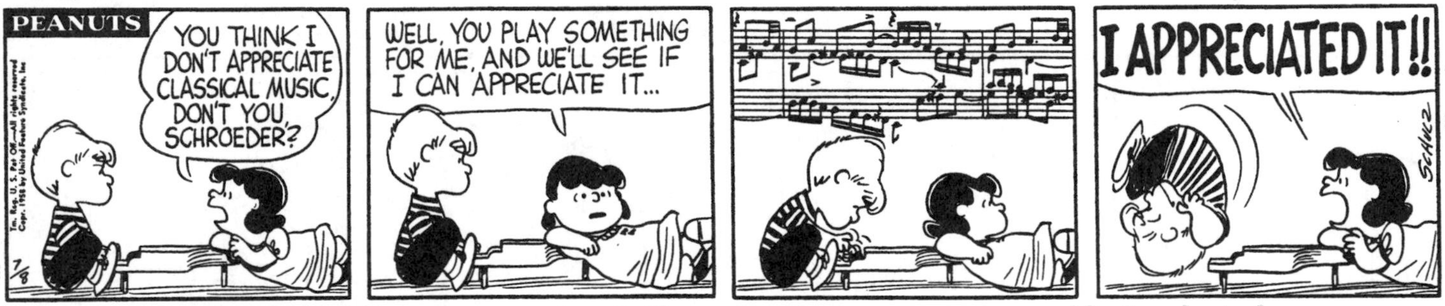
PEANUTS
Tm. Reg. U. S. Pat. Off.—All rights reserved
Copr. 1958 by United Feature Syndicate, Inc
7/8
YOU THINK I DON'T APPRECIATE CLASSICAL MUSIC, DON'T YOU, SCHROEDER?
WELL, YOU PLAY SOMETHING FOR ME, AND WE'LL SEE IF I CAN APPRECIATE IT...
I APPRECIATED IT!!
SCHULZ

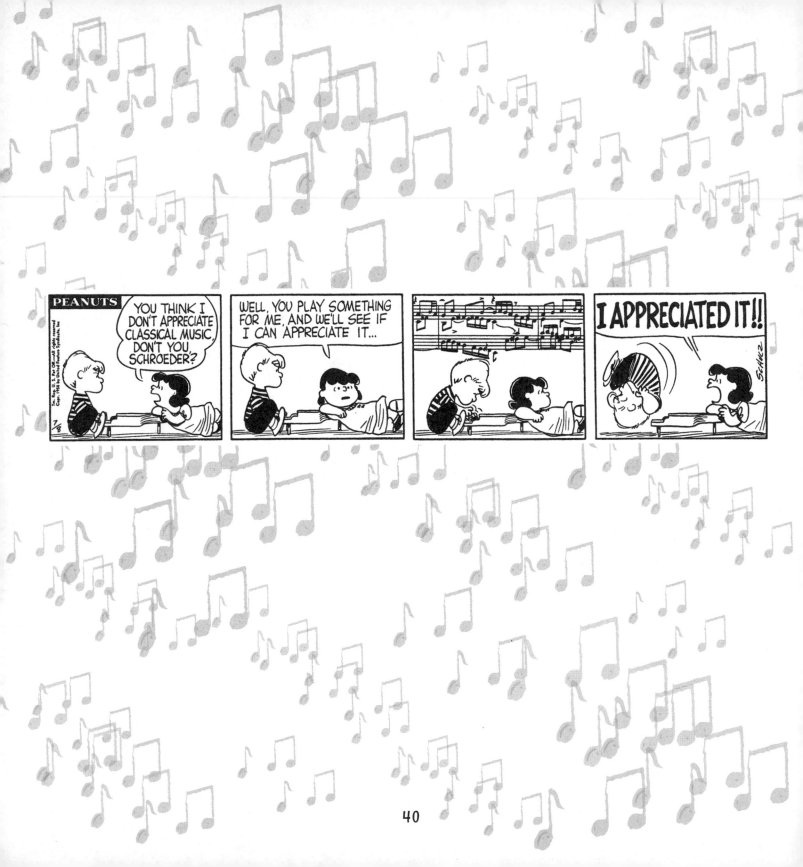

PEANUTS®
by SCHULZ
8-31
Tm. Reg. U. S. Pat Off.—All rights reserved
Copr. 1958 by United Feature Syndicate, Inc.
WAP!
SCHULZ

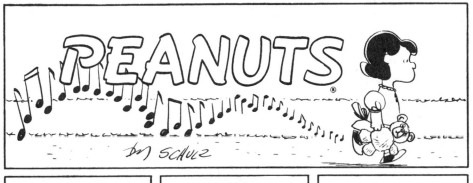

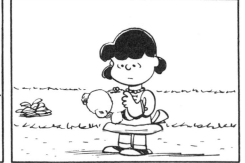

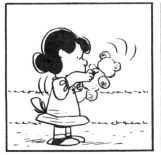

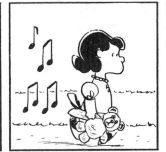

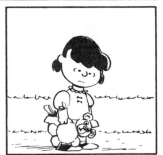

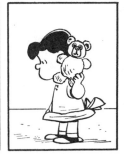

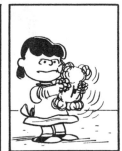

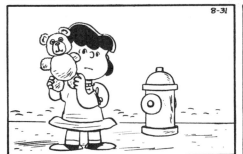

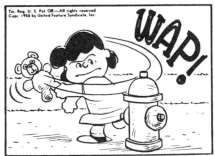

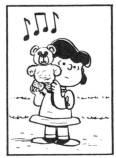

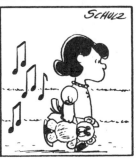

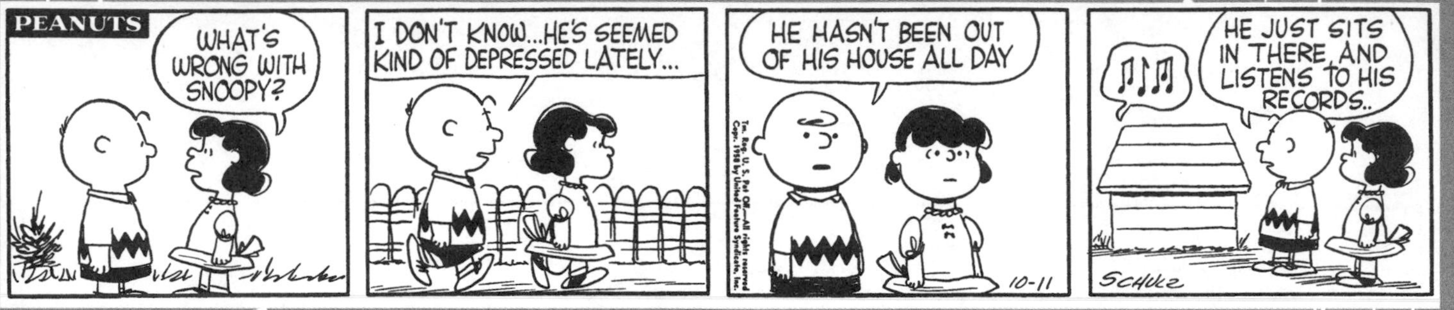
PEANUTS
WHAT'S WRONG WITH SNOOPY?
I DON'T KNOW...HE'S SEEMED KIND OF DEPRESSED LATELY...
HE HASN'T BEEN OUT OF HIS HOUSE ALL DAY
Tm. Reg. U. S. Pat. Off.—All rights reserved Copr. 1958 by United Feature Syndicate, Inc.
10-11
HE JUST SITS IN THERE, AND LISTENS TO HIS RECORDS..
SCHULZ

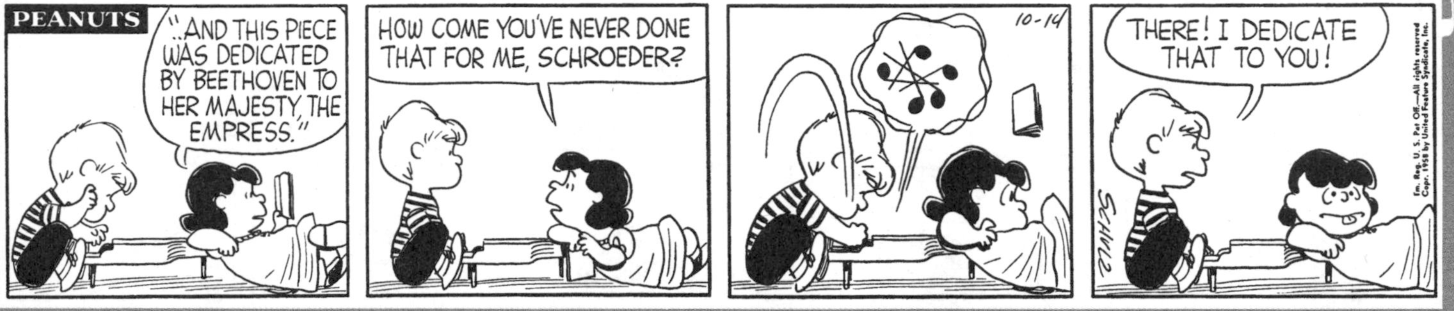
PEANUTS
"..AND THIS PIECE WAS DEDICATED BY BEETHOVEN TO HER MAJESTY, THE EMPRESS."
HOW COME YOU'VE NEVER DONE THAT FOR ME, SCHROEDER?
10-14
THERE! I DEDICATE THAT TO YOU!
SCHULZ
Tm. Reg. U. S. Pat. Off.—All rights reserved Copr. 1958 by United Feature Syndicate, Inc.

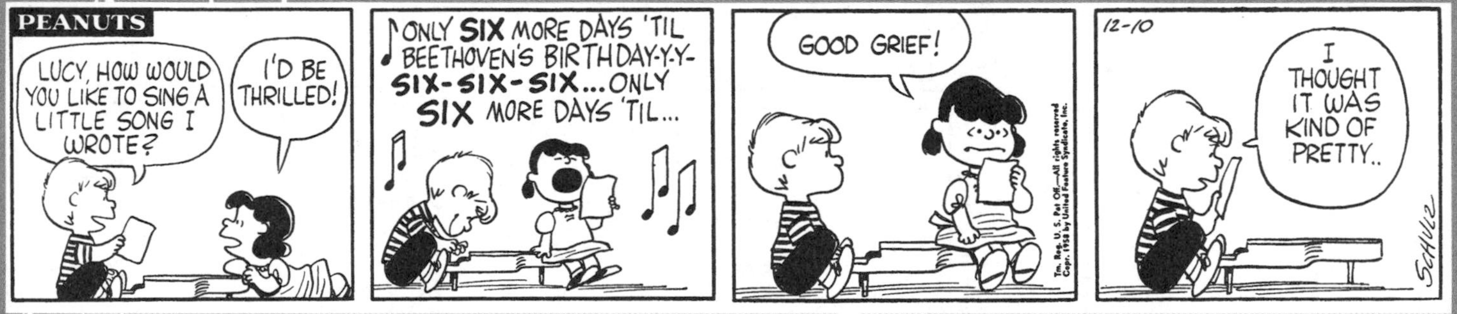
PEANUTS
LUCY, HOW WOULD YOU LIKE TO SING A LITTLE SONG I WROTE?
I'D BE THRILLED!
ONLY SIX MORE DAYS 'TIL BEETHOVEN'S BIRTHDAY-Y-Y-SIX-SIX-SIX...ONLY SIX MORE DAYS 'TIL...
GOOD GRIEF!
Tm. Reg. U. S. Pat. Off.—All rights reserved Copr. 1958 by United Feature Syndicate, Inc.
12-10
I THOUGHT IT WAS KIND OF PRETTY..
SCHULZ

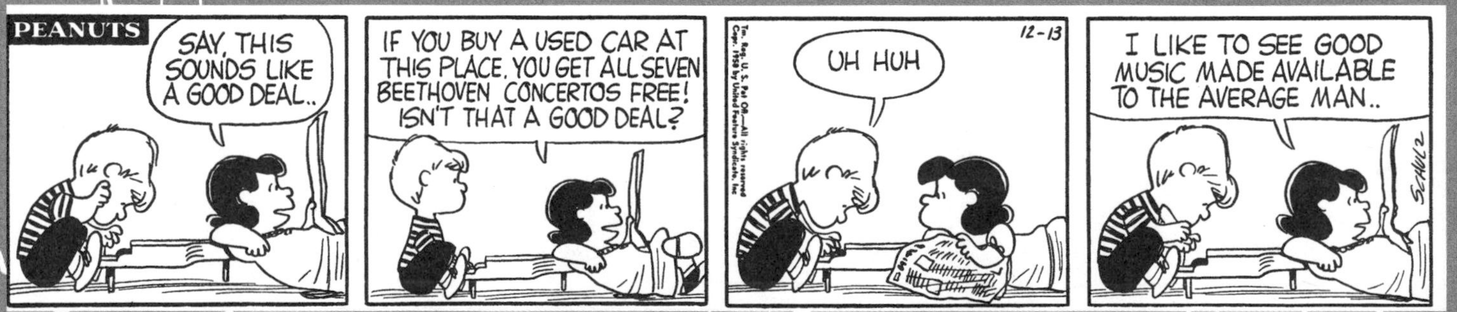
PEANUTS
SAY, THIS SOUNDS LIKE A GOOD DEAL..
IF YOU BUY A USED CAR AT THIS PLACE, YOU GET ALL SEVEN BEETHOVEN CONCERTOS FREE! ISN'T THAT A GOOD DEAL?
Tm. Reg. U. S. Pat. Off.—All rights reserved Copr. 1958 by United Feature Syndicate, Inc.
12-13
UH HUH
I LIKE TO SEE GOOD MUSIC MADE AVAILABLE TO THE AVERAGE MAN..
SCHULZ

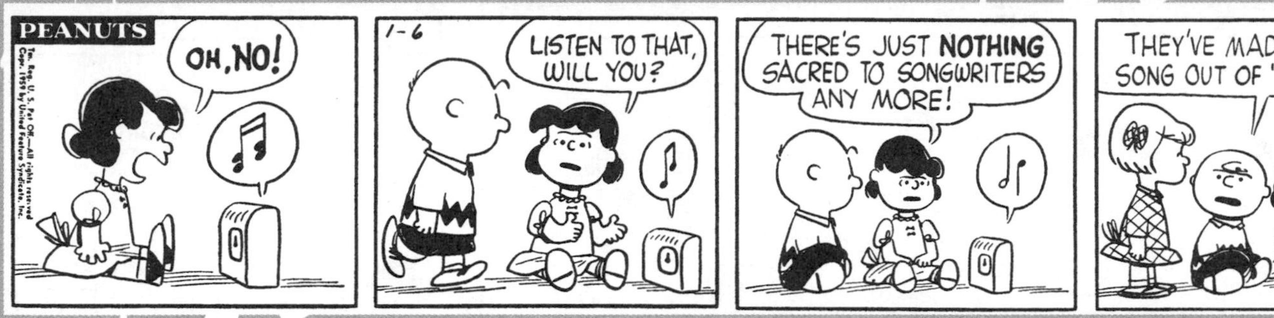
PEANUTS
OH, NO!
1-6
LISTEN TO THAT, WILL YOU?
THERE'S JUST **NOTHING** SACRED TO SONGWRITERS ANY MORE!
THEY'VE MADE A POPULAR SONG OUT OF "STARDUST"!
SCHULZ

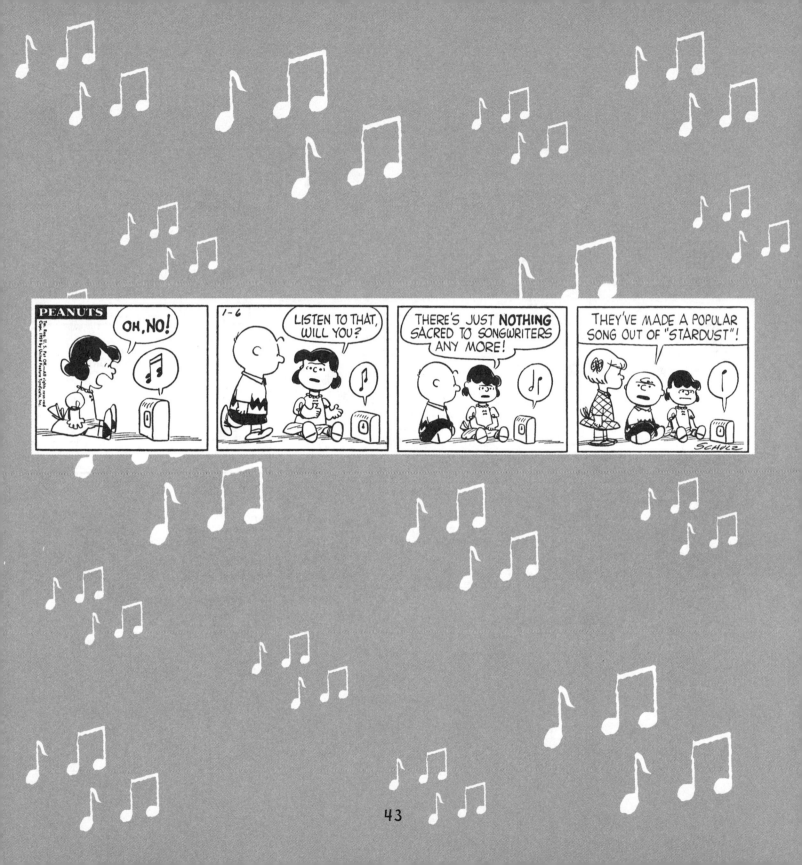

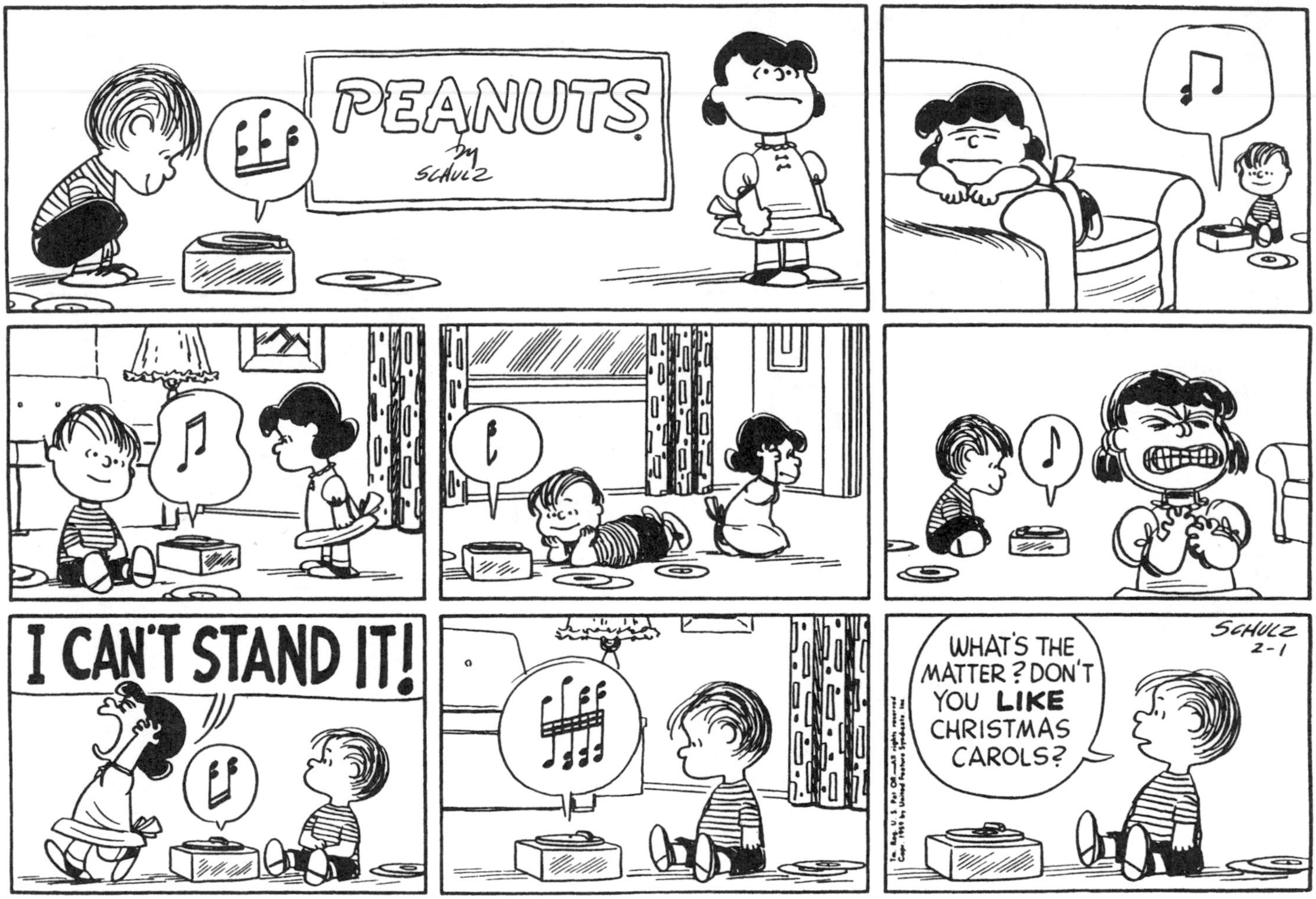
PEANUTS
by
SCHULZ
I CAN'T STAND IT!
SCHULZ
2-1
WHAT'S THE MATTER? DON'T YOU LIKE CHRISTMAS CAROLS?

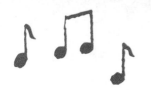

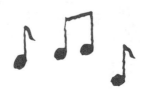

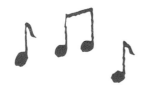

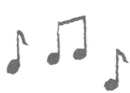

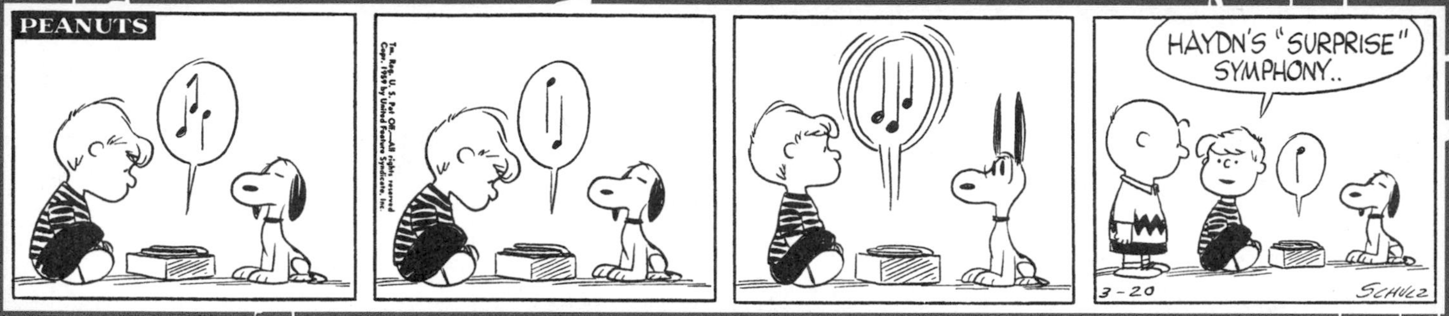
PEANUTS
HAYDN'S "SURPRISE" SYMPHONY..
3-20
SCHULZ

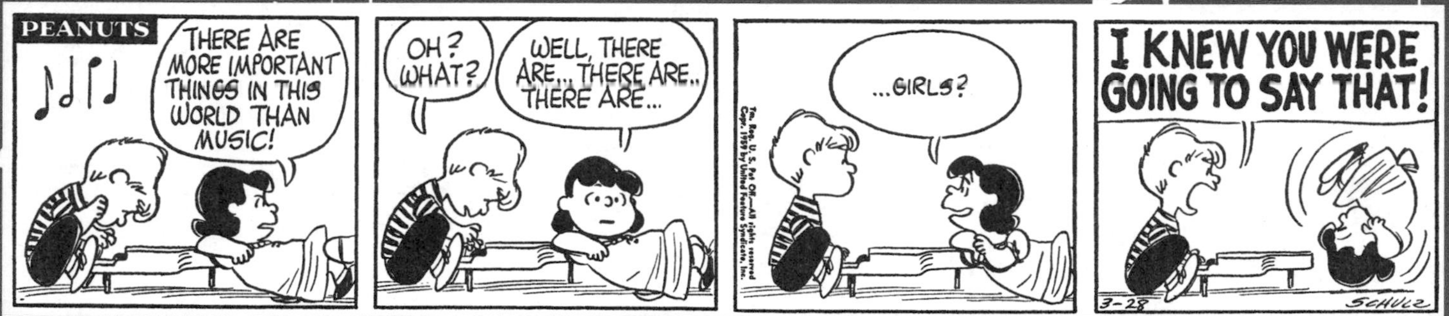
PEANUTS
THERE ARE MORE IMPORTANT THINGS IN THIS WORLD THAN MUSIC!
OH? WHAT?
WELL, THERE ARE... THERE ARE.. THERE ARE...
...GIRLS?
I KNEW YOU WERE GOING TO SAY THAT!
3-28
SCHULZ

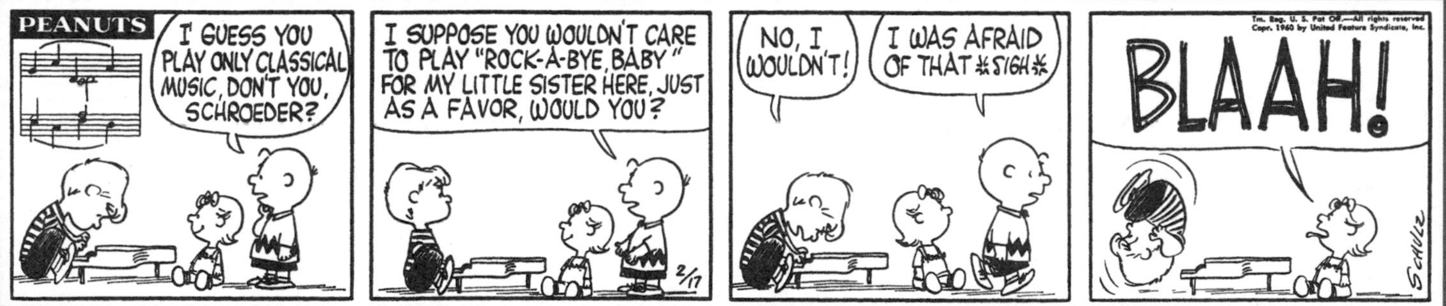
PEANUTS
I GUESS YOU PLAY ONLY CLASSICAL MUSIC, DON'T YOU, SCHROEDER?
I SUPPOSE YOU WOULDN'T CARE TO PLAY "ROCK-A-BYE, BABY" FOR MY LITTLE SISTER HERE, JUST AS A FAVOR, WOULD YOU?
2/17
NO, I WOULDN'T!
I WAS AFRAID OF THAT *SIGH*
Tm. Reg. U. S. Pat. Off.—All rights reserved Copr. 1960 by United Feature Syndicate, Inc.
BLAAH!
SCHULZ

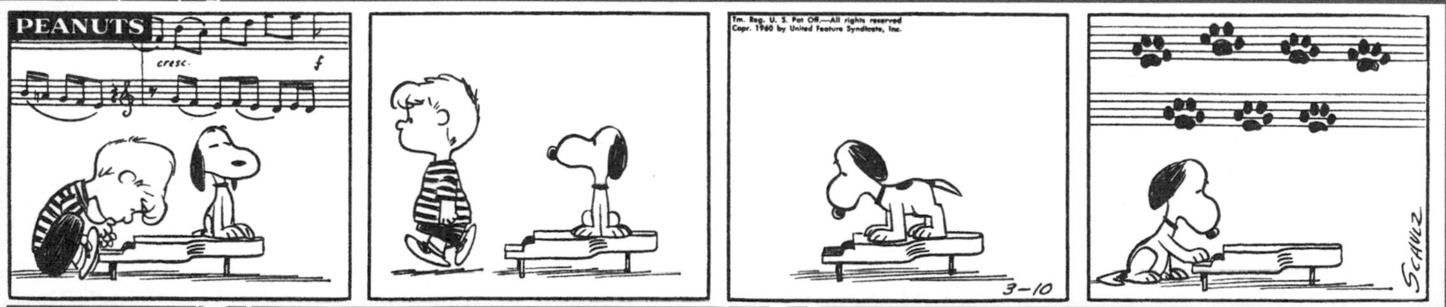
PEANUTS
cresc.
f
Tm. Reg. U. S. Pat. Off.—All rights reserved Copr. 1960 by United Feature Syndicate, Inc.
3-10
SCHULZ

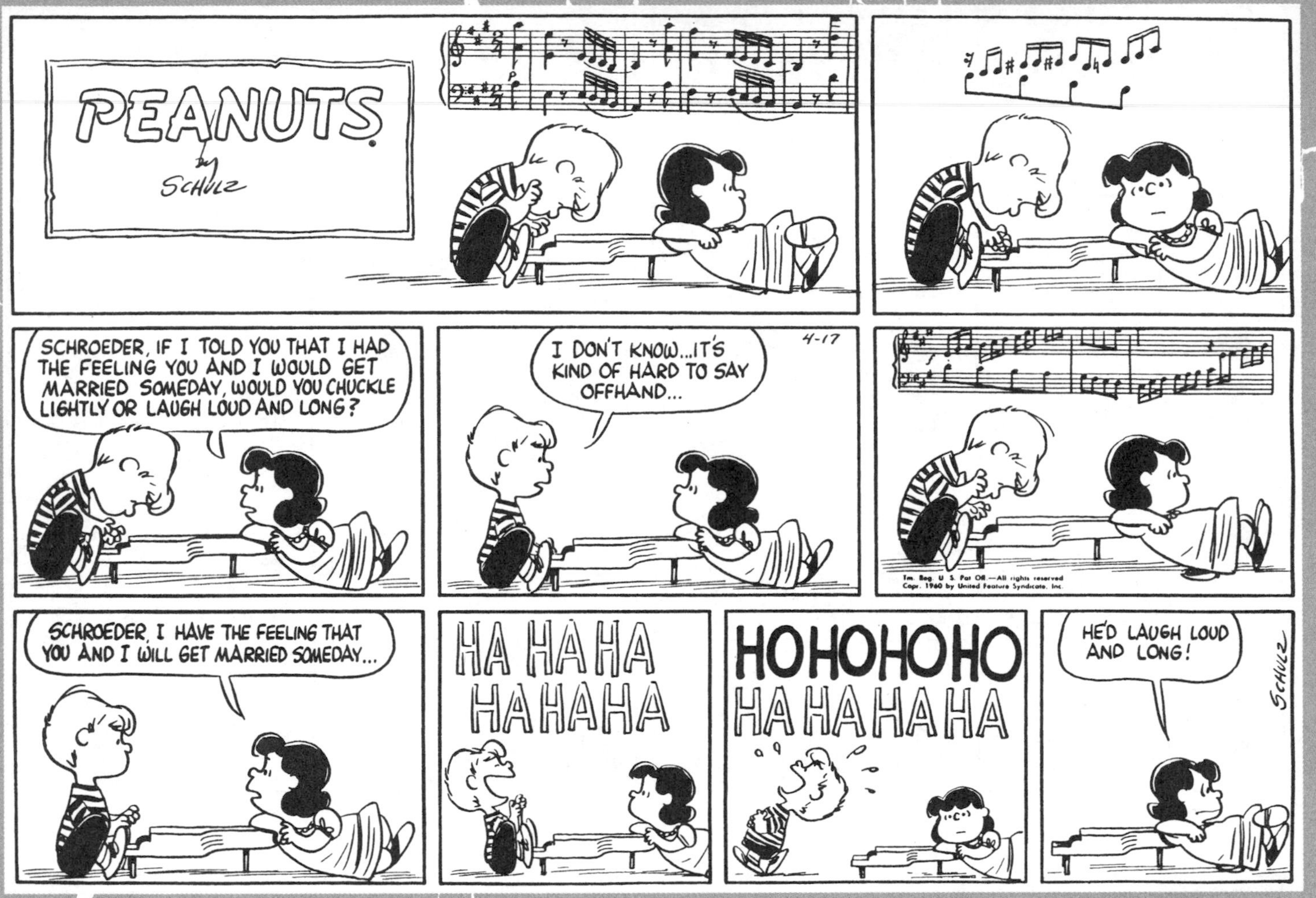
PEANUTS
by SCHULZ
SCHROEDER, IF I TOLD YOU THAT I HAD THE FEELING YOU AND I WOULD GET MARRIED SOMEDAY, WOULD YOU CHUCKLE LIGHTLY OR LAUGH LOUD AND LONG?
I DON'T KNOW...IT'S KIND OF HARD TO SAY OFFHAND...
4-17
Tm. Reg. U. S. Pat. Off.—All rights reserved
Copr. 1960 by United Feature Syndicate, Inc.
SCHROEDER, I HAVE THE FEELING THAT YOU AND I WILL GET MARRIED SOMEDAY...
HA HA HA HA
HA HA HA
HOHOHOHOHO
HA HA HA HA HA
HE'D LAUGH LOUD AND LONG!
SCHULZ

PEANUTS
I THINK YOU AND I ARE GROWING CLOSER TOGETHER SCHROEDER..
AS YOU WERE PLAYING THAT PIECE BY BEETHOVEN, I THOUGHT TO MYSELF, "HOW BEAUTIFUL!"
5-6
AND THEN I THOUGHT, "IF HE LIKES BEETHOVEN AND I LIKE BEETHOVEN, WHAT A WONDERFUL EXPERIENCE TO SHARE!"
SCHULZ
THAT WAS BY BRAHMS!
Tm. Reg. U. S. Pat. Off.—All rights reserved
Copr. 1960 by United Feature Syndicate, Inc.

PEANUTS
9-27
THAT WAS VERY BEAUTIFUL, SCHROEDER...WHAT WAS IT?
Tm. Reg. U. S. Pat. Off.—All rights reserved
Copr. 1960 by United Feature Syndicate, Inc.
THAT WAS BEETHOVEN'S SONATA NO. 11, OPUS 22
NOW YOU HAVE ME WORRIED...
LITTLE BY LITTLE BEETHOVEN IS SNEAKING AROUND, OVER AND UNDER MY MENTAL BLOCK!
SCHULZ

PEANUTS
WHAT ARE YOU GOING TO GET ME FOR BEETHOVEN'S BIRTHDAY, SCHROEDER?
A MILLION-DOLLAR DIAMOND NECKLACE!
Tm. Reg. U. S. Pat. Off.—All rights reserved
Copr. 1960 by United Feature Syndicate, Inc.
THAT WILL BE NICE
11/15
I LOVE GEMS!
SCHULZ

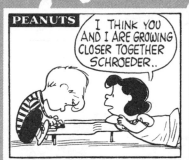

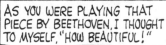

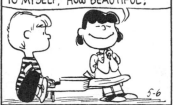

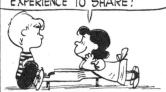

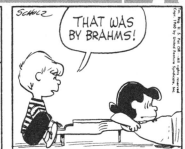

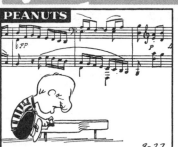

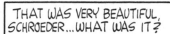

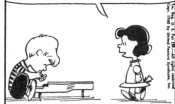

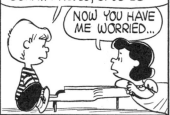

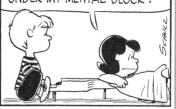

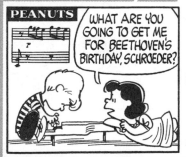

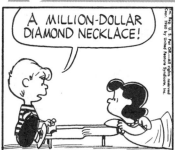

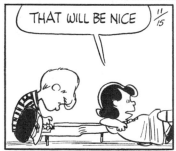

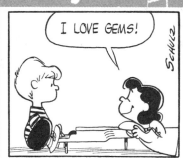

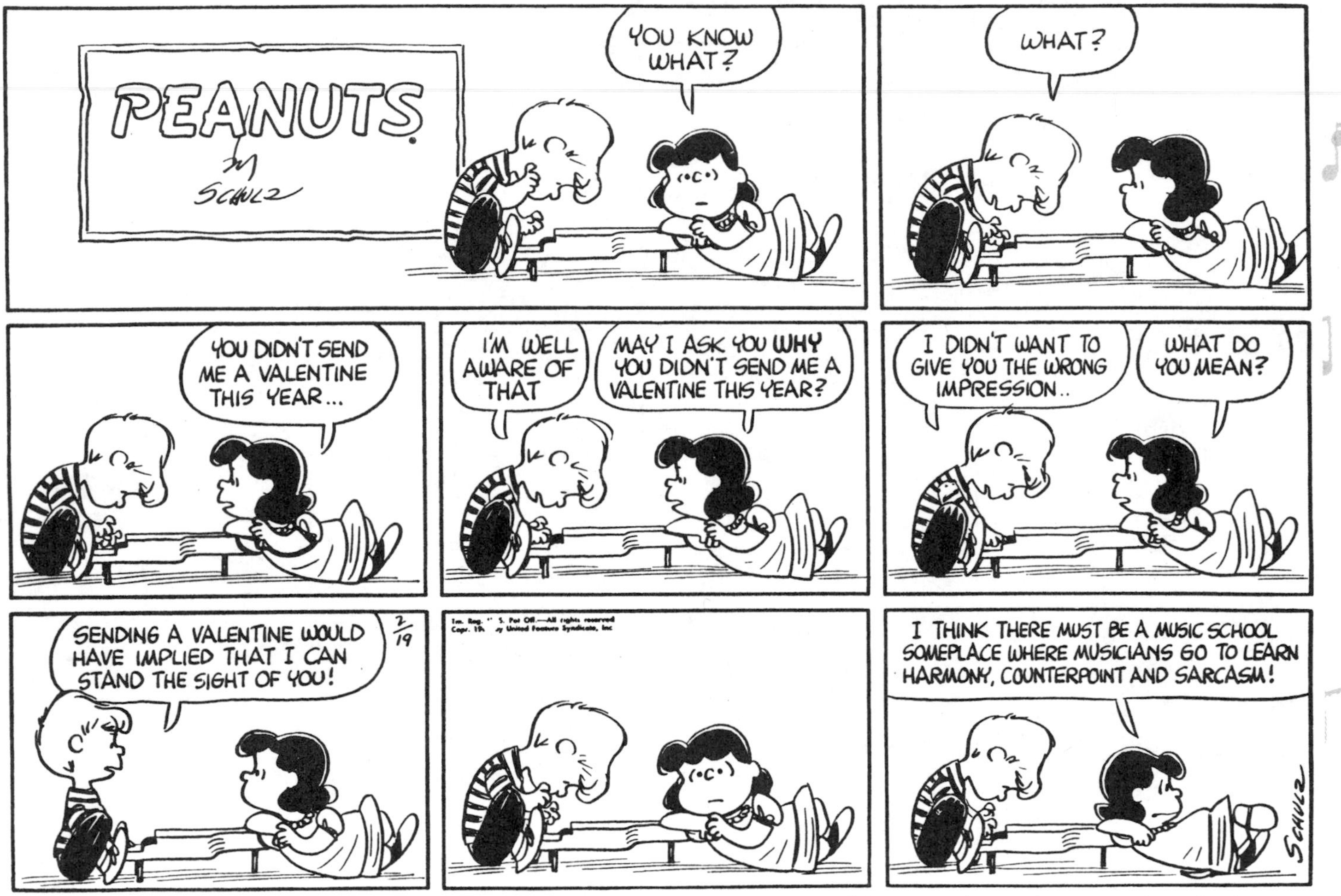
PEANUTS
SCHULZ
YOU KNOW WHAT?
WHAT?
YOU DIDN'T SEND ME A VALENTINE THIS YEAR...
I'M WELL AWARE OF THAT
MAY I ASK YOU **WHY** YOU DIDN'T SEND ME A VALENTINE THIS YEAR?
I DIDN'T WANT TO GIVE YOU THE WRONG IMPRESSION..
WHAT DO YOU MEAN?
SENDING A VALENTINE WOULD HAVE IMPLIED THAT I CAN STAND THE SIGHT OF YOU!
2/19
I THINK THERE MUST BE A MUSIC SCHOOL SOMEPLACE WHERE MUSICIANS GO TO LEARN HARMONY, COUNTERPOINT AND SARCASM!
SCHULZ

PEANUTS
ALL YOU EVER THINK OF IS THIS STUPID PIANO!
I SUPPOSE YOU THINK YOU'RE GOING TO BE ANOTHER BEETHOVEN!
I'M GOING TO BE MORE THAN THAT...
Tm. Reg. U. S. Pat. Off.—All rights reserved
Copr. 1961 by United Feature Syndicate, Inc.
I'M GOING TO BE THE **SAM SNEAD** OF MUSIC!!!
SCHULZ
6/1

PEANUTS
BOOM BIDDY BOOM
BOOM BIDDY BOOM
Tm. Reg. U. S. Pat. Off.—All rights reserved
Copr. 1961 by United Feature Syndicate, Inc.
UM PAW UM PAW UM PAW PAW
9-4
UM PAW PAW?
SCHULZ

PEANUTS
I HAVE A FRIEND WHO PLAYS THE ACCORDION..
HE CAN PLAY POLKAS, WALTZES, SCHOTTISHES...ALL SORTS OF THINGS..YOU KNOW, THE KIND OF TUNES THAT PEOPLE LIKE TO HEAR
5/9
AAUGH!
Tm. Reg. U. S. Pat. Off.—All rights reserved Copr. 1962 by United Feature Syndicate, Inc.
I KNEW THAT WOULD GET HIM!
SCHULZ

PEANUTS
YOU WANT TO HEAR SOME **REAL** MUSIC? LISTEN TO THIS!
Tm. Reg. U. S. Pat. Off.—All rights reserved Copr. 1962 by United Feature Syndicate, Inc.
POLKAS, SCHOTTISHES AND WALTZES
POLKAS, SCHOTTISHES AND WALTZES
SEE? THAT'S REAL MUSIC! THAT'S THE SORT OF MUSIC THAT PEOPLE LIKE! NOT THAT OL' BEETHOVEN STUFF!
5-10
I CAN'T STAND IT! I JUST CAN'T STAND IT!
POLKAS, SCHOTTISHES AND WALTZES
POLKAS, SCHOTTISHES AND WALTZES
SCHULZ

PEANUTS
YOU DON'T WANNA PLAY BALL, HUH?
NOPE!
ALL RIGHT... I'LL GO FIND SOMEONE ELSE..
SORRY..
Tm. Reg. U. S. Pat. Off.—All rights reserved
Copr. 1962 by United Feature Syndicate, Inc.
5-11
POLKAS, SCHOTTISHES AND WALTZES
POLKAS, SCHOTTISHES AND WALTZES
ALL I CARE ABOUT IS MY MUSIC!
SCHULZ

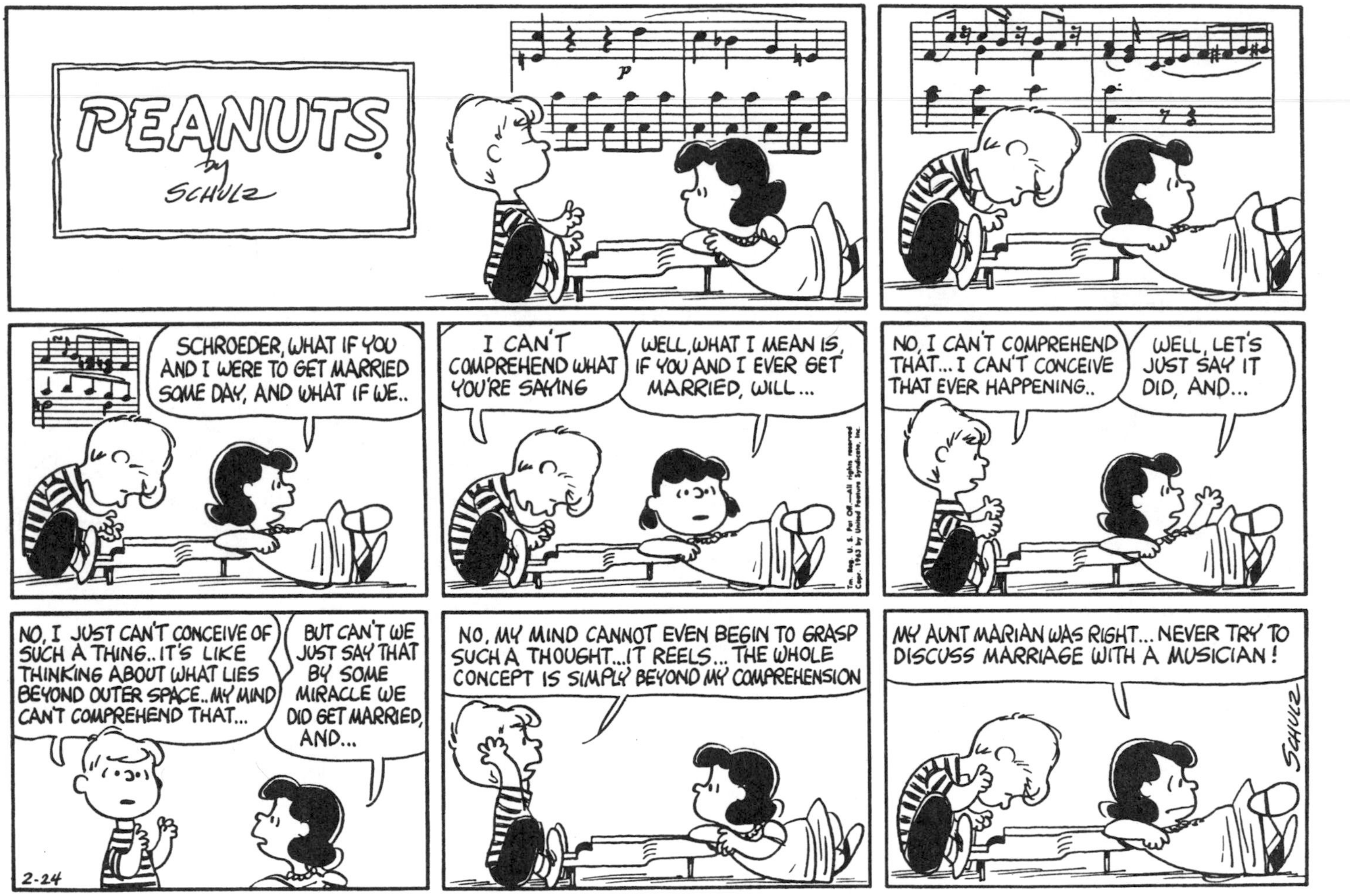
PEANUTS
by SCHULZ
SCHROEDER, WHAT IF YOU AND I WERE TO GET MARRIED SOME DAY, AND WHAT IF WE..
I CAN'T COMPREHEND WHAT YOU'RE SAYING
WELL, WHAT I MEAN IS, IF YOU AND I EVER GET MARRIED, WILL...
NO, I CAN'T COMPREHEND THAT... I CAN'T CONCEIVE THAT EVER HAPPENING..
WELL, LET'S JUST SAY IT DID, AND...
NO, I JUST CAN'T CONCEIVE OF SUCH A THING.. IT'S LIKE THINKING ABOUT WHAT LIES BEYOND OUTER SPACE.. MY MIND CAN'T COMPREHEND THAT...
BUT CAN'T WE JUST SAY THAT BY SOME MIRACLE WE DID GET MARRIED, AND...
2-24
NO, MY MIND CANNOT EVEN BEGIN TO GRASP SUCH A THOUGHT... IT REELS... THE WHOLE CONCEPT IS SIMPLY BEYOND MY COMPREHENSION
MY AUNT MARIAN WAS RIGHT... NEVER TRY TO DISCUSS MARRIAGE WITH A MUSICIAN!
SCHULZ

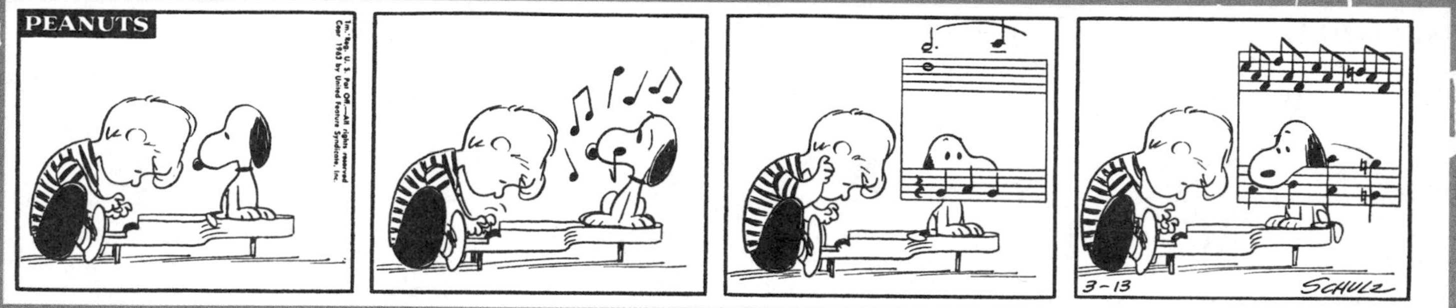
PEANUTS
3-13
SCHULZ

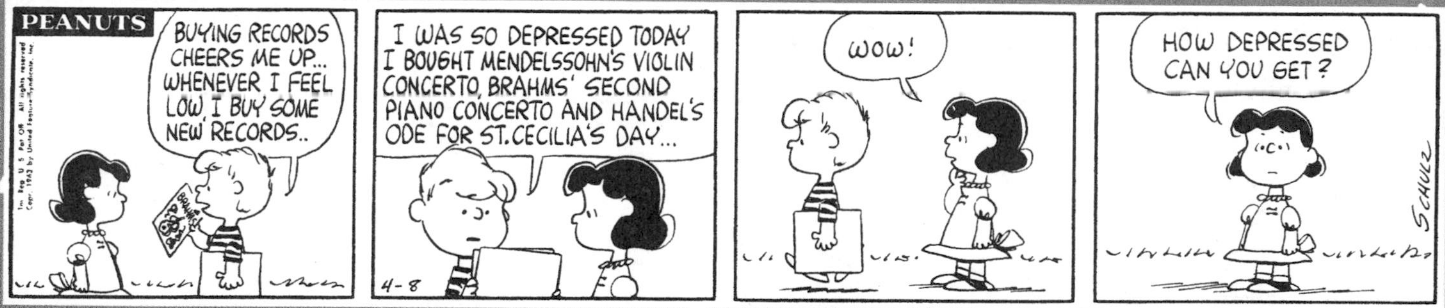
PEANUTS
BUYING RECORDS CHEERS ME UP... WHENEVER I FEEL LOW, I BUY SOME NEW RECORDS..
I WAS SO DEPRESSED TODAY I BOUGHT MENDELSSOHN'S VIOLIN CONCERTO, BRAHMS' SECOND PIANO CONCERTO AND HANDEL'S ODE FOR ST. CECILIA'S DAY...
WOW!
HOW DEPRESSED CAN YOU GET?
SCHULZ

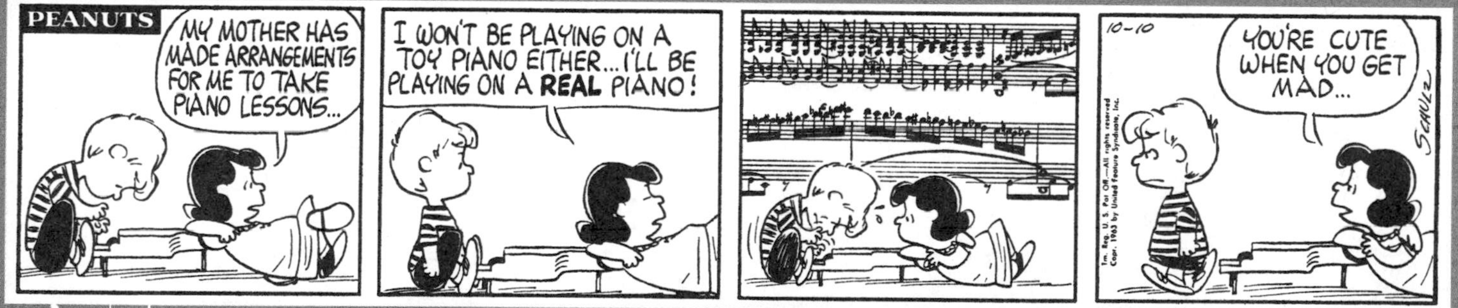
PEANUTS
MY MOTHER HAS MADE ARRANGEMENTS FOR ME TO TAKE PIANO LESSONS...
I WON'T BE PLAYING ON A TOY PIANO EITHER... I'LL BE PLAYING ON A REAL PIANO!
10-10
YOU'RE CUTE WHEN YOU GET MAD...
SCHULZ

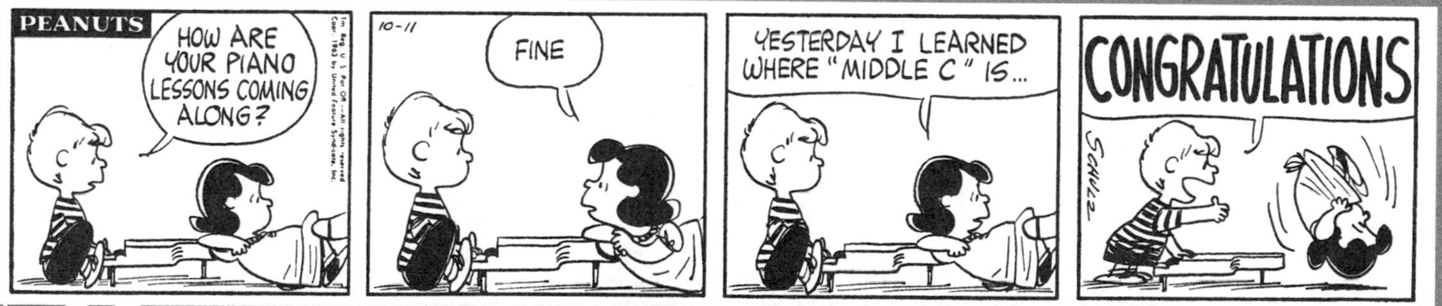
PEANUTS
HOW ARE YOUR PIANO LESSONS COMING ALONG?
10-11
FINE
YESTERDAY I LEARNED WHERE "MIDDLE C" IS...
CONGRATULATIONS
SCHULZ

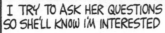

PEANUTS | I THINK MY PIANO TEACHER IS QUITE IMPRESSED BY ME.. | I TRY TO ASK HER QUESTIONS SO SHE'LL KNOW I'M INTERESTED | WHAT SORT OF QUESTIONS? | I ASKED HER IF SHE HAD EVER HEARD OF BEETHOVEN..

PEANUTS | | | THERE! I PLAYED IT ALL THE WAY THROUGH WITHOUT A SINGLE MISTAKE! | LUCK!

PEANUTS | I'LL GIVE YOU THREE NAMES... I'LL BET YOU CAN'T IDENTIFY THEM.. | C.G.NEEFE, ANTONIO SALIERI AND J.G. ALBRECHTSBERGER... | THOSE WERE THREE OF BEETHOVEN'S MUSIC TEACHERS | YOU DRIVE ME CRAZY!

PEANUTS | I DON'T THINK YOU MUSICIANS KNOW WHAT LOVE IS! | ALL YOU EVER THINK ABOUT IS YOUR STUPID MUSIC! ALL YOU THINK ABOUT IS YOUR MUSIC AND YOURSELVES! | YOU DON'T CARE ANYTHING ABOUT OTHER PEOPLE! YOU DON'T CARE ABOUT LOVE OR TENDERNESS OR..

PEANUTS
BEETHOVEN HAD A LOT OF PROBLEMS, DIDN'T HE?
I SUPPOSE IN THOSE DAYS THERE WERE NO SYNDICATED ADVICE COLUMNS FROM WHICH HE COULD GET HELP...
8/27
NO, I DON'T SUPPOSE THERE WERE...
Tm. Reg. U. S. Pat. Off.—All rights reserved
Copr. 1964 by United Feature Syndicate, Inc.
IT'S AMAZING THAT HE DID AS WELL AS HE DID!

PEANUTS
Tm. Reg. U. S. Pat. Off.—All rights reserved
© 1965 by United Feature Syndicate, Inc.
Z
FORTUNATELY, I'M PRACTICING A PIECE WHERE I CAN PLAY **AROUND** HIS NOSE!
Z
1-12
SCHULZ

PEANUTS
4-27
Tm. Reg. U. S. Pat. Off.—All rights reserved
© 1965 by United Feature Syndicate, Inc.
Z
SCHULZ

PEANUTS
I LIKE BEETHOVEN, BUT BRAHMS MAKES ME GLAD I'M ALIVE..
I THINK I'LL GO HOME, AND LISTEN TO BRAHMS' FOURTH...
I FEEL THE NEED TO HAVE THE FEELING THAT IT'S GOOD TO BE ALIVE..
I KNOW WHAT YOU MEAN...
8-17
THAT'S A TERRIBLE FEELING TO HAVE THE NEED OF HAVING THE FEELING OF HAVING...
SCHULZ

PEANUTS
LISTEN..
1-29
DON'T YOU THINK SOME NICE MUSIC IN THE MORNING IS A GOOD WAY TO START THE DAY?
I NEVER WORRY ABOUT HOW I START THE DAY...
IT'S HOW IT ENDS UP THAT BOTHERS ME!
SCHULZ

PEANUTS
YOU THINK BEETHOVEN WAS GREAT...
Tm. Reg. U.S. Pat. Off.—All rights reserved ©1966 by United Feature Syndicate, Inc.
WELL, WHAT ABOUT CHOPIN, BACH, MOZART, BLOCH, BARTOK, BERLIOZ, BIZET, BRAHMS, DELIUS, DEBUSSY AND DVORAK?
WHAT ABOUT ELGAR, FRANCK, GLINKA, GRIEG, HANDEL, HAYDN, HUMPERDINCK, LISZT, MAHLER, MENDELSSOHN, RAVEL, RACHMANINOFF, SCHUBERT, SIBELIUS, TSCHAIKOWSKY AND VIVALDI?
8-20
THEY WERE GREAT, TOO..
RATS! FOR ONE BRIEF MOMENT I THOUGHT I HAD HIM!
SCHULZ

PEANUTS
HI! I HEAR YOU'RE MY CATCHER..
WELL, WE WON'T NEED ANY SIGNALS...I'LL JUST FOG IT BY 'EM, AND YOU CATCH 'EM, OKAY? BY THE WAY, WHAT WAS THAT YOU WERE WHISTLING?
JUST A LITTLE SOMETHING BY BEETHOVEN
OH...
I COME CLEAR ACROSS TOWN TO PLAY BALL, AND WHO DO I GET FOR A CATCHER? A MINIATURE LEONARD BERNSTEIN!
SCHULZ

PEANUTS
HERE'S THE WORLD WAR I FLYING ACE ZOOMING THROUGH THE AIR IN HIS SOPWITH CAMEL..
OVER THERE! OVER THERE!
PACK UP YOUR TROUBLES IN YOUR OLD KIT BAG....
HOW IN THE WORLD AM I GOING TO GET MY TROUBLES IN A "KIT BAG"?
SCHULZ

PEANUTS
THIS IS THE SORT OF DREARY FALL RAIN THAT MAKES YOU WANT TO SIT INSIDE ALL DAY, AND STARE OUT THE WINDOW, AND DRINK TEA AND PLAY SAD SONGS ON THE STEREO
SO WHY AM I LYING HERE?

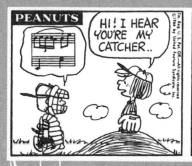

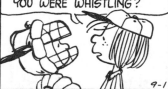

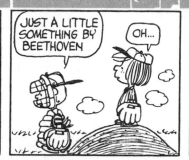

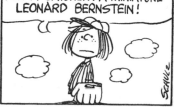

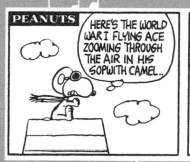

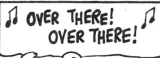

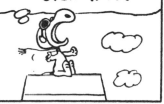

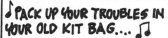

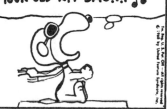

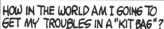

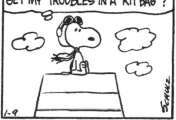

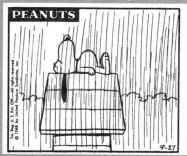

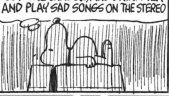

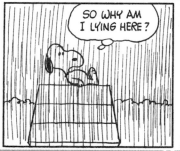

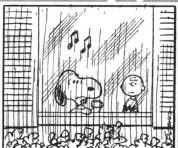

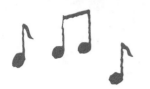

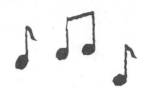

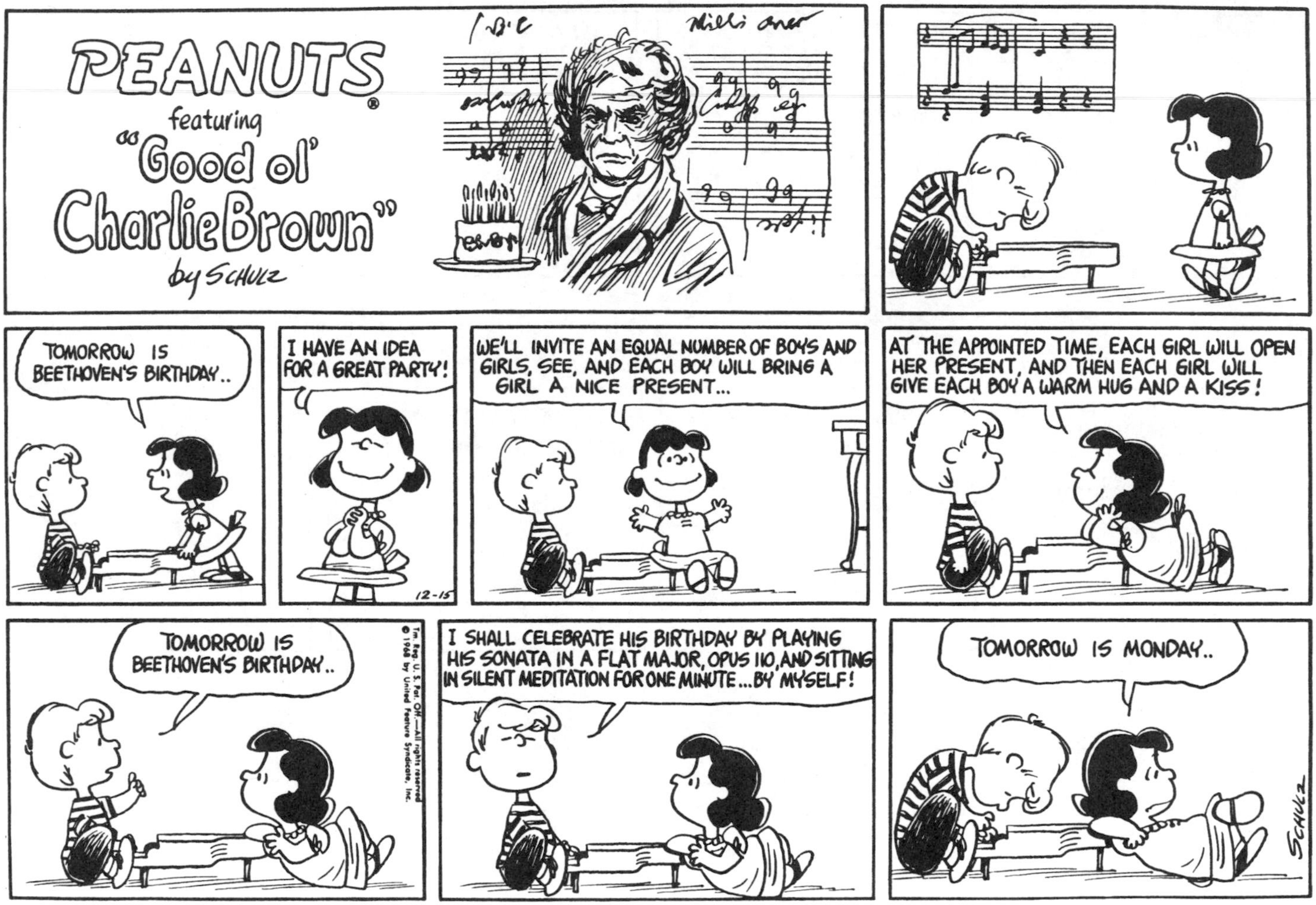
PEANUTS®
featuring
"Good ol' Charlie Brown"
by SCHULZ
TOMORROW IS BEETHOVEN'S BIRTHDAY..
I HAVE AN IDEA FOR A GREAT PARTY!
WE'LL INVITE AN EQUAL NUMBER OF BOYS AND GIRLS, SEE, AND EACH BOY WILL BRING A GIRL A NICE PRESENT...
12-15
AT THE APPOINTED TIME, EACH GIRL WILL OPEN HER PRESENT, AND THEN EACH GIRL WILL GIVE EACH BOY A WARM HUG AND A KISS!
TOMORROW IS BEETHOVEN'S BIRTHDAY..
Tm. Reg. U.S. Pat. Off.—All rights reserved © 1968 by United Feature Syndicate, Inc.
I SHALL CELEBRATE HIS BIRTHDAY BY PLAYING HIS SONATA IN A FLAT MAJOR, OPUS 110, AND SITTING IN SILENT MEDITATION FOR ONE MINUTE...BY MYSELF!
TOMORROW IS MONDAY..
SCHULZ

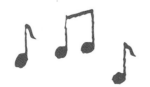

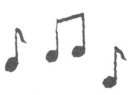

PEANUTS
12-30
Tm. Reg. U. S. Pat. Off.—All rights reserved
© 1968 by United Feature Syndicate, Inc.

PEANUTS
Tm. Reg. U. S. Pat. Off.—All rights reserved
© 1969 by United Feature Syndicate, Inc.
I'M LOOKING FOR THE ANSWER TO LIFE, SCHROEDER.. WHAT DO YOU THINK IS THE ANSWER?
BEETHOVEN!
3-20
BEETHOVEN IS IT, CLEAR AND SIMPLE!! DO YOU UNDERSTAND?
GOOD GRIEF!
SCHULZ

PEANUTS
Tm. Reg. U. S. Pat. Off.—All rights reserved
© 1969 by United Feature Syndicate, Inc.
I HEAR YOU SKINNED YOUR KNEES ROLLER SKATING
IT ISN'T FUNNY!
I NEVER SAID IT WAS FUNNY..
WELL, IT'S NOT FUNNY.. IT HURTS!
7-3
I'M SORRY I SAID ANYTHING
I HATE THE WHOLE WORLD...
THIS IS A LITTLE PIECE CALLED "MUSIC FOR SKINNED KNEES"
I CAN'T STAND IT!
SCHULZ

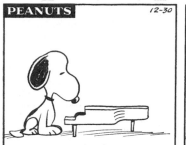

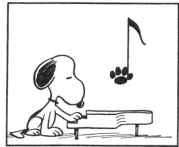

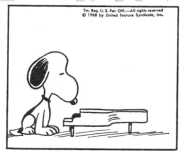

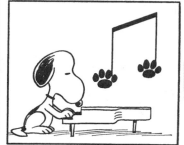

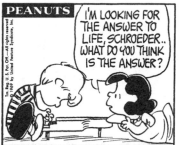

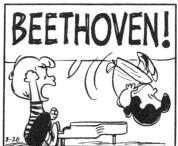

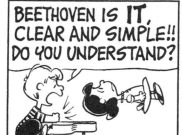

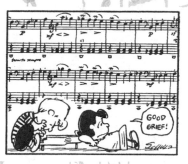

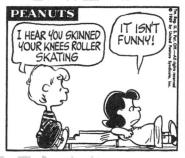

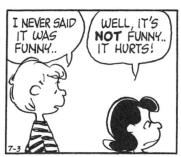

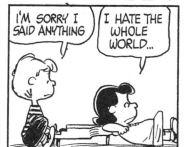

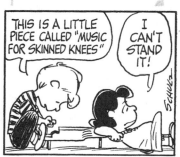

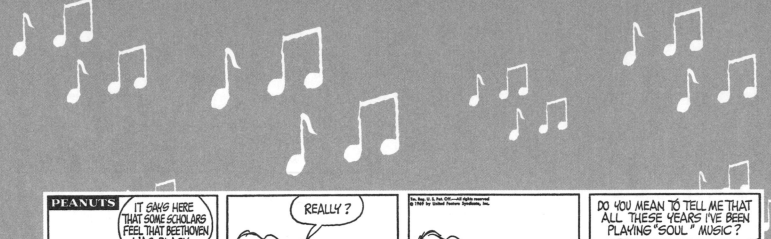

PEANUTS
IT SAYS HERE THAT SOME SCHOLARS FEEL THAT BEETHOVEN WAS BLACK
REALLY?
Tm. Reg. U. S. Pat. Off.—All rights reserved © 1969 by United Feature Syndicate, Inc.
DO YOU MEAN TO TELL ME THAT ALL THESE YEARS I'VE BEEN PLAYING "SOUL" MUSIC?
SCHULZ
7-7

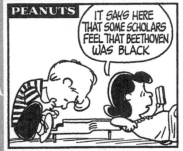

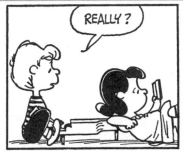

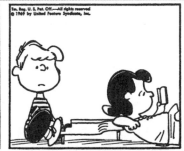

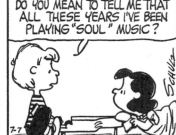

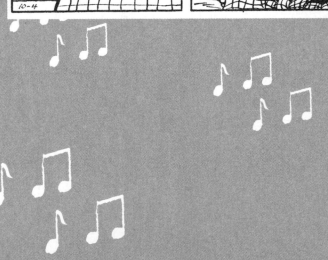

PEANUTS
SOMETIMES I LIE AWAKE AT NIGHT AND THINK ABOUT THAT LITTLE RED-HAIRED GIRL...
10-4
I DON'T EVER WANT TO FORGET HER FACE, BUT IF I DON'T FORGET HER FACE, I'LL GO CRAZY...
HOW CAN I REMEMBER THE FACE I CAN'T FORGET?
SUDDENLY I'M WRITING COUNTRY WESTERN MUSIC!
SCHULZ

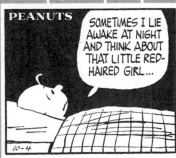

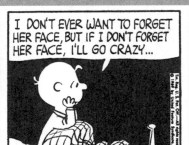

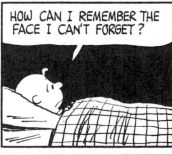

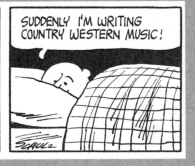

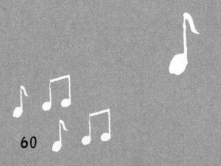

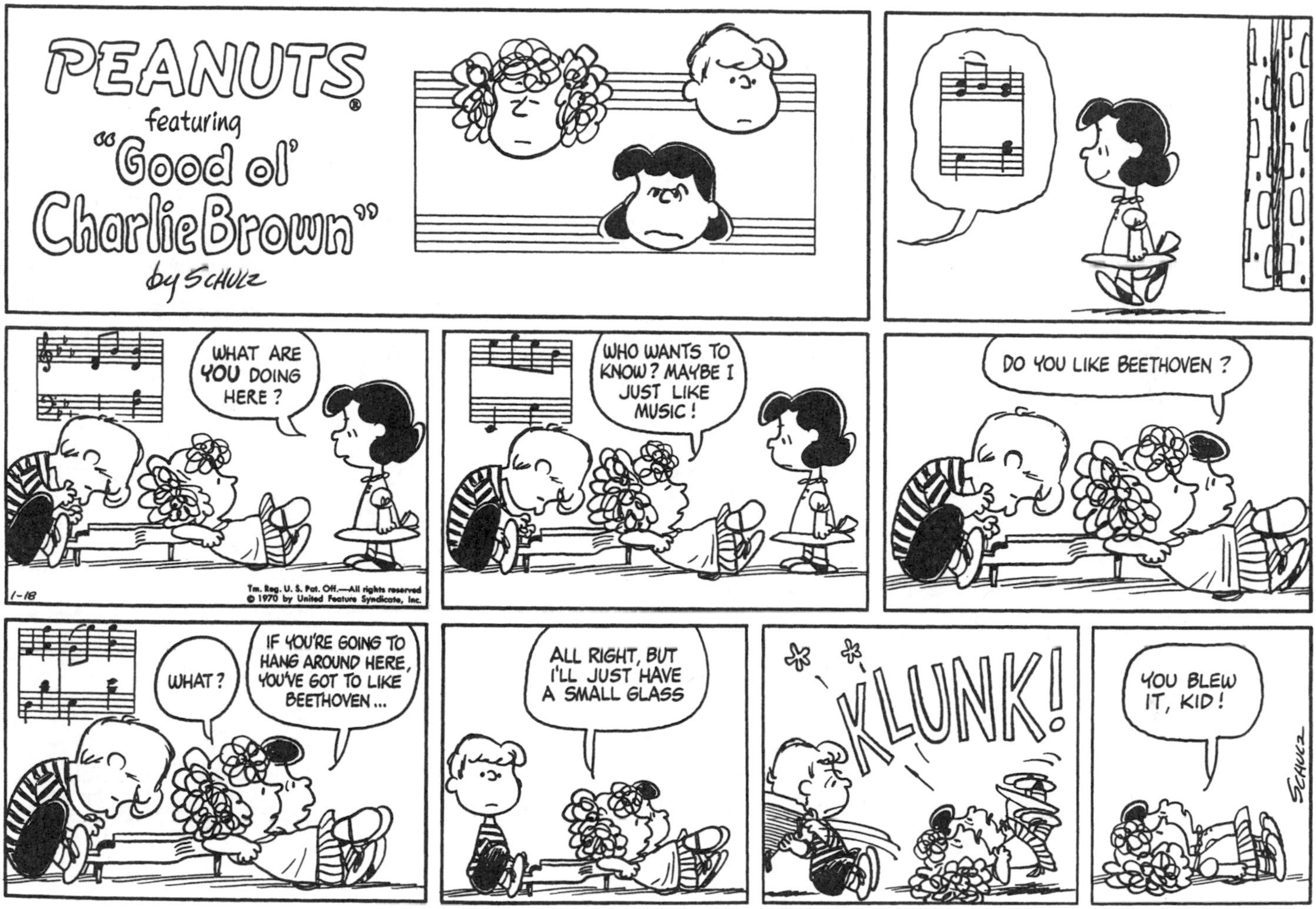
PEANUTS®
featuring
"Good ol' Charlie Brown"
by SCHULZ
WHAT ARE YOU DOING HERE?
1-18
Tm. Reg. U. S. Pat. Off.—All rights reserved © 1970 by United Feature Syndicate, Inc.
WHO WANTS TO KNOW? MAYBE I JUST LIKE MUSIC!
DO YOU LIKE BEETHOVEN?
WHAT?
IF YOU'RE GOING TO HANG AROUND HERE, YOU'VE GOT TO LIKE BEETHOVEN...
ALL RIGHT, BUT I'LL JUST HAVE A SMALL GLASS
KLUNK!
YOU BLEW IT, KID!
SCHULZ

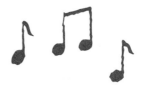

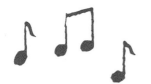

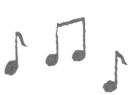

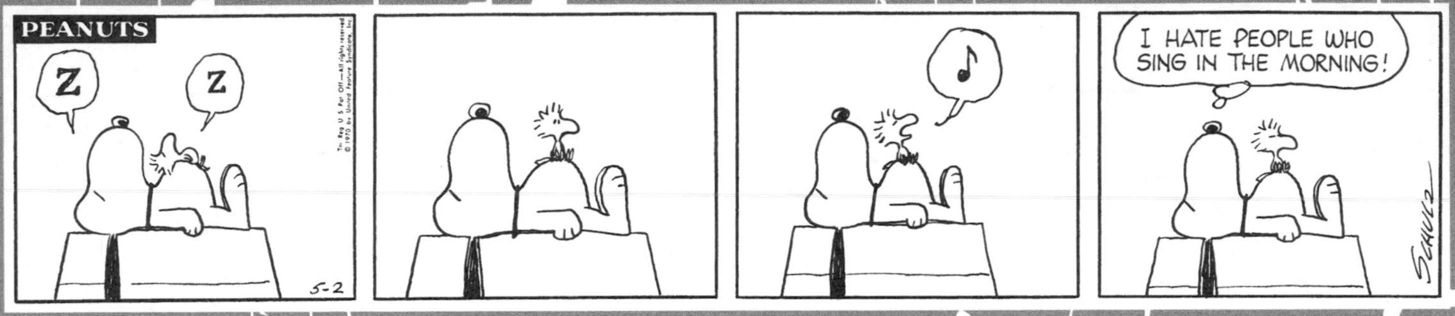
PEANUTS
Z
Z
5-2
♪
I HATE PEOPLE WHO SING IN THE MORNING!
SCHULZ

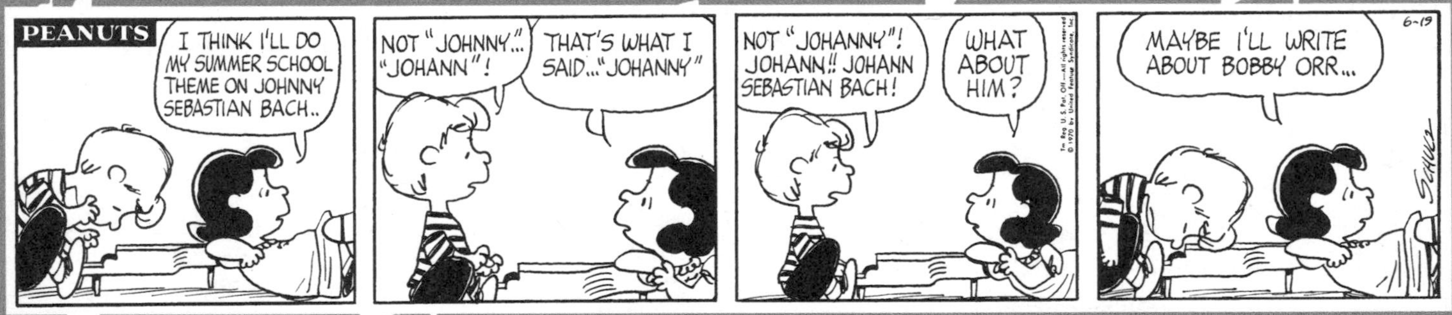
PEANUTS
I THINK I'LL DO MY SUMMER SCHOOL THEME ON JOHNNY SEBASTIAN BACH..
NOT "JOHNNY"... "JOHANN"!
THAT'S WHAT I SAID..."JOHANNY"
NOT "JOHANNY"! JOHANN!! JOHANN SEBASTIAN BACH!
WHAT ABOUT HIM?
6-15
MAYBE I'LL WRITE ABOUT BOBBY ORR...
SCHULZ

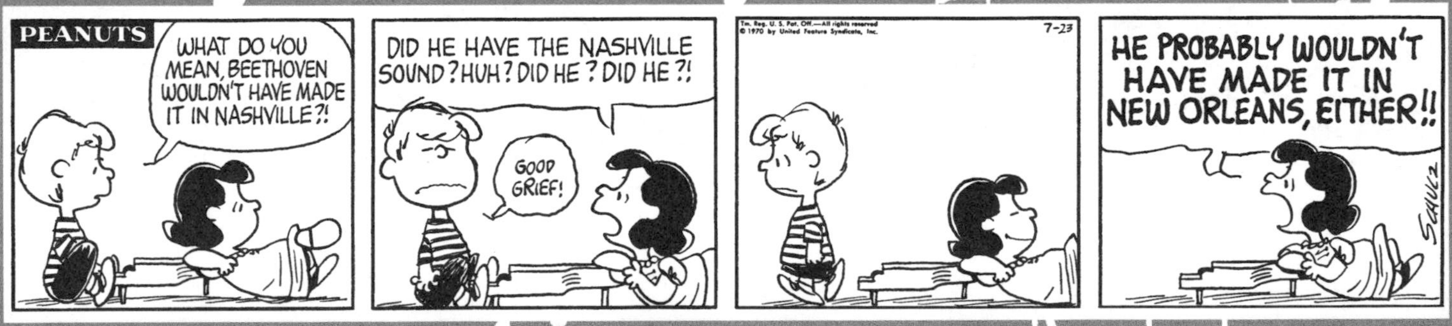
PEANUTS
WHAT DO YOU MEAN, BEETHOVEN WOULDN'T HAVE MADE IT IN NASHVILLE?!
DID HE HAVE THE NASHVILLE SOUND? HUH? DID HE? DID HE?!
GOOD GRIEF!
Tm. Reg. U. S. Pat. Off.—All rights reserved © 1970 by United Feature Syndicate, Inc.
7-23
HE PROBABLY WOULDN'T HAVE MADE IT IN NEW ORLEANS, EITHER!!
SCHULZ

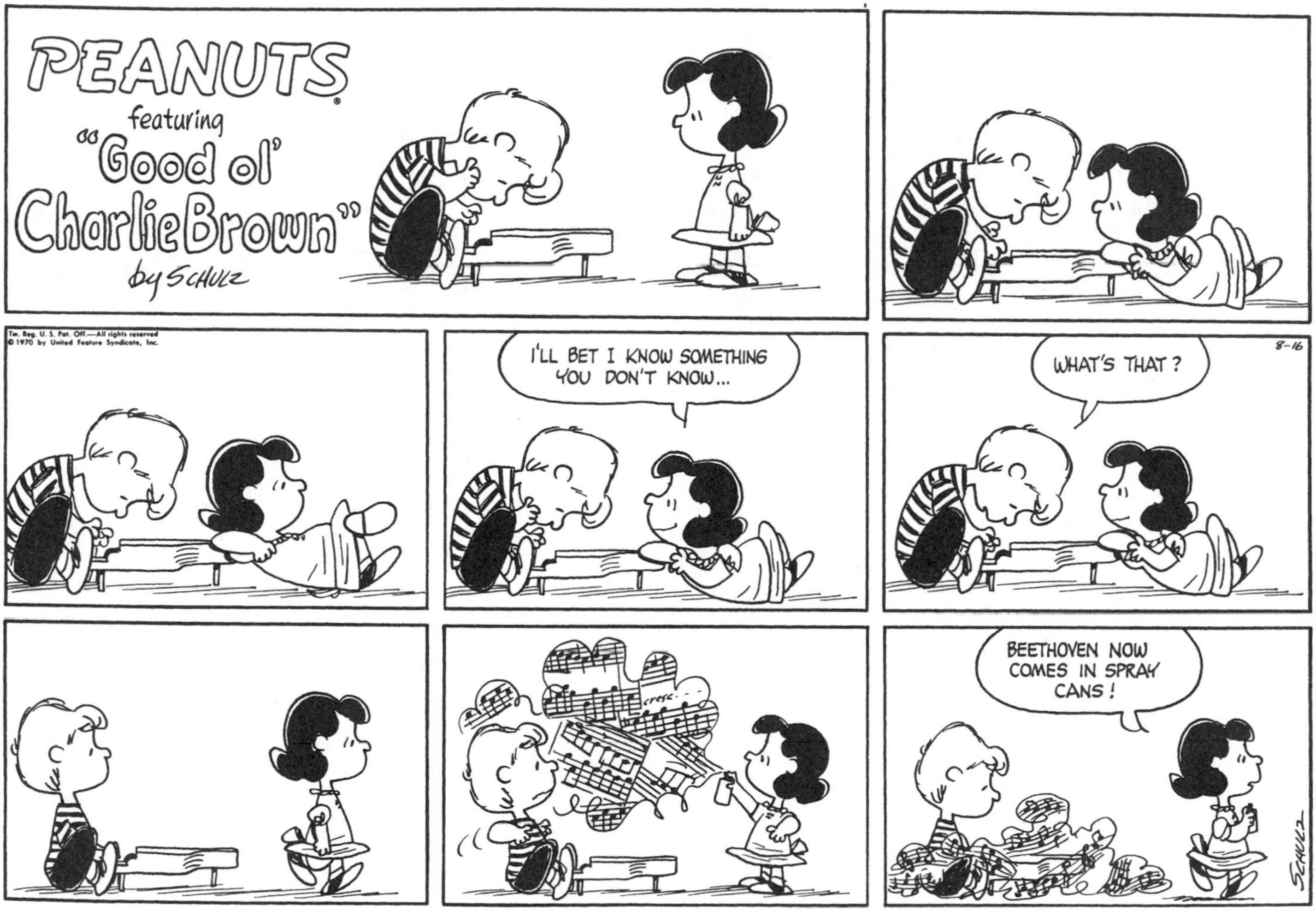
PEANUTS
featuring
"Good ol' Charlie Brown"
by SCHULZ
Tm. Reg. U. S. Pat. Off.—All rights reserved
© 1970 by United Feature Syndicate, Inc.
I'LL BET I KNOW SOMETHING YOU DON'T KNOW...
8-16
WHAT'S THAT?
cresc.
BEETHOVEN NOW COMES IN SPRAY CANS!
SCHULZ

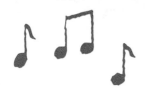

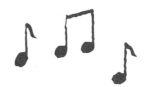

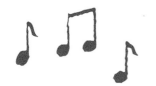

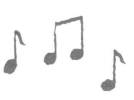

PEANUTS
DO YOU THINK IF TWO PEOPLE LIKED THE SAME THING, IT COULD BRING THEM CLOSER TOGETHER?
CERTAINLY...TAKE CLASSICAL MUSIC, FOR INSTANCE...TWO PEOPLE WHO SHARED A LOVE FOR BEETHOVEN COULD BECOME VERY CLOSE...
Tm. Reg. U. S. Pat. Off.—All rights reserved © 1971 by United Feature Syndicate, Inc.
1-25
HOW ABOUT TV?
SCHULZ

PEANUTS
Tm. Reg. U.S. Pat. Off.—All rights reserved © 1971 by United Feature Syndicate, Inc
♫
3-24
HE JUST STOPPED BY TO SAY ♫
SCHULZ

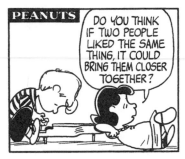

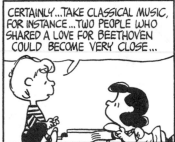

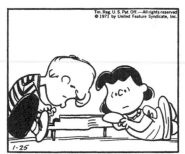

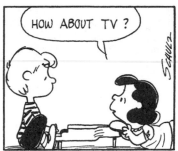

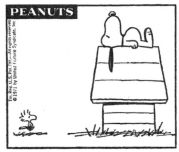

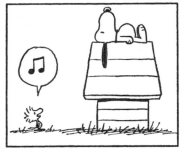

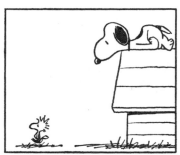

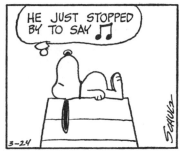

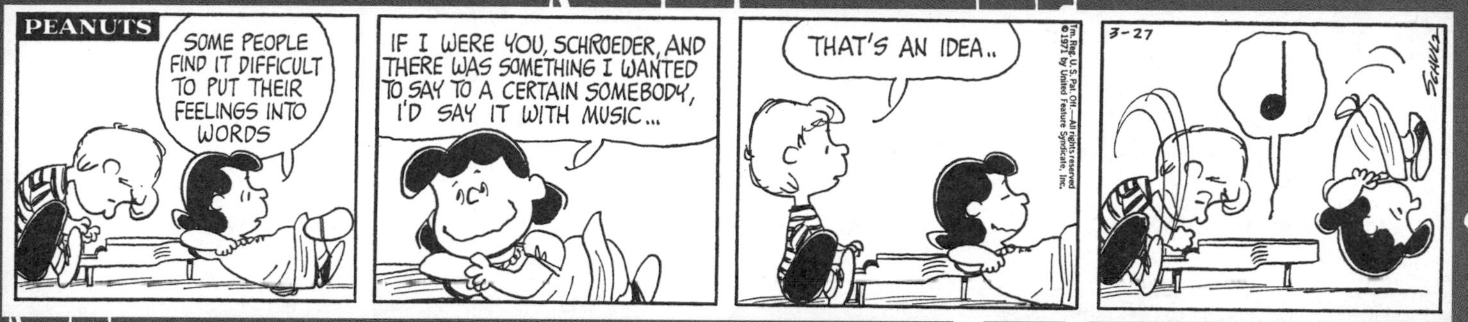
PEANUTS
SOME PEOPLE FIND IT DIFFICULT TO PUT THEIR FEELINGS INTO WORDS
IF I WERE YOU, SCHROEDER, AND THERE WAS SOMETHING I WANTED TO SAY TO A CERTAIN SOMEBODY, I'D SAY IT WITH MUSIC...
THAT'S AN IDEA..
Tm. Reg. U.S. Pat. Off.—All rights reserved © 1971 by United Feature Syndicate, Inc.
3-27
SCHULZ

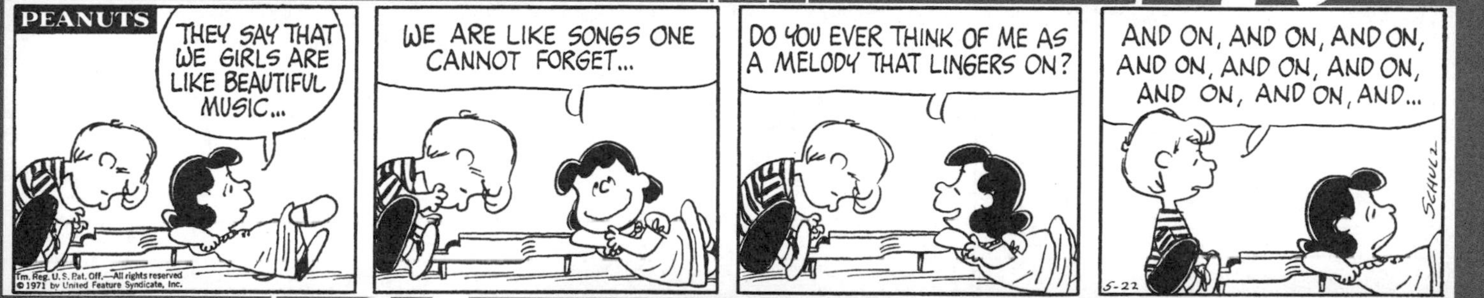
PEANUTS
THEY SAY THAT WE GIRLS ARE LIKE BEAUTIFUL MUSIC...
WE ARE LIKE SONGS ONE CANNOT FORGET...
DO YOU EVER THINK OF ME AS A MELODY THAT LINGERS ON?
AND ON, AND ON, AND ON, AND ON, AND ON, AND ON, AND ON, AND ON, AND...
Tm. Reg. U.S. Pat. Off.—All rights reserved © 1971 by United Feature Syndicate, Inc.
SCHULZ
5-22

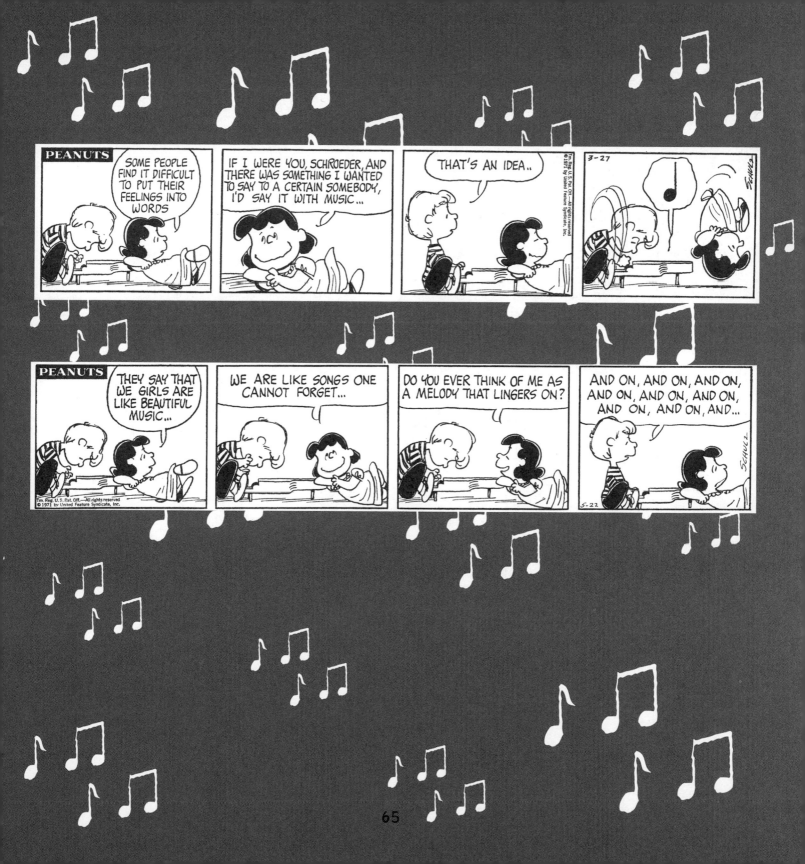

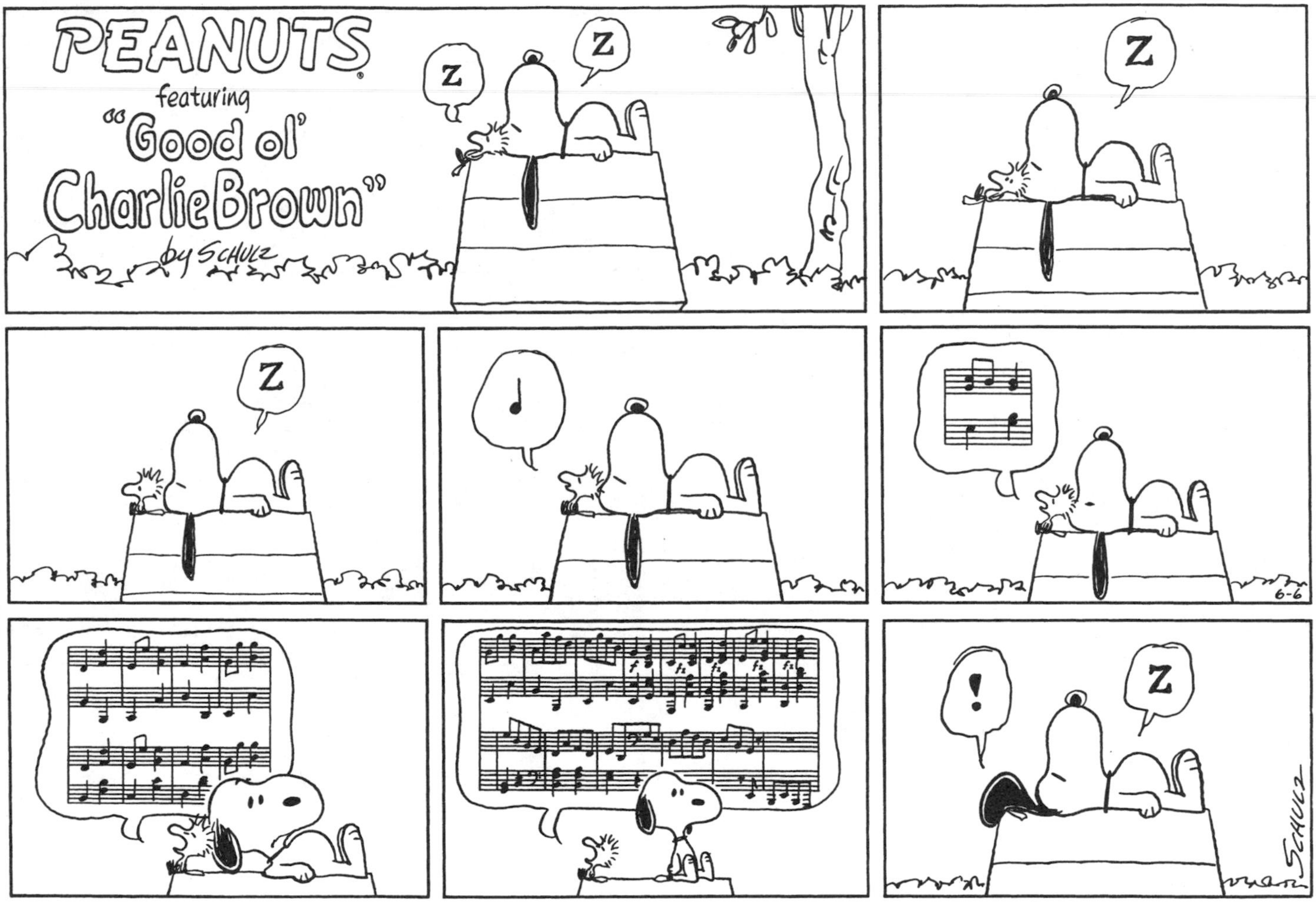
PEANUTS
featuring
"Good ol' Charlie Brown"
by SCHULZ
Z
Z
Z
Z
!
Z
6-6
SCHULZ

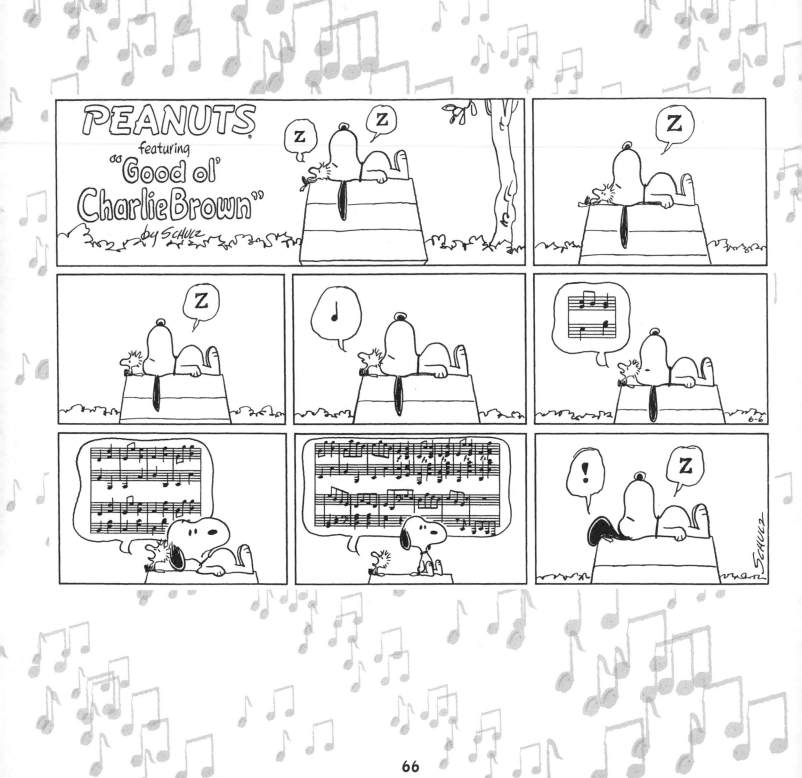

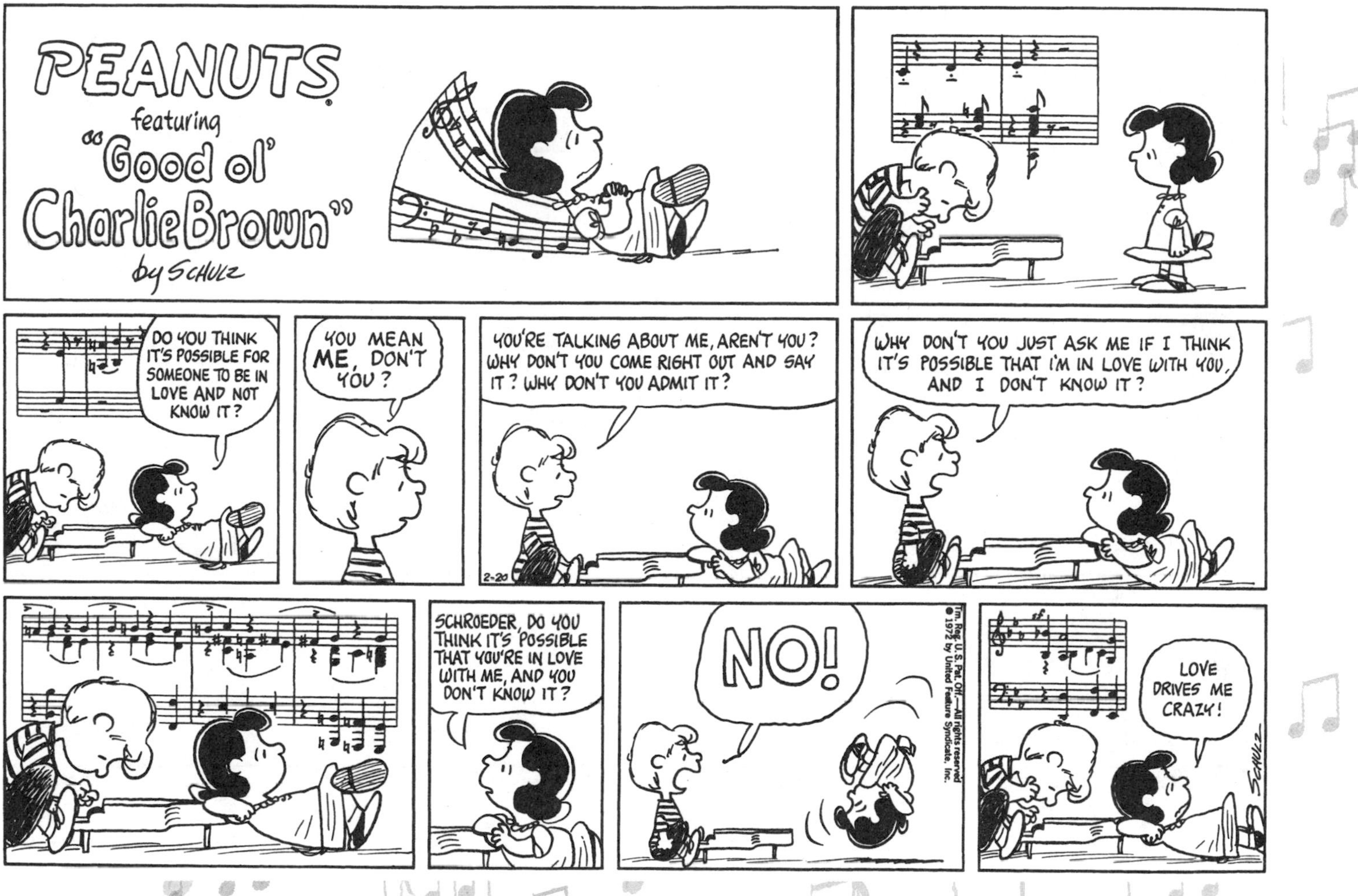
PEANUTS
featuring
"Good ol' CharlieBrown"
by SCHULZ
DO YOU THINK IT'S POSSIBLE FOR SOMEONE TO BE IN LOVE AND NOT KNOW IT?
YOU MEAN ME, DON'T YOU?
YOU'RE TALKING ABOUT ME, AREN'T YOU? WHY DON'T YOU COME RIGHT OUT AND SAY IT? WHY DON'T YOU ADMIT IT?
2-20
WHY DON'T YOU JUST ASK ME IF I THINK IT'S POSSIBLE THAT I'M IN LOVE WITH YOU, AND I DON'T KNOW IT?
SCHROEDER, DO YOU THINK IT'S POSSIBLE THAT YOU'RE IN LOVE WITH ME, AND YOU DON'T KNOW IT?
NO!
Tm. Reg. U.S. Pat. Off.—All rights reserved
© 1972 by United Feature Syndicate, Inc.
LOVE DRIVES ME CRAZY!
SCHULZ

PEANUTS
BEETHOVEN WROTE NINE SYMPHONIES
I KNOW THAT
HE ALSO WROTE A LOT OF THOSE INDIVIDUAL THINGIES
Tm. Reg. U.S. Pat. Off.—All rights reserved © 1972 by United Feature Syndicate, Inc.
SONATAS
THAT'S THE WORD
SCHULZ

PEANUTS
GUESS WHAT I JUST DID
I JUST LISTENED TO PART OF AN OPERA ON THE RADIO
I SURPRISED MYSELF... I KIND OF LIKED IT
Tm. Reg. U.S. Pat. Off.—All rights reserved © 1972 by United Feature Syndicate, Inc.
I'LL BET IF I LISTENED ENOUGH, I COULD BECOME A REAL OPERETTA
SCHULZ

PEANUTS
WOODSTOCK LIKES TO LISTEN TO MY STEREO..
Tm. Reg. U.S. Pat. Off.—All rights reserved © 1972 by United Feature Syndicate, Inc.
"AMERICAN PIE" OVER AND OVER AND OVER AND OVER...
SCHULZ

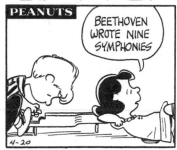

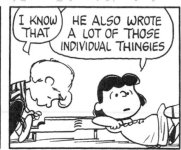

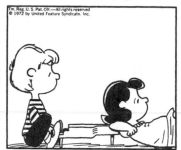

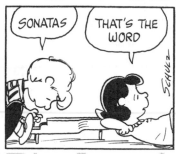

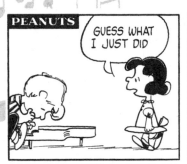

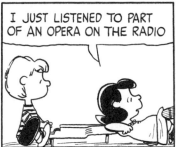

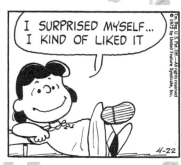

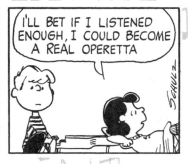

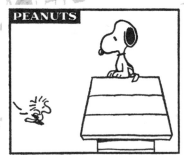

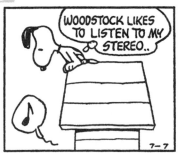

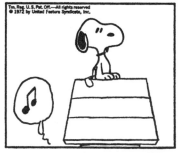

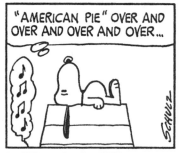

PEANUTS
Tm. Reg. U. S. Pat. Off.—All rights reserved © 1972 by United Feature Syndicate, Inc.
Z
10-16
SCHULZ

PEANUTS
WHAT HAPPENS IF YOU PRACTICE FOR TWENTY YEARS, AND THEN END UP NOT BEING RICH AND FAMOUS?
1-27
THE JOY IS IN THE PLAYING
Tm. Reg. U. S. Pat. Off.—All rights reserved © 1973 by United Feature Syndicate, Inc.
YOU'RE KIDDING!
SCHULZ

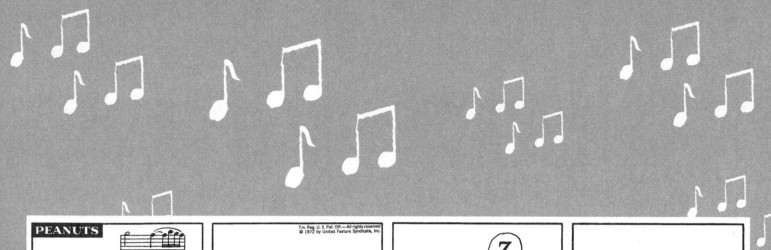

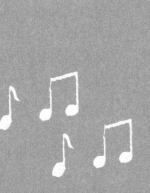

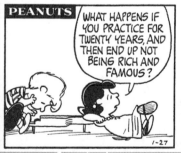

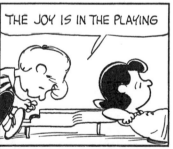

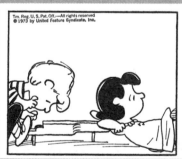

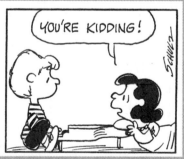

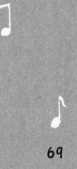

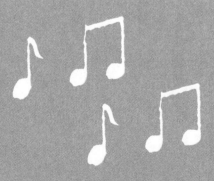

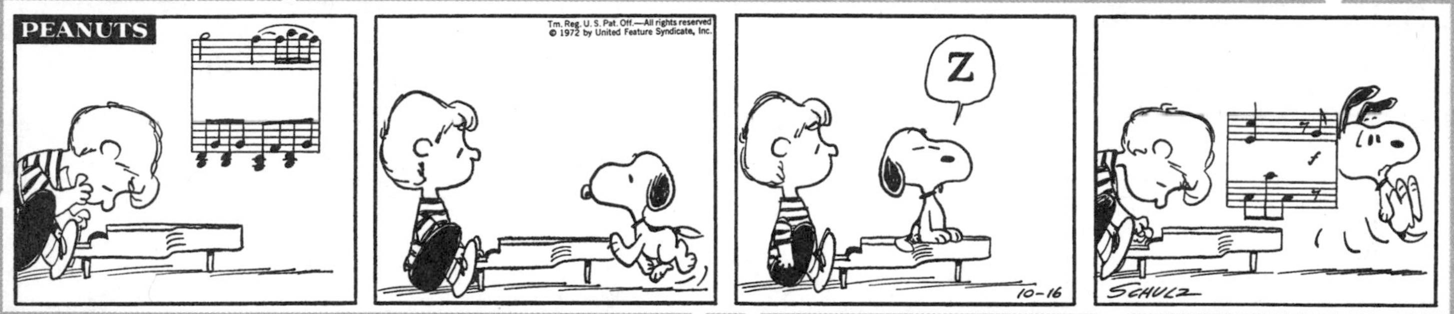

PEANUTS
featuring
"Good ol' Charlie Brown"
by SCHULZ
YAWN
Z
TELEPHONE
Tm. Reg. U. S. Pat. Off.—All rights reserved
© 1973 by United Feature Syndicate, Inc.
8-19
SCHULZ

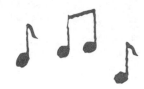

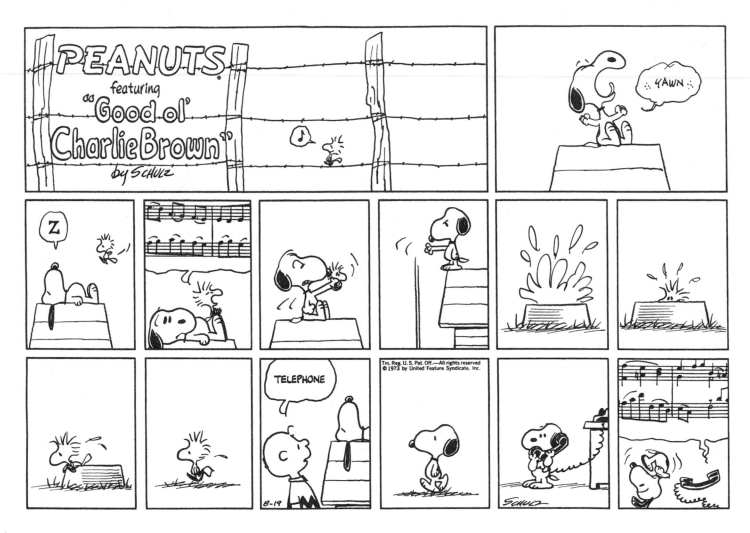

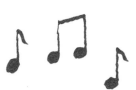

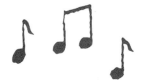

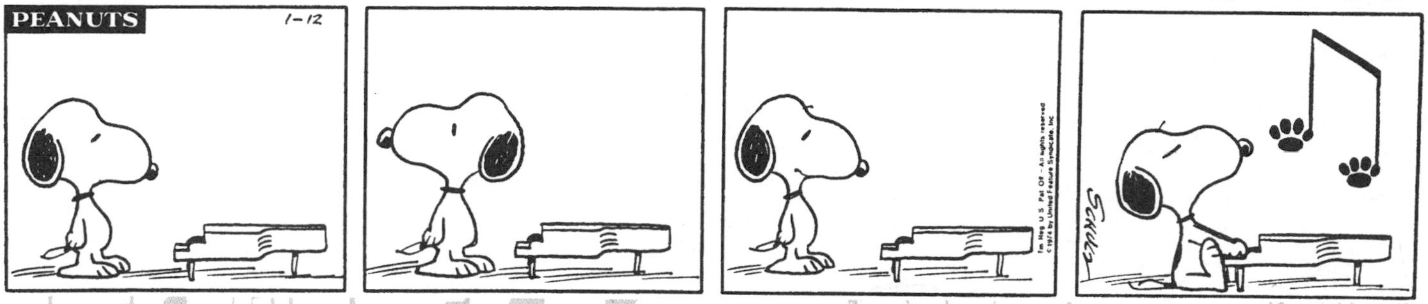
PEANUTS
1-12

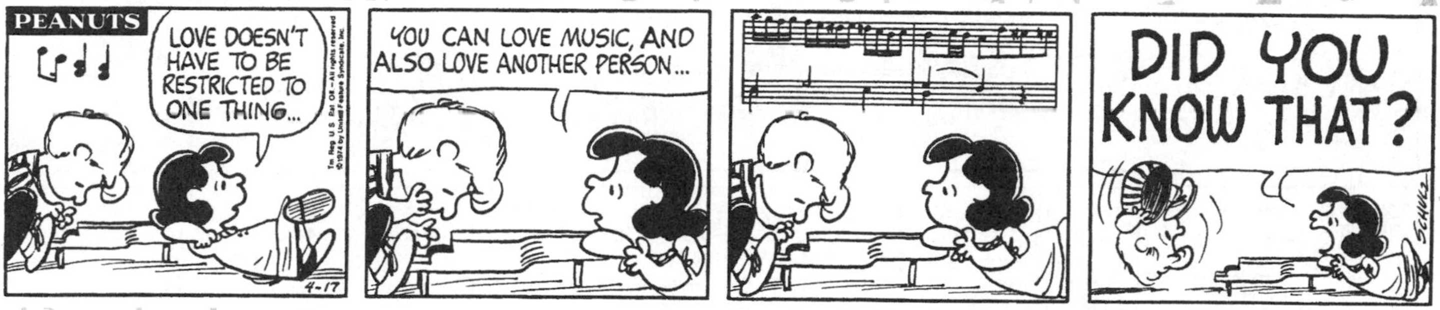
PEANUTS
LOVE DOESN'T HAVE TO BE RESTRICTED TO ONE THING...
4-17
YOU CAN LOVE MUSIC, AND ALSO LOVE ANOTHER PERSON...
DID YOU KNOW THAT?

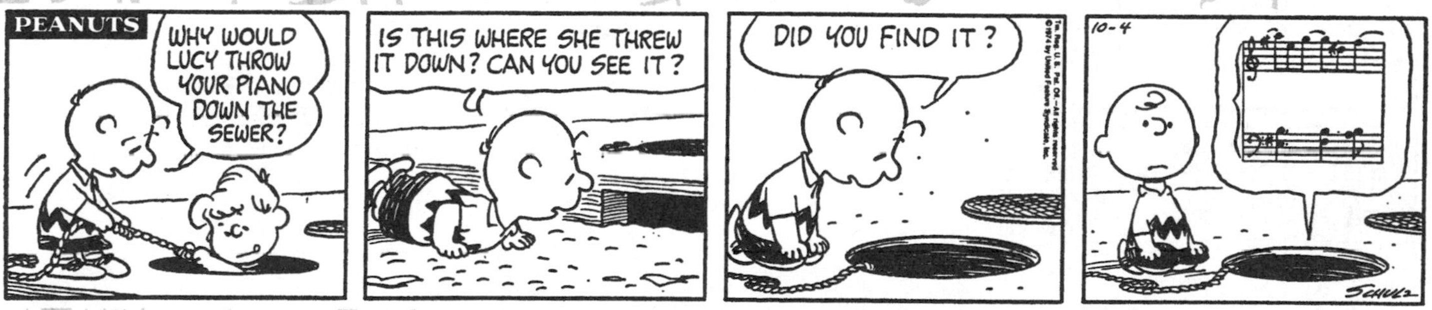
PEANUTS
WHY WOULD LUCY THROW YOUR PIANO DOWN THE SEWER?
IS THIS WHERE SHE THREW IT DOWN? CAN YOU SEE IT?
DID YOU FIND IT?
10-4

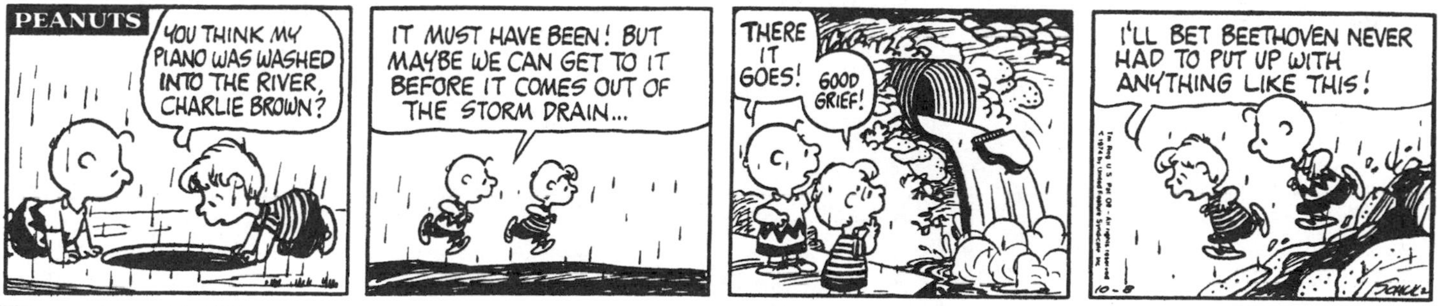
PEANUTS
YOU THINK MY PIANO WAS WASHED INTO THE RIVER, CHARLIE BROWN?
IT MUST HAVE BEEN! BUT MAYBE WE CAN GET TO IT BEFORE IT COMES OUT OF THE STORM DRAIN...
THERE IT GOES!
GOOD GRIEF!
I'LL BET BEETHOVEN NEVER HAD TO PUT UP WITH ANYTHING LIKE THIS!
10-8

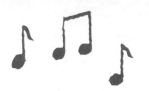

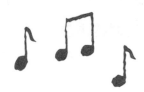

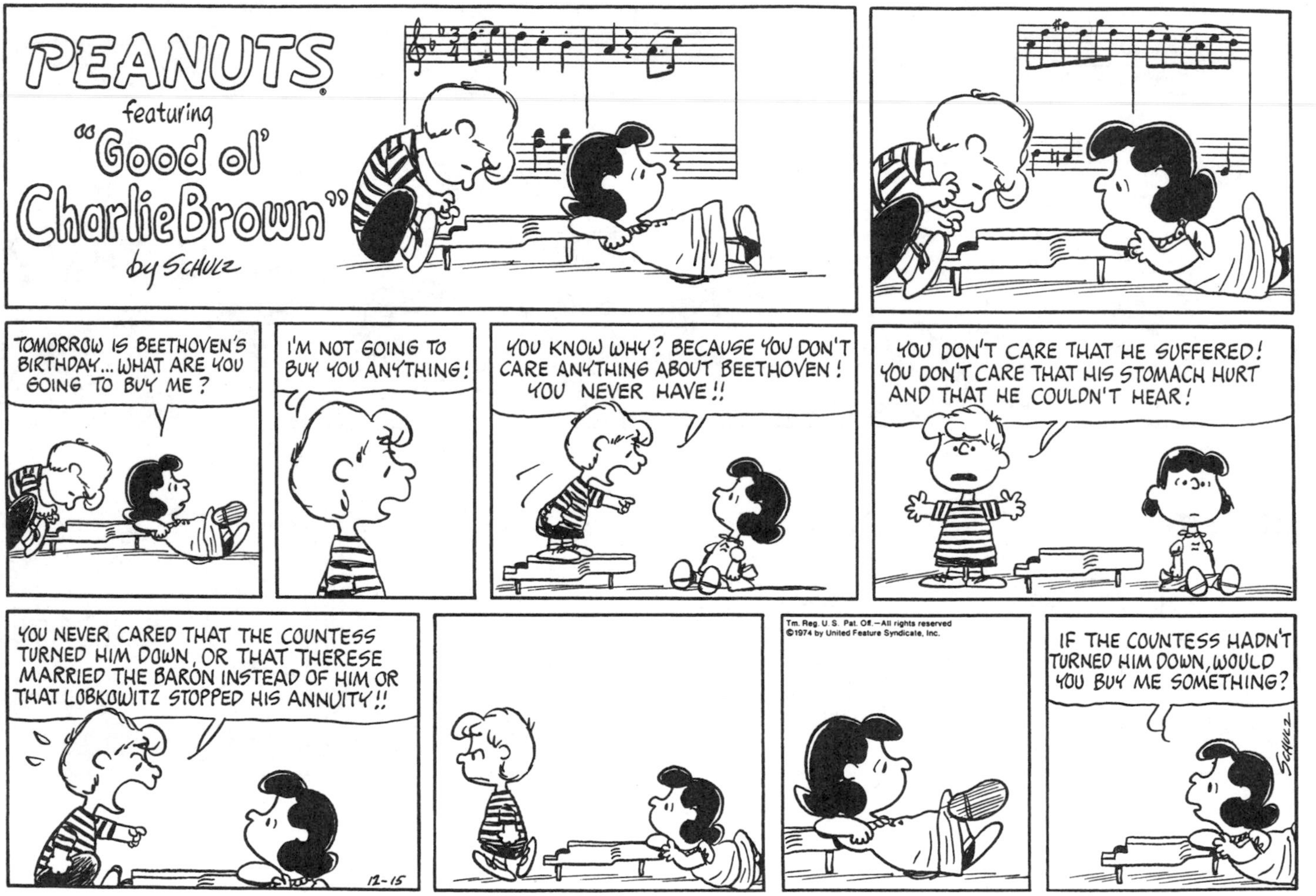
PEANUTS
featuring "Good ol' Charlie Brown"
by SCHULZ
TOMORROW IS BEETHOVEN'S BIRTHDAY... WHAT ARE YOU GOING TO BUY ME?
I'M NOT GOING TO BUY YOU ANYTHING!
YOU KNOW WHY? BECAUSE YOU DON'T CARE ANYTHING ABOUT BEETHOVEN! YOU NEVER HAVE!!
YOU DON'T CARE THAT HE SUFFERED! YOU DON'T CARE THAT HIS STOMACH HURT AND THAT HE COULDN'T HEAR!
YOU NEVER CARED THAT THE COUNTESS TURNED HIM DOWN, OR THAT THERESE MARRIED THE BARON INSTEAD OF HIM OR THAT LOBKOWITZ STOPPED HIS ANNUITY!!
12-15
Tm. Reg. U.S. Pat. Off.—All rights reserved
©1974 by United Feature Syndicate, Inc.
IF THE COUNTESS HADN'T TURNED HIM DOWN, WOULD YOU BUY ME SOMETHING?
SCHULZ

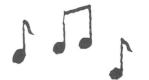

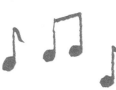

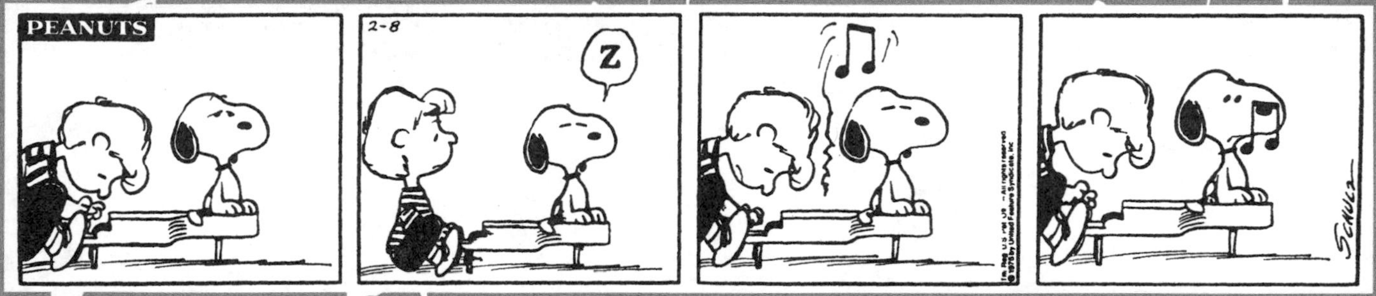
PEANUTS
2-8
Z
Tm. Reg. U.S. Pat. Off.—All rights reserved
© 1976 by United Feature Syndicate, Inc.
SCHULZ

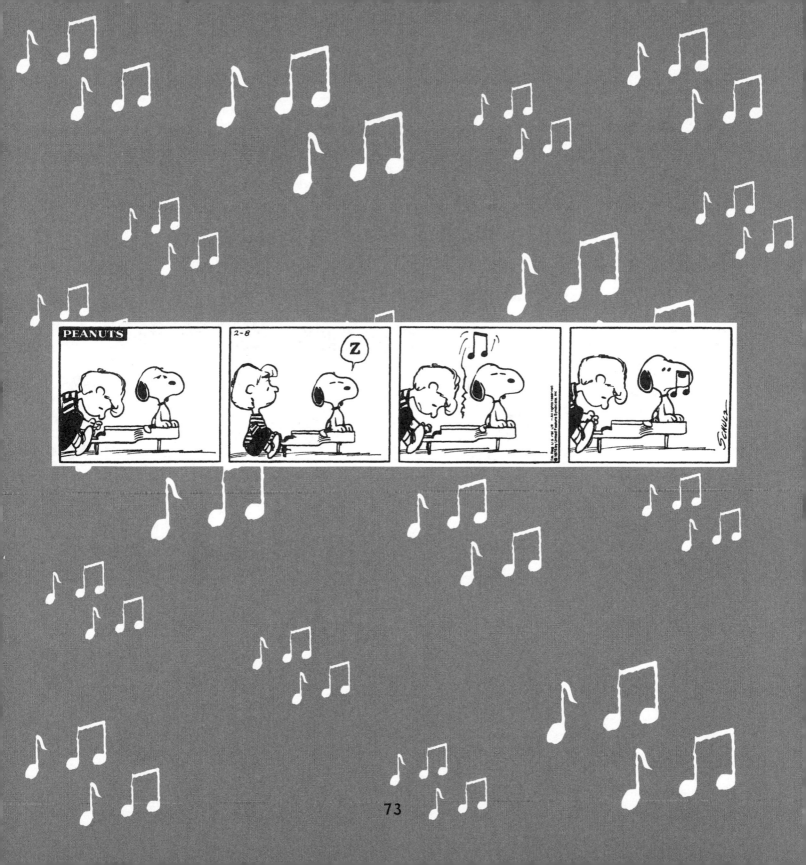

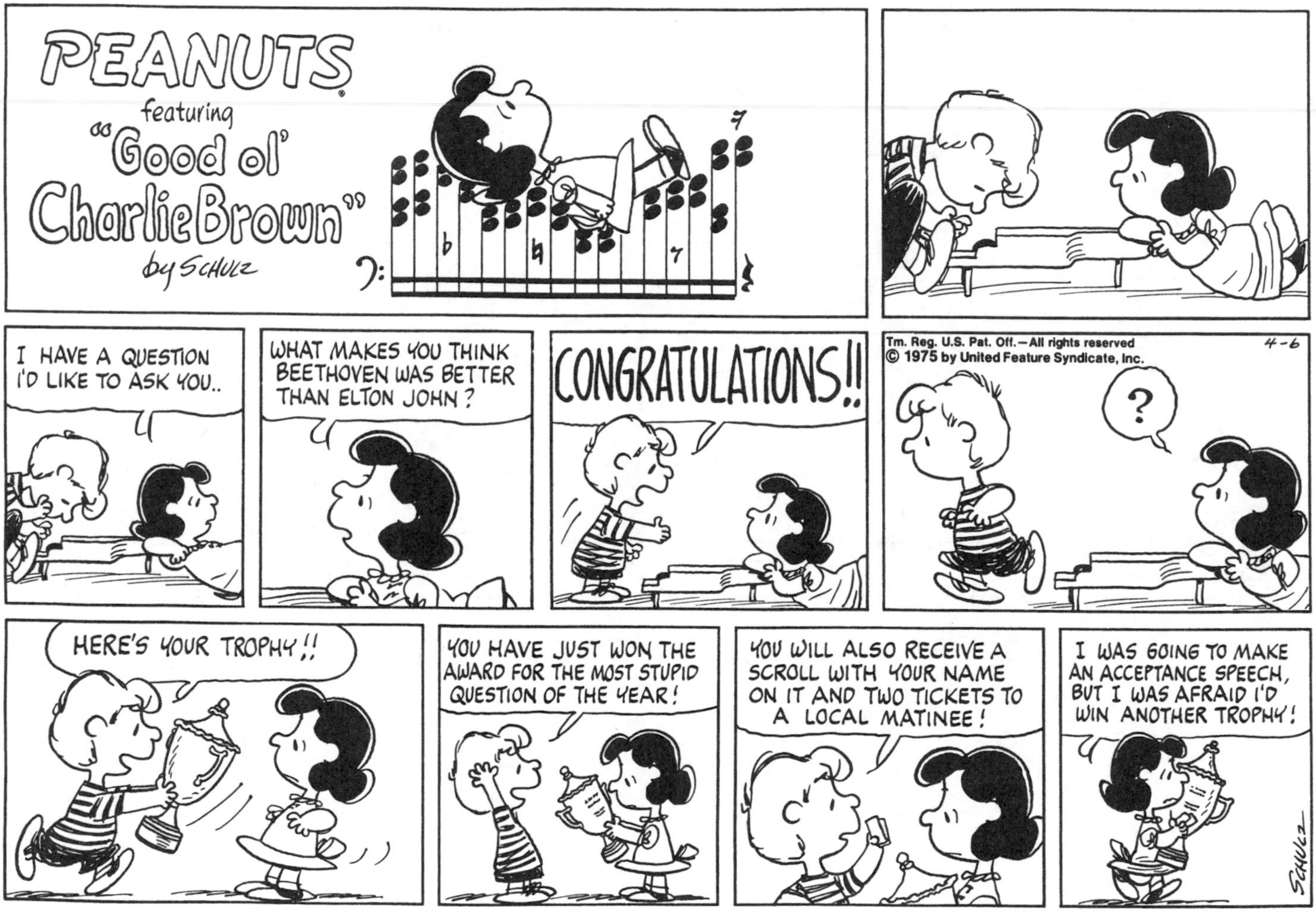

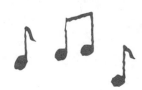

PEANUTS
featuring
"Good ol' CharlieBrown"
by SCHULZ
I HAVE A QUESTION I'D LIKE TO ASK YOU..
WHAT MAKES YOU THINK BEETHOVEN WAS BETTER THAN ELTON JOHN?
CONGRATULATIONS!!
Tm. Reg. U.S. Pat. Off.—All rights reserved
© 1975 by United Feature Syndicate, Inc.
4-6
?
HERE'S YOUR TROPHY!!
YOU HAVE JUST WON THE AWARD FOR THE MOST STUPID QUESTION OF THE YEAR!
YOU WILL ALSO RECEIVE A SCROLL WITH YOUR NAME ON IT AND TWO TICKETS TO A LOCAL MATINEE!
I WAS GOING TO MAKE AN ACCEPTANCE SPEECH, BUT I WAS AFRAID I'D WIN ANOTHER TROPHY!
SCHULZ

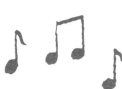

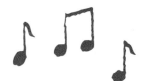

PEANUTS
Z
Tm. Reg. U.S. Pat. Off.—All rights reserved
© 1975 by United Feature Syndicate, Inc.
5-1
SCHULZ

PEANUTS
Tm. Reg. U.S. Pat. Off.—All rights reserved
© 1975 by United Feature Syndicate, Inc.
5-14
SCHULZ

PEANUTS
I'VE JUST COME UP WITH THE PERFECT THEORY
IT'S MY THEORY THAT BEETHOVEN WOULD HAVE WRITTEN EVEN BETTER MUSIC IF HE HAD BEEN MARRIED!
7-16
WHAT'S SO PERFECT ABOUT THAT THEORY?
Tm. Reg. U.S. Pat. Off.—All rights reserved
©1975 by United Feature Syndicate, Inc.
IT CAN'T BE PROVED ONE WAY OR THE OTHER!
SCHULZ

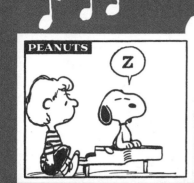

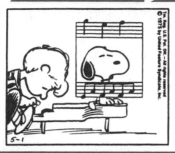

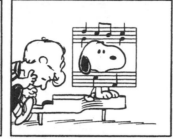

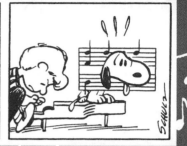

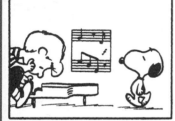

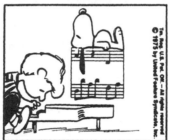

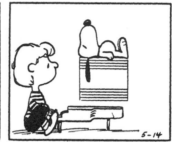

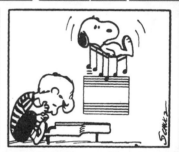

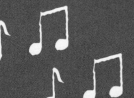

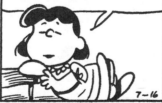

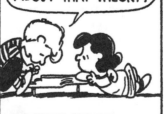

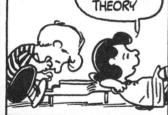

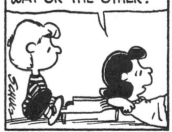

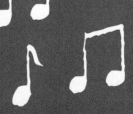

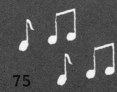

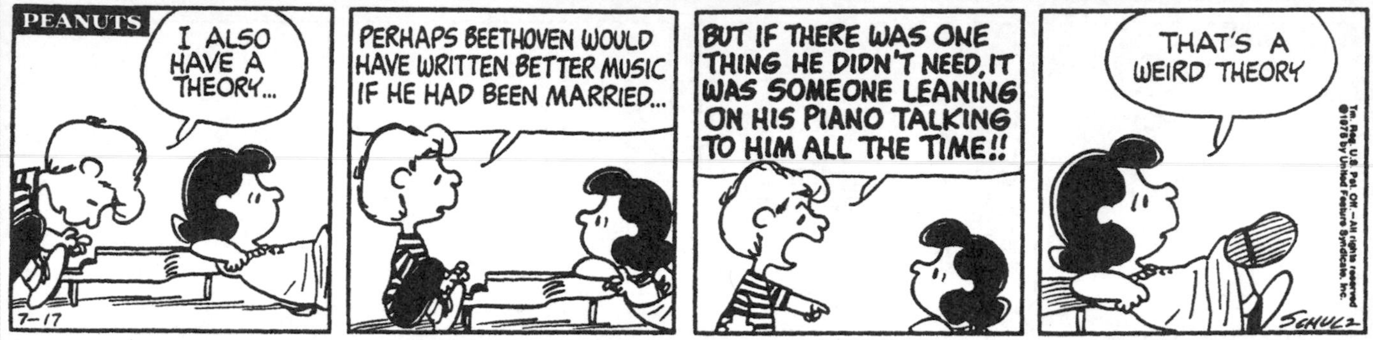
PEANUTS
I ALSO HAVE A THEORY...
7-17
PERHAPS BEETHOVEN WOULD HAVE WRITTEN BETTER MUSIC IF HE HAD BEEN MARRIED...
BUT IF THERE WAS ONE THING HE DIDN'T NEED, IT WAS SOMEONE LEANING ON HIS PIANO TALKING TO HIM ALL THE TIME!!
THAT'S A WEIRD THEORY
Tm. Reg. U.S. Pat. Off.—All rights reserved ©1975 by United Feature Syndicate, Inc.
SCHULZ

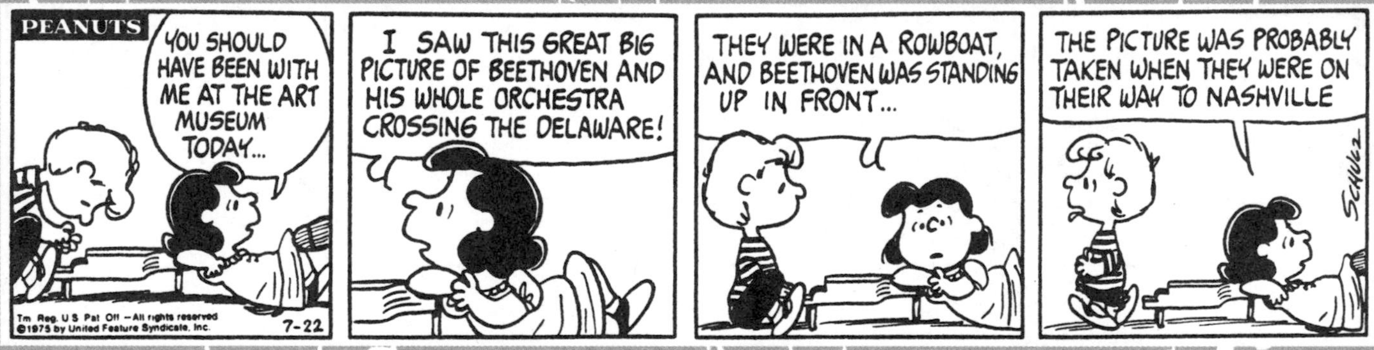
PEANUTS
YOU SHOULD HAVE BEEN WITH ME AT THE ART MUSEUM TODAY...
Tm Reg. U.S Pat Off —All rights reserved ©1975 by United Feature Syndicate, Inc.
7-22
I SAW THIS GREAT BIG PICTURE OF BEETHOVEN AND HIS WHOLE ORCHESTRA CROSSING THE DELAWARE!
THEY WERE IN A ROWBOAT, AND BEETHOVEN WAS STANDING UP IN FRONT...
THE PICTURE WAS PROBABLY TAKEN WHEN THEY WERE ON THEIR WAY TO NASHVILLE
SCHULZ

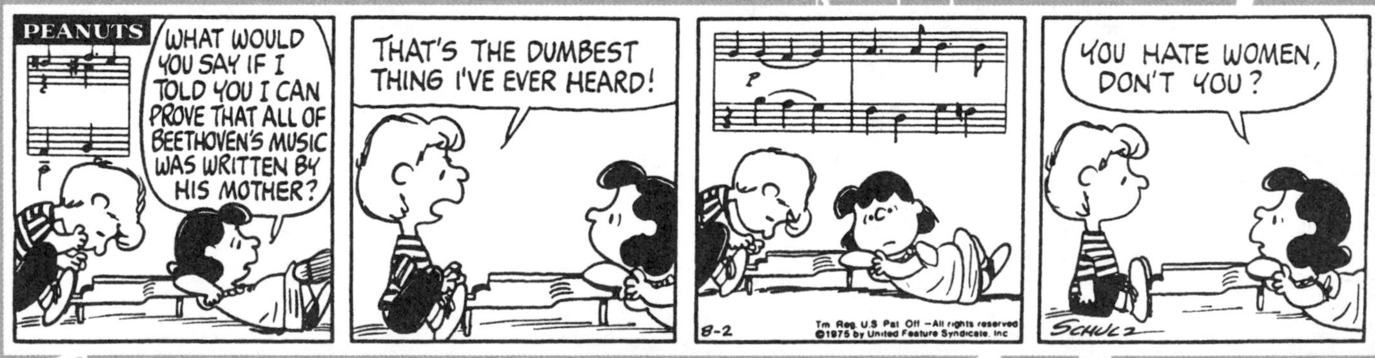
PEANUTS
WHAT WOULD YOU SAY IF I TOLD YOU I CAN PROVE THAT ALL OF BEETHOVEN'S MUSIC WAS WRITTEN BY HIS MOTHER?
THAT'S THE DUMBEST THING I'VE EVER HEARD!
8-2
Tm Reg. U.S Pat Off —All rights reserved ©1975 by United Feature Syndicate, Inc
YOU HATE WOMEN, DON'T YOU?
SCHULZ

Tm. Reg. U.S. Pat. Off. — All rights reserved.
©1975 by United Feature Syndicate, Inc.

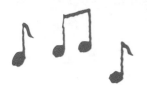

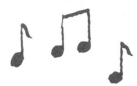

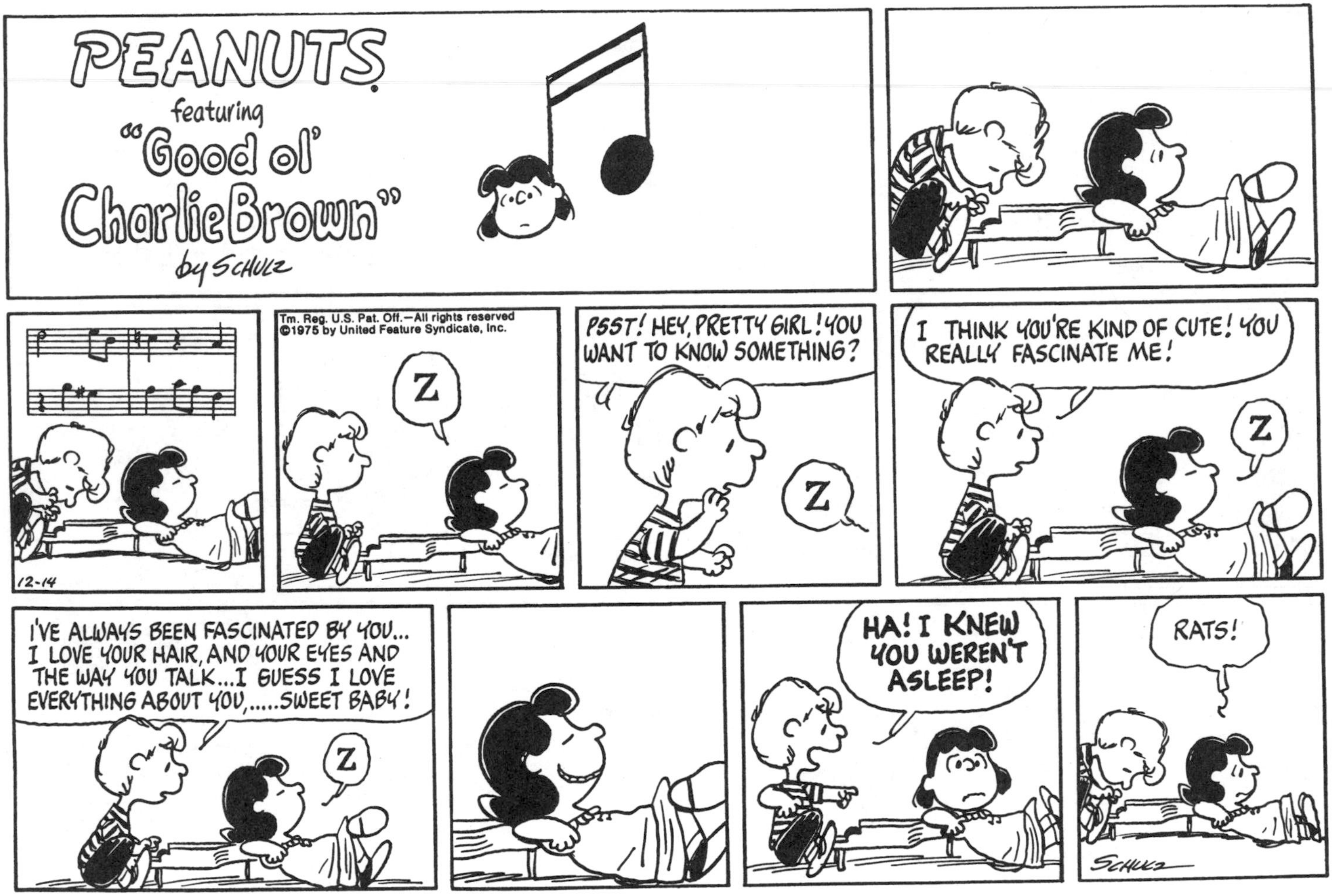
PEANUTS
featuring
"Good ol' CharlieBrown"
by SCHULZ
12-14
Tm. Reg. U.S. Pat. Off.—All rights reserved
©1975 by United Feature Syndicate, Inc.
Z
PSST! HEY, PRETTY GIRL! YOU WANT TO KNOW SOMETHING?
Z
I THINK YOU'RE KIND OF CUTE! YOU REALLY FASCINATE ME!
Z
I'VE ALWAYS BEEN FASCINATED BY YOU... I LOVE YOUR HAIR, AND YOUR EYES AND THE WAY YOU TALK...I GUESS I LOVE EVERYTHING ABOUT YOU,.....SWEET BABY!
Z
HA! I KNEW YOU WEREN'T ASLEEP!
RATS!
SCHULZ

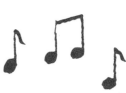

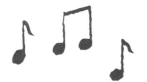

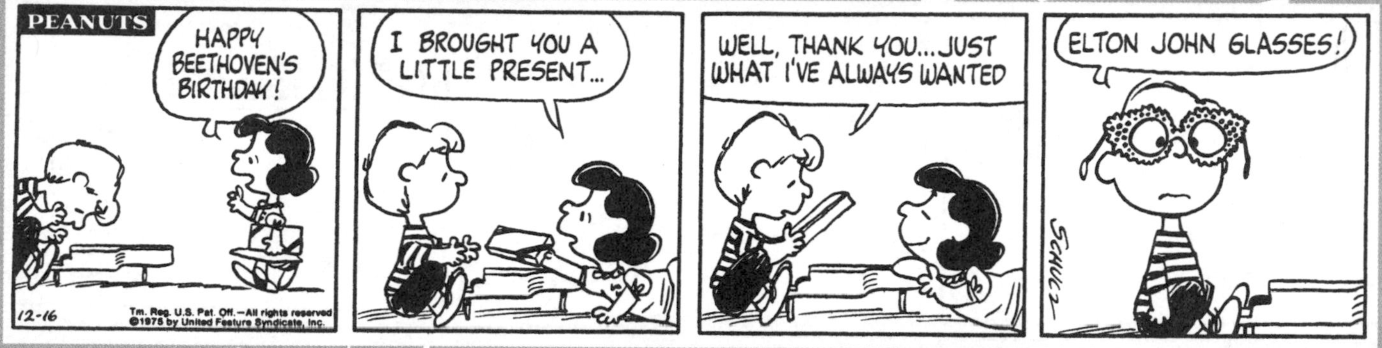
PEANUTS
HAPPY BEETHOVEN'S BIRTHDAY!
I BROUGHT YOU A LITTLE PRESENT...
WELL, THANK YOU...JUST WHAT I'VE ALWAYS WANTED
ELTON JOHN GLASSES!
12-16
Tm. Reg. U.S. Pat. Off.—All rights reserved ©1975 by United Feature Syndicate, Inc.
SCHULZ

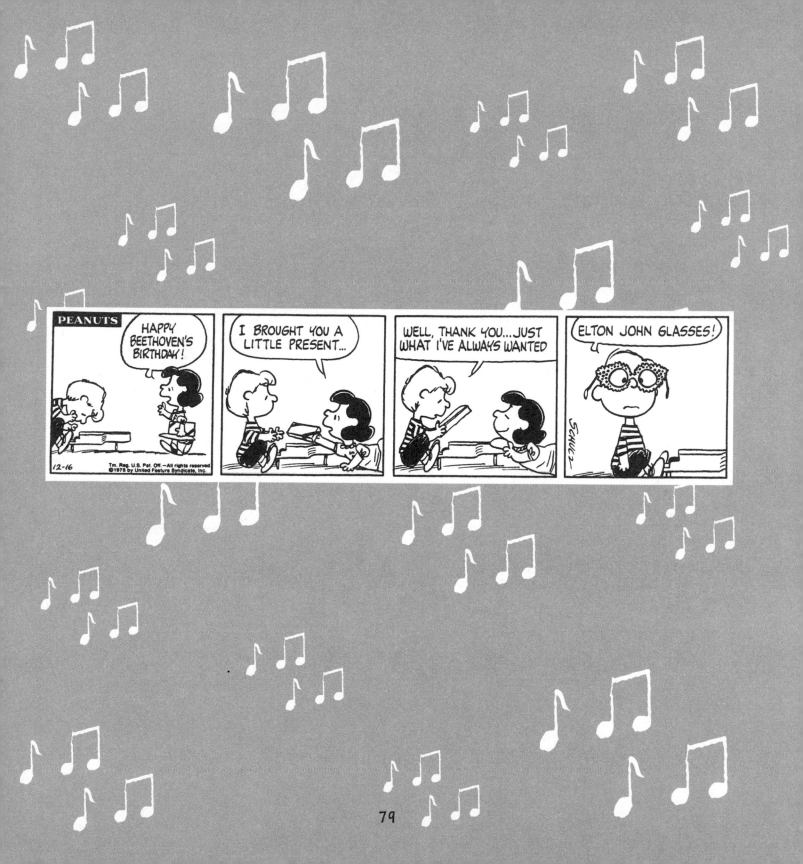

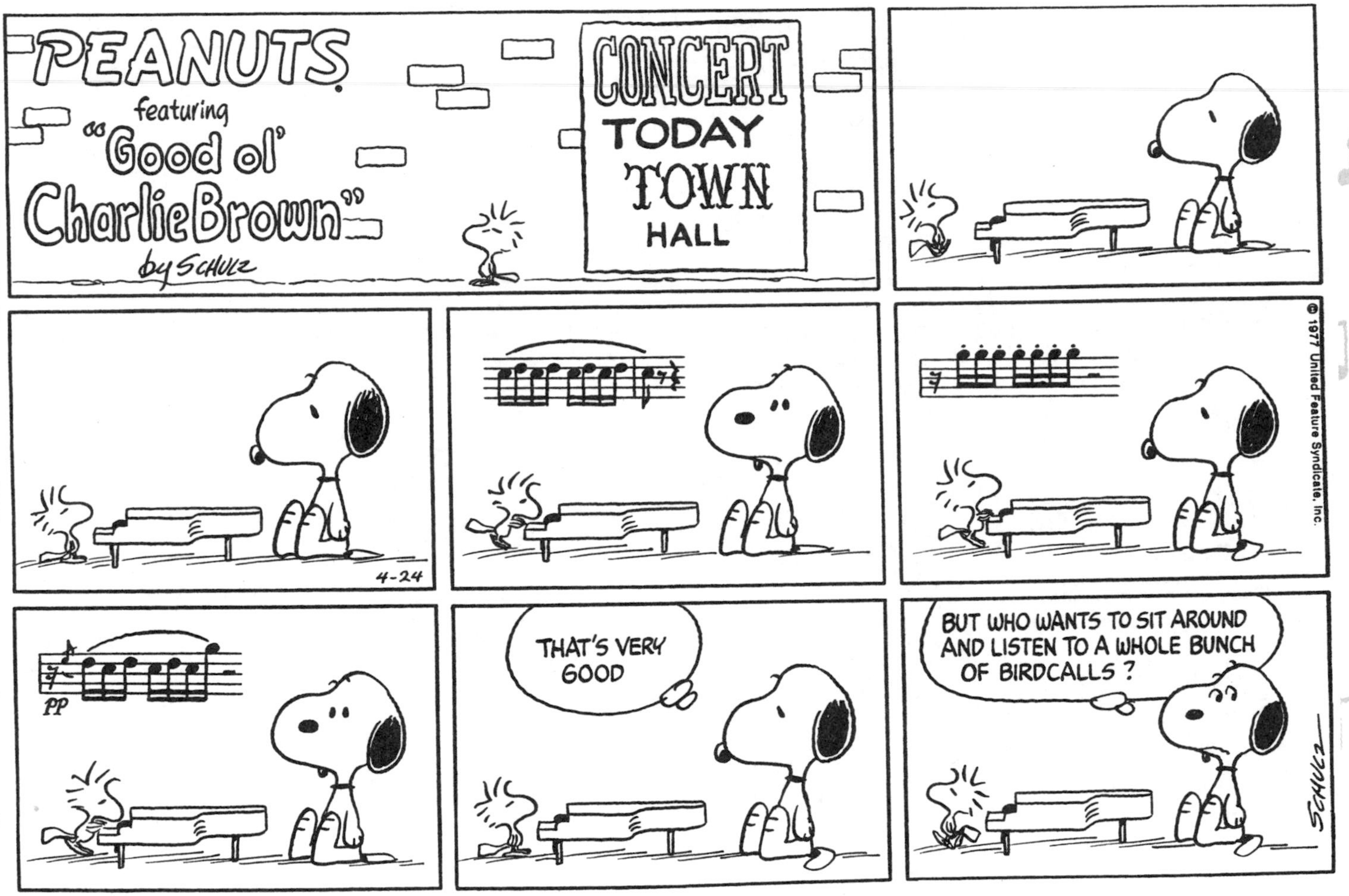
PEANUTS
featuring
"Good ol' CharlieBrown"
by SCHULZ
CONCERT
TODAY
TOWN
HALL
4-24
© 1977 United Feature Syndicate, Inc.
pp
THAT'S VERY GOOD
BUT WHO WANTS TO SIT AROUND AND LISTEN TO A WHOLE BUNCH OF BIRDCALLS?
SCHULZ

© 1977 United Feature Syndicate, Inc.
4-26
SCHULZ

SIGH
© 1977 United Feature Syndicate, Inc.
I GUESS I'M FINALLY BEGINNING TO REALIZE THAT YOU'LL ALWAYS LOVE YOUR PIANO MORE THAN YOU'LL EVER LOVE ME...
THAT'S TRUE
4-29
SCHULZ

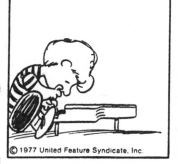

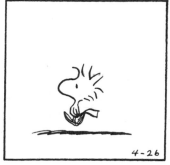

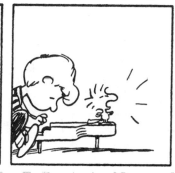

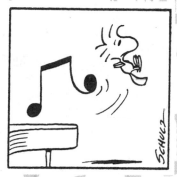

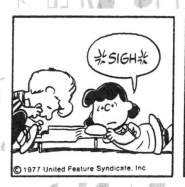

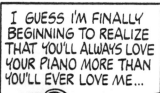

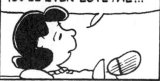

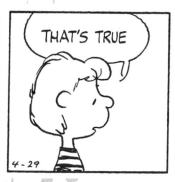

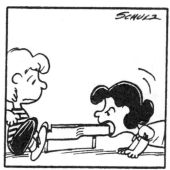

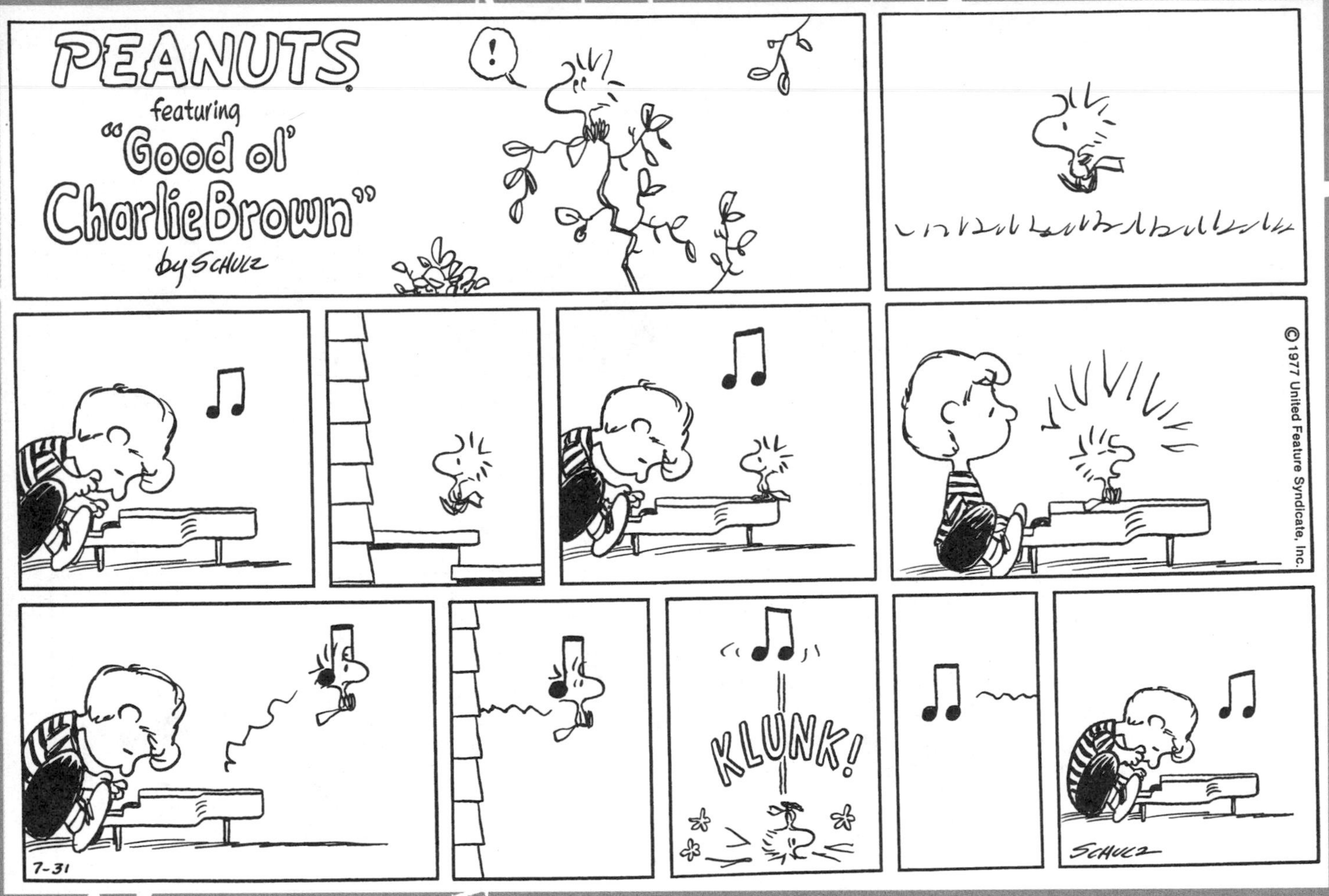
PEANUTS
featuring
"Good ol' CharlieBrown"
by SCHULZ
!
© 1977 United Feature Syndicate, Inc.
7-31
KLUNK!
SCHULZ

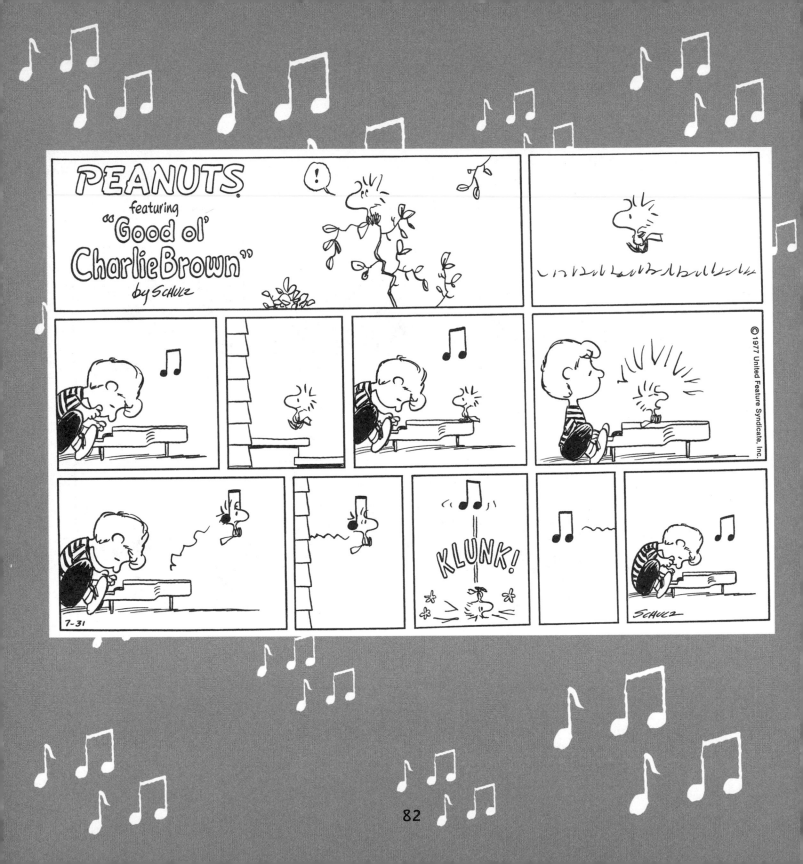

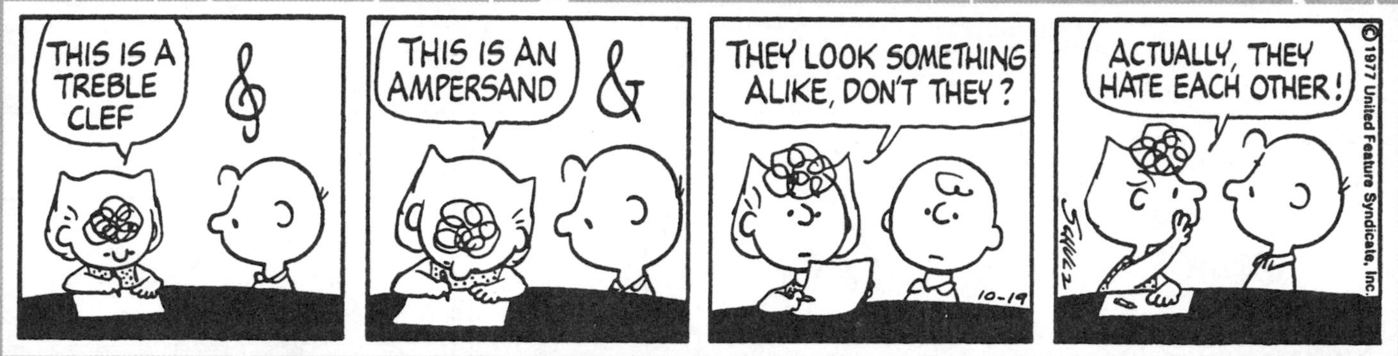
THIS IS A TREBLE CLEF
THIS IS AN AMPERSAND
THEY LOOK SOMETHING ALIKE, DON'T THEY ?
ACTUALLY, THEY HATE EACH OTHER!
© 1977 United Feature Syndicate, Inc.

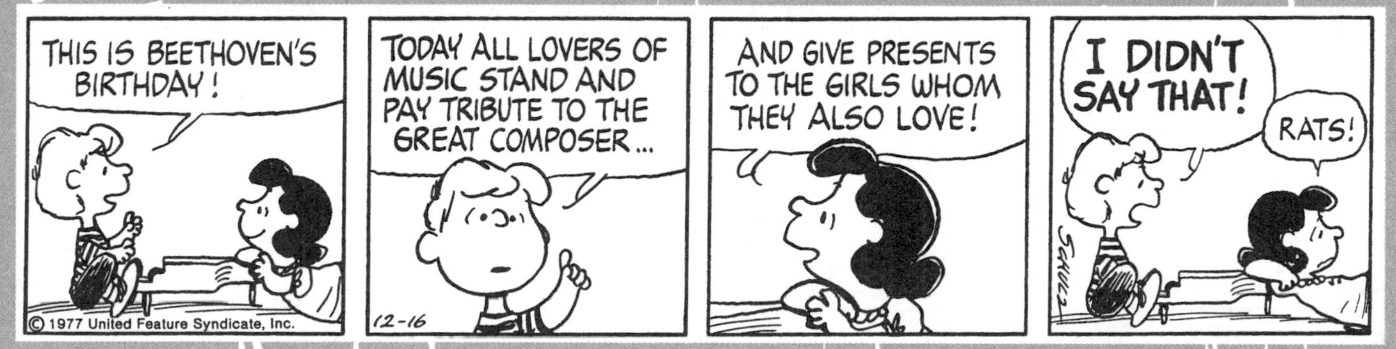
THIS IS BEETHOVEN'S BIRTHDAY!
© 1977 United Feature Syndicate, Inc.
TODAY ALL LOVERS OF MUSIC STAND AND PAY TRIBUTE TO THE GREAT COMPOSER...
AND GIVE PRESENTS TO THE GIRLS WHOM THEY ALSO LOVE!
I DIDN'T SAY THAT!
RATS!

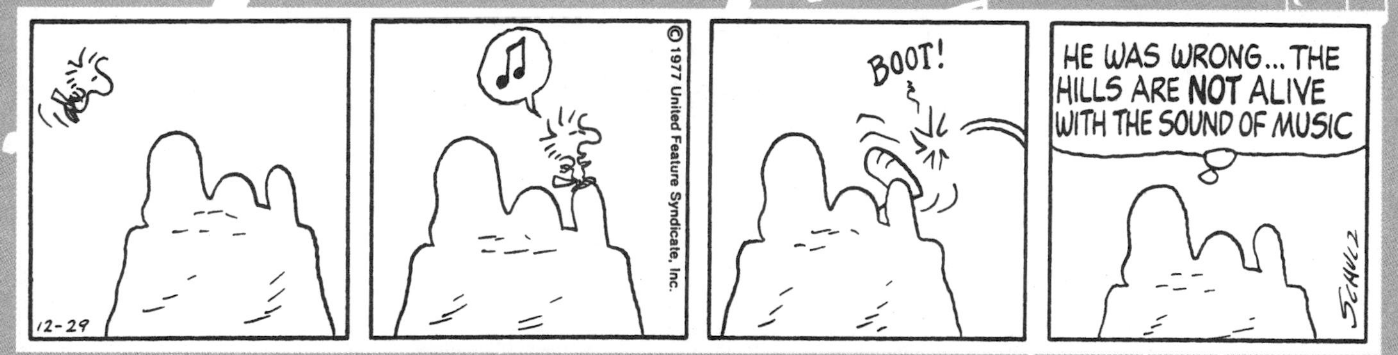
© 1977 United Feature Syndicate, Inc.
BOOT!
HE WAS WRONG... THE HILLS ARE NOT ALIVE WITH THE SOUND OF MUSIC

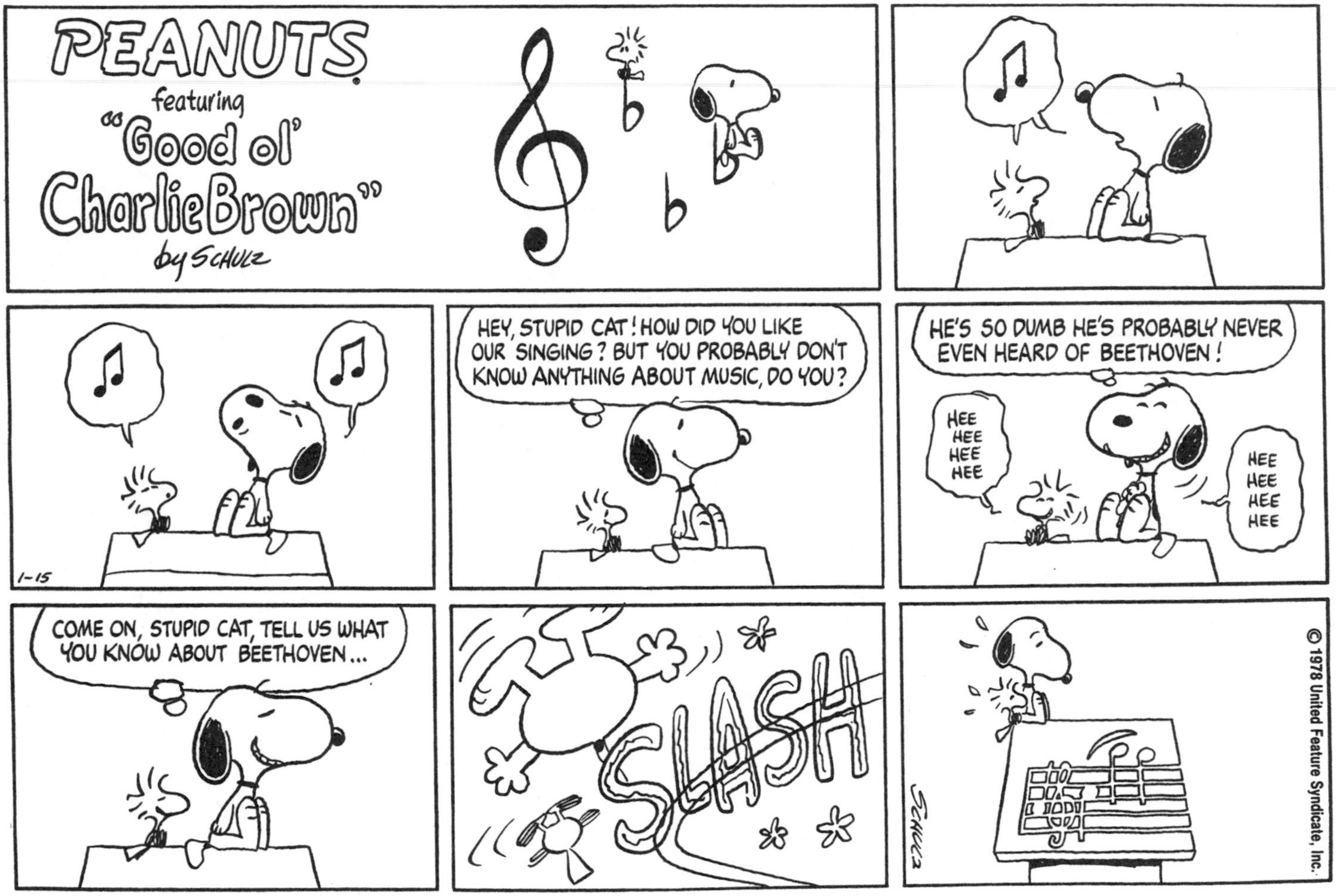
PEANUTS
featuring
"Good ol' CharlieBrown"
by SCHULZ
1-15
HEY, STUPID CAT! HOW DID YOU LIKE OUR SINGING? BUT YOU PROBABLY DON'T KNOW ANYTHING ABOUT MUSIC, DO YOU?
HE'S SO DUMB HE'S PROBABLY NEVER EVEN HEARD OF BEETHOVEN!
HEE HEE HEE HEE
HEE HEE HEE HEE
COME ON, STUPID CAT, TELL US WHAT YOU KNOW ABOUT BEETHOVEN...
SLASH
SCHULZ
© 1978 United Feature Syndicate, Inc.

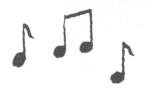

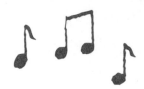

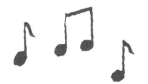

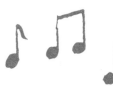

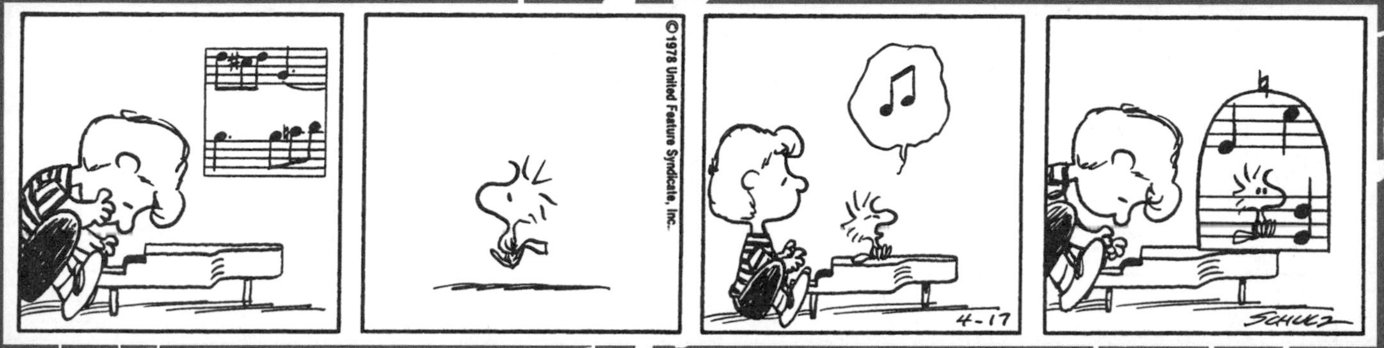
© 1978 United Feature Syndicate, Inc.
4-17
SCHULZ

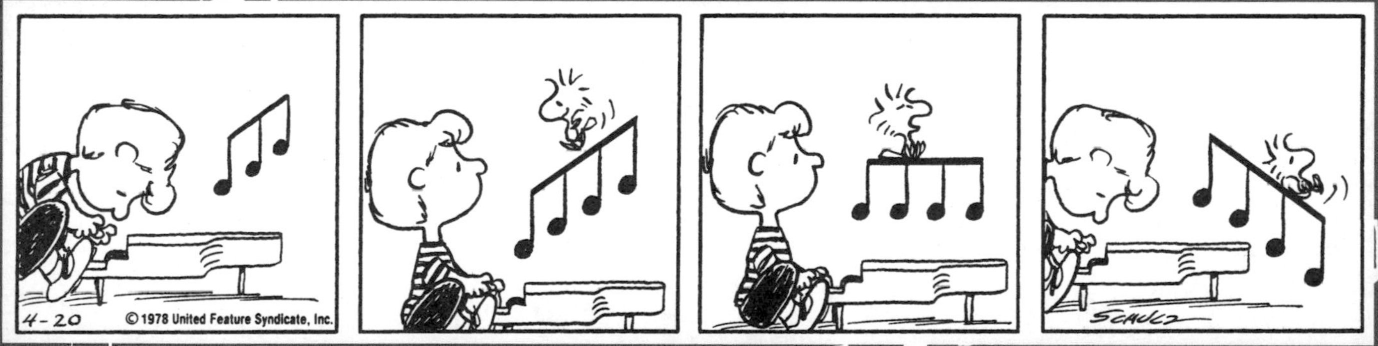
4-20
© 1978 United Feature Syndicate, Inc.
SCHULZ

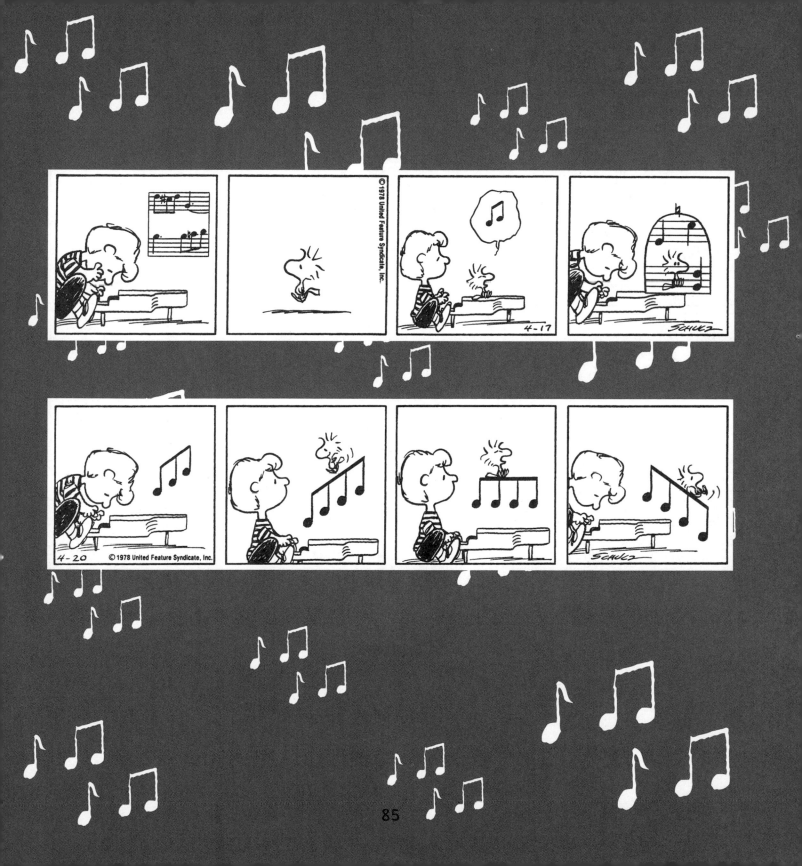

PEANUTS
featuring "Good ol' CharlieBrown"
by SCHULZ
THEATRE ROYAL
COVENT GARDEN
WOODSTOCK
IN CONCERT
BOXES 7s
PIT 3s·6d.
Galleries 2s
SIGH
WHY NOT?
SURE, YOU COULD! YOU'D BE VERY GOOD AT IT
© 1978 United Feature Syndicate, Inc.
4-30
HEY, STUPID CAT! MY LITTLE FRIEND HERE WANTS TO LEARN HOW TO PLAY THE VIOLIN...
YOU DON'T HAPPEN TO KNOW WHERE WE COULD ROUND UP A GOOD FIDDLE, DO YOU?
BUT WHY AM I ASKING YOU? YOU'RE SO STUPID YOU WOULDN'T KNOW A VIOLIN FROM A BASS DRUM...
SLASH
A 1727 PAGANINI! HOW NICE!
SCHULZ

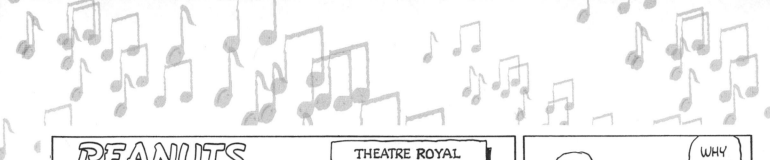

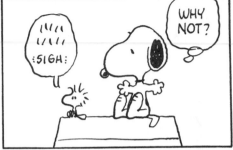

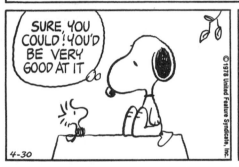

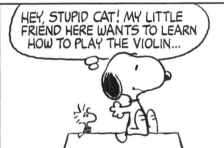

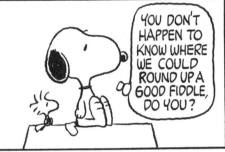

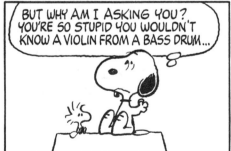

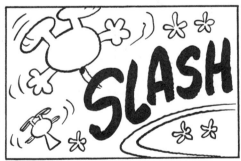

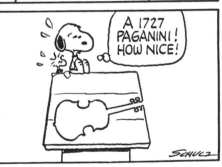

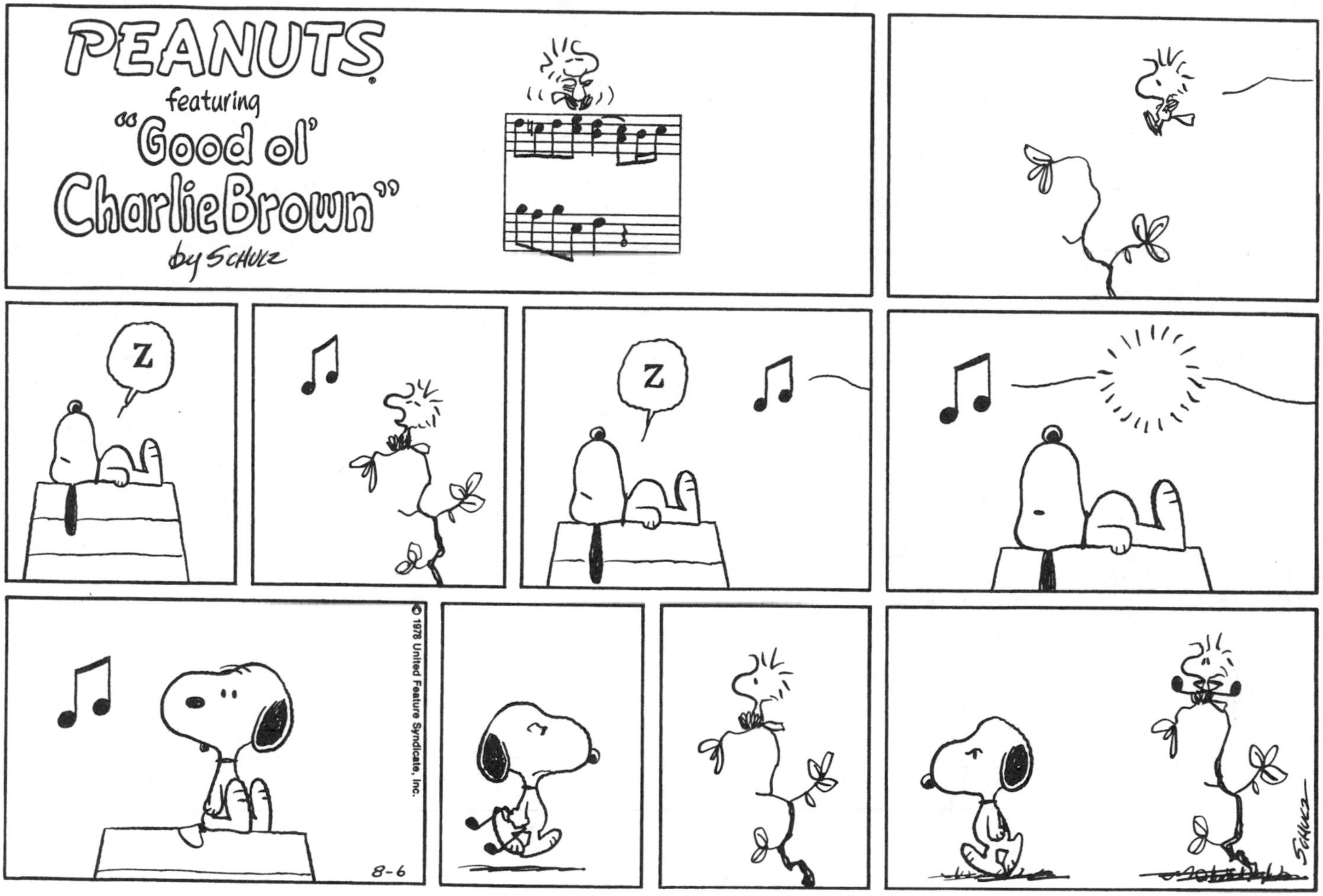
PEANUTS
featuring
"Good ol' Charlie Brown"
by SCHULZ
Z
Z
© 1978 United Feature Syndicate, Inc.
8-6
SCHULZ

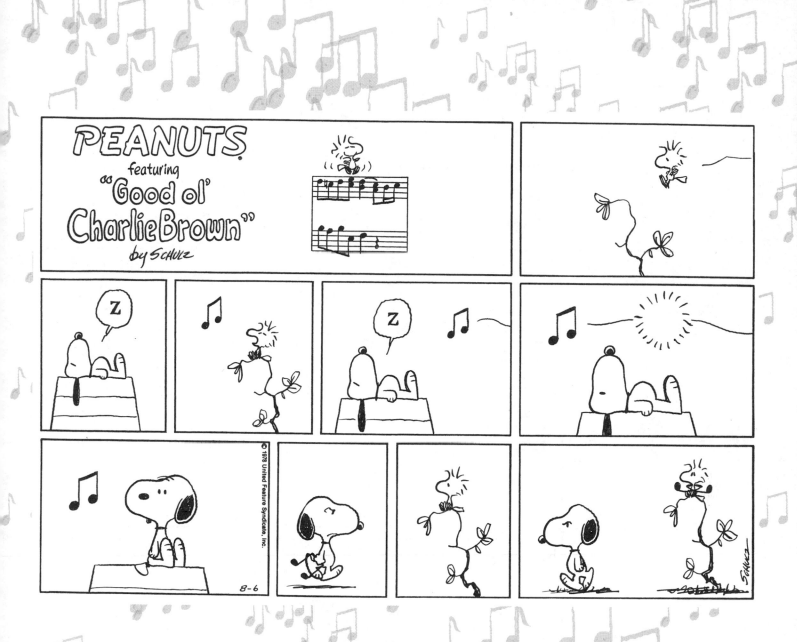

I'M WRITING A BOOK ABOUT BEETHOVEN
THERE'S THIS GIRL WHO LIKES HIM, SEE, BUT HE WON'T PAY ANY ATTENTION TO HER...SO YOU KNOW WHAT SHE DOES? GUESS!
12-4
SHE KICKS HIS PIANO!
"'WHAT DO YOU THINK OF THAT?' SHE SAID"
SCHULZ
© 1978 United Feature Syndicate, Inc.

I'M STILL WORKING ON MY BOOK ABOUT THE LIFE OF BEETHOVEN
© 1978 United Feature Syndicate, Inc.
REMEMBER HOW IN CHAPTER ONE THERE WAS THIS FRUSTRATED GIRL WHO KICKED HIS PIANO?
12-5
WELL, GUESS WHAT HAPPENS IN CHAPTER TWO
SHE DOES IT AGAIN!
SCHULZ

IN MY BOOK ABOUT BEETHOVEN, I'VE MADE A FEW IMPROVEMENTS
FOR INSTANCE, INSTEAD OF PLAYING THE PIANO, I HAVE HIM PLAYING AN ELECTRIC GUITAR...
12-6
ALSO, IN MY BOOK HE DOESN'T HAVE STOMACH PAINS..
© 1978 United Feature Syndicate, Inc.
I'VE UPDATED IT TO TENNIS ELBOW!
SCHULZ

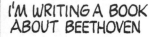

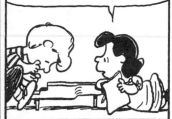

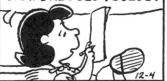

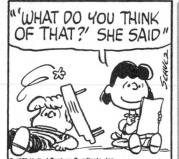

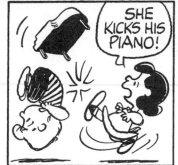

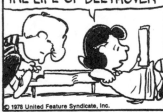

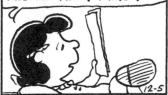

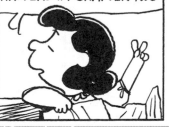

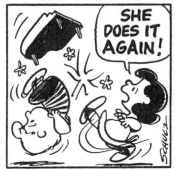

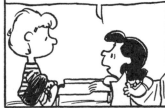

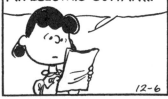

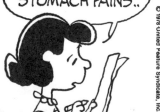

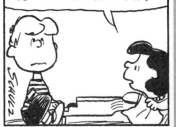

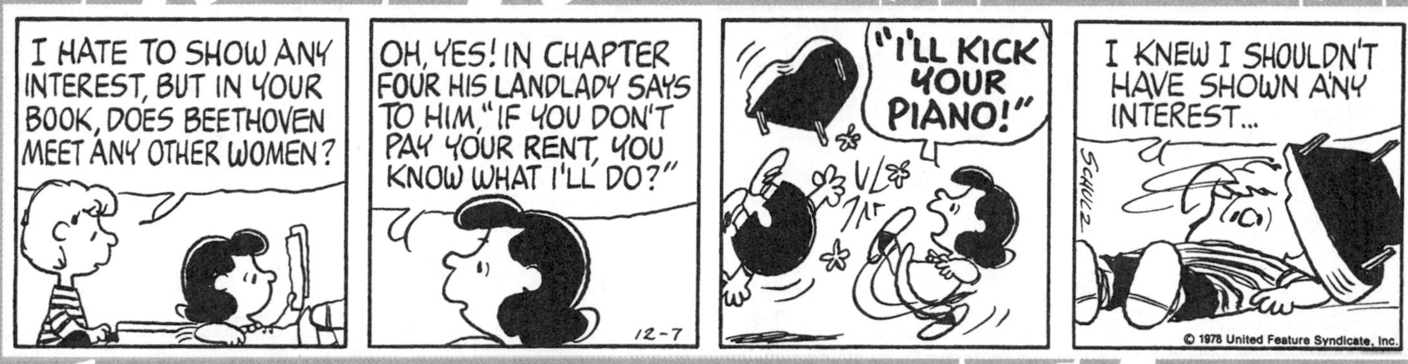
I HATE TO SHOW ANY INTEREST, BUT IN YOUR BOOK, DOES BEETHOVEN MEET ANY OTHER WOMEN?
OH, YES! IN CHAPTER FOUR HIS LANDLADY SAYS TO HIM, "IF YOU DON'T PAY YOUR RENT, YOU KNOW WHAT I'LL DO?"
12-7
"I'LL KICK YOUR PIANO!"
I KNEW I SHOULDN'T HAVE SHOWN ANY INTEREST...
SCHULZ
© 1978 United Feature Syndicate, Inc.

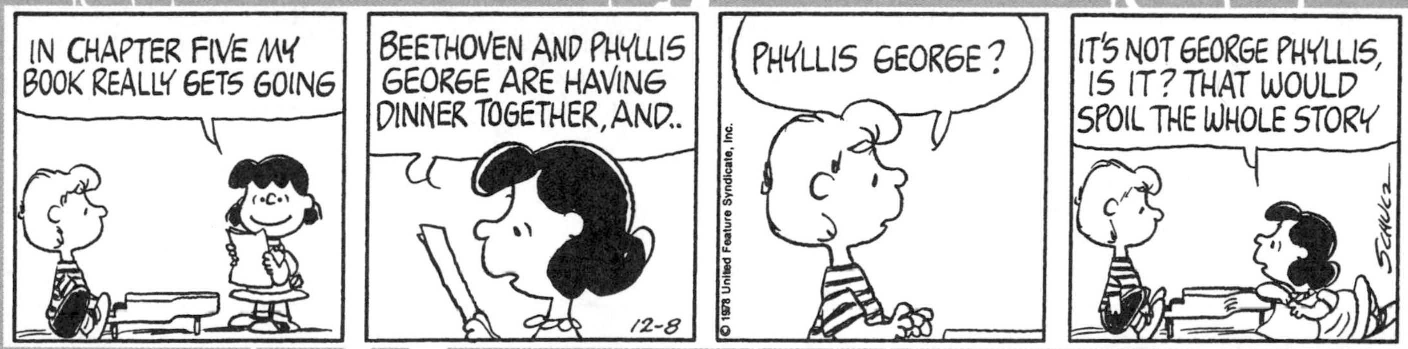
IN CHAPTER FIVE MY BOOK REALLY GETS GOING
BEETHOVEN AND PHYLLIS GEORGE ARE HAVING DINNER TOGETHER, AND..
12-8
© 1978 United Feature Syndicate, Inc.
PHYLLIS GEORGE?
IT'S NOT GEORGE PHYLLIS, IS IT? THAT WOULD SPOIL THE WHOLE STORY
SCHULZ

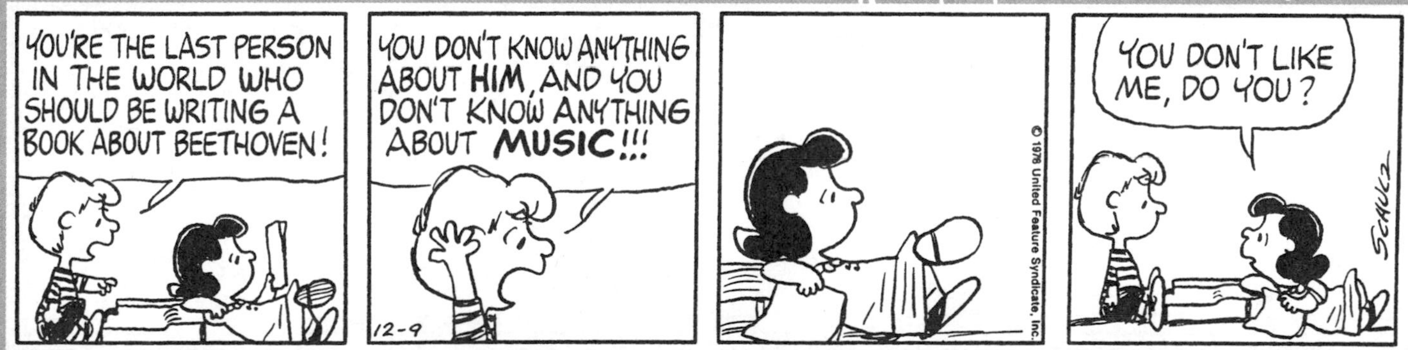
YOU'RE THE LAST PERSON IN THE WORLD WHO SHOULD BE WRITING A BOOK ABOUT BEETHOVEN!
YOU DON'T KNOW ANYTHING ABOUT HIM, AND YOU DON'T KNOW ANYTHING ABOUT MUSIC!!!
12-9
© 1978 United Feature Syndicate, Inc.
YOU DON'T LIKE ME, DO YOU?
SCHULZ

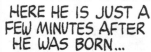

Panel 1: I'M MAKING ILLUSTRATIONS FOR MY BOOK ABOUT THE LIFE OF BEETHOVEN

Panel 2: HERE HE IS JUST A FEW MINUTES AFTER HE WAS BORN...

12-11

Panel 3: AND HERE HE IS JUST BEFORE HE DIED

© 1978 United Feature Syndicate, Inc.

Panel 4: THAT'S ENOUGH!

SCHULZ

Panel 5: OKAY, YOU STUPID BEAGLE...

Panel 6: I HAVE A JOB FOR YOU

© 1978 United Feature Syndicate, Inc.

Panel 7: I WANT YOU TO TYPE THIS MANUSCRIPT FOR ME, AND IF YOU DON'T DO A PERFECT JOB, I'M GONNA PUNCH YOUR LIGHTS OUT!

Panel 8: THEY NEVER TOLD US ABOUT HER KIND IN TYPING CLASS...

12-12

Panel 9: NOW, LOOK, YOU STUPID BEAGLE...

© 1978 United Feature Syndicate, Inc.

12-13

Panel 10: BEETHOVEN'S BIRTHDAY IS THIS SATURDAY! I WANT MY BOOK IN ALL THE STORES BY THEN

Panel 11: SO GET TYPING!!

Panel 12: IF WE CHANGED THE NAME TO BACH, IT WOULD GO FASTER

SCHULZ

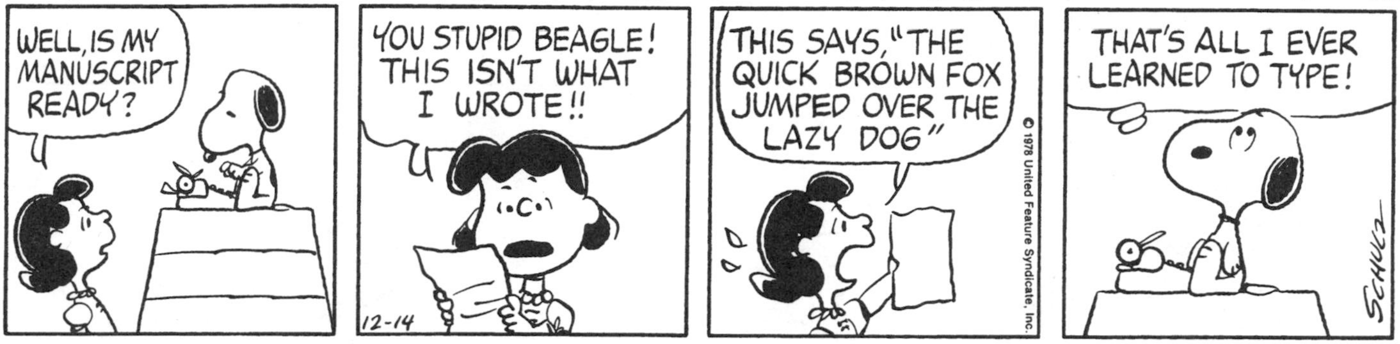
WELL, IS MY MANUSCRIPT READY?
YOU STUPID BEAGLE! THIS ISN'T WHAT I WROTE!!
12-14
THIS SAYS, "THE QUICK BROWN FOX JUMPED OVER THE LAZY DOG"
© 1978 United Feature Syndicate, Inc.
THAT'S ALL I EVER LEARNED TO TYPE!
SCHULZ

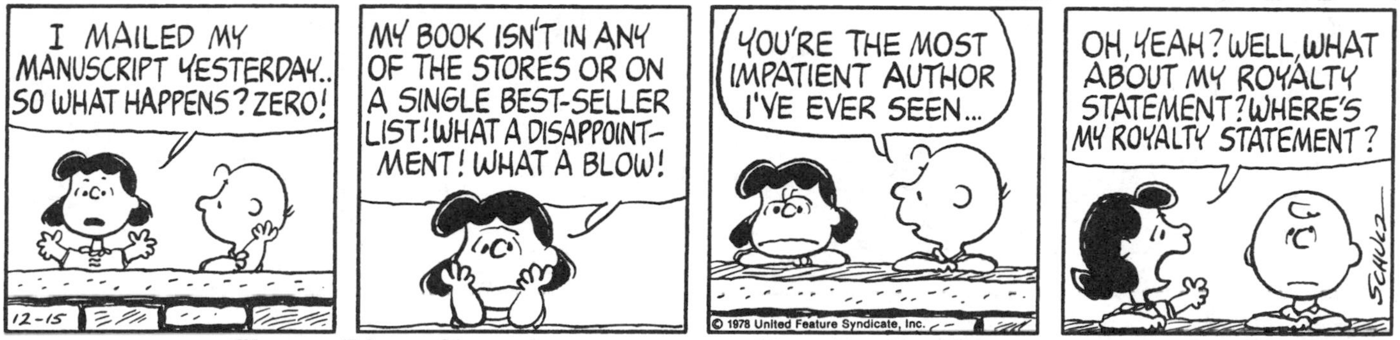
I MAILED MY MANUSCRIPT YESTERDAY.. SO WHAT HAPPENS? ZERO!
12-15
MY BOOK ISN'T IN ANY OF THE STORES OR ON A SINGLE BEST-SELLER LIST! WHAT A DISAPPOINTMENT! WHAT A BLOW!
YOU'RE THE MOST IMPATIENT AUTHOR I'VE EVER SEEN...
© 1978 United Feature Syndicate, Inc.
OH, YEAH? WELL, WHAT ABOUT MY ROYALTY STATEMENT? WHERE'S MY ROYALTY STATEMENT?
SCHULZ

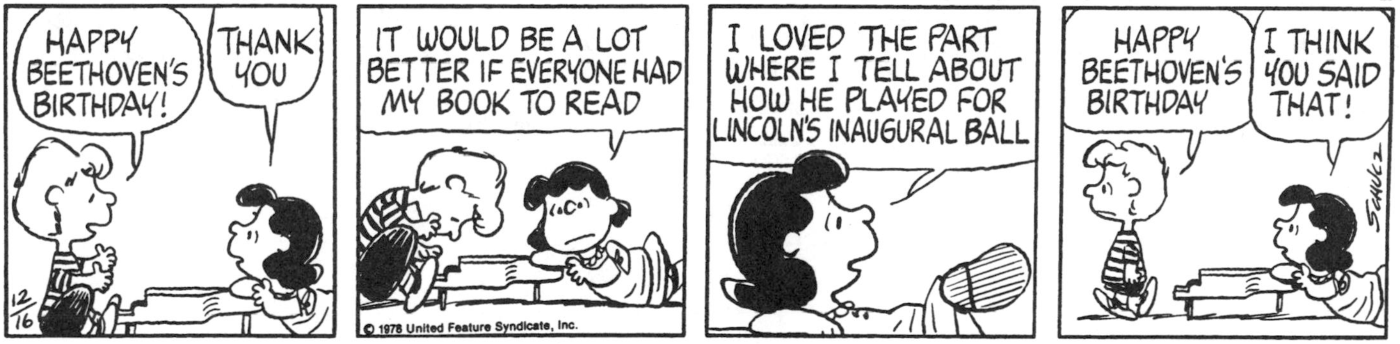
HAPPY BEETHOVEN'S BIRTHDAY!
THANK YOU
12/16
IT WOULD BE A LOT BETTER IF EVERYONE HAD MY BOOK TO READ
© 1978 United Feature Syndicate, Inc.
I LOVED THE PART WHERE I TELL ABOUT HOW HE PLAYED FOR LINCOLN'S INAUGURAL BALL
HAPPY BEETHOVEN'S BIRTHDAY
I THINK YOU SAID THAT!
SCHULZ

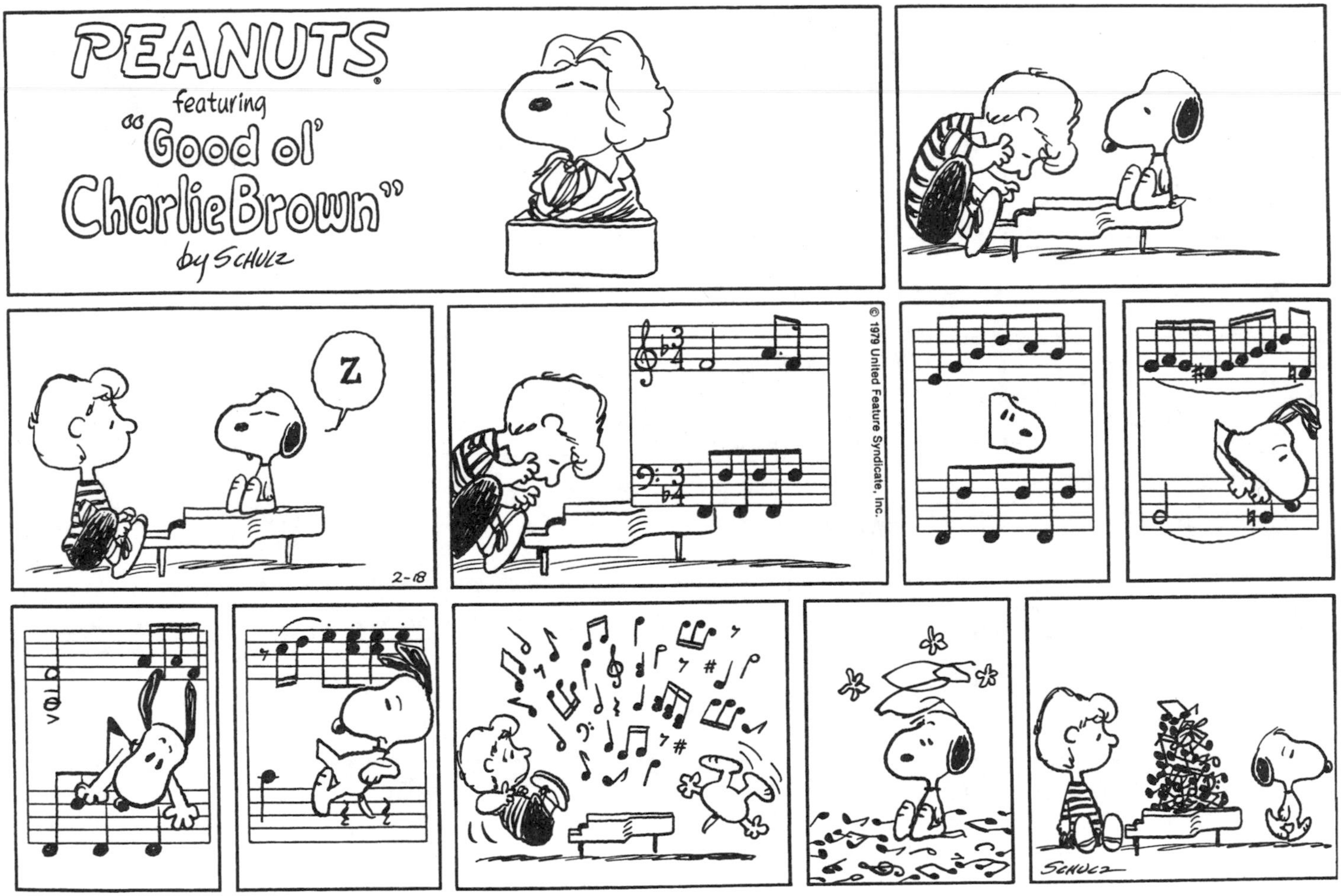
PEANUTS
featuring
"Good ol' CharlieBrown"
by SCHULZ
Z
2-18
© 1979 United Feature Syndicate, Inc.
SCHULZ

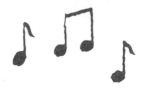

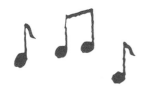

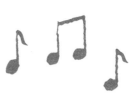

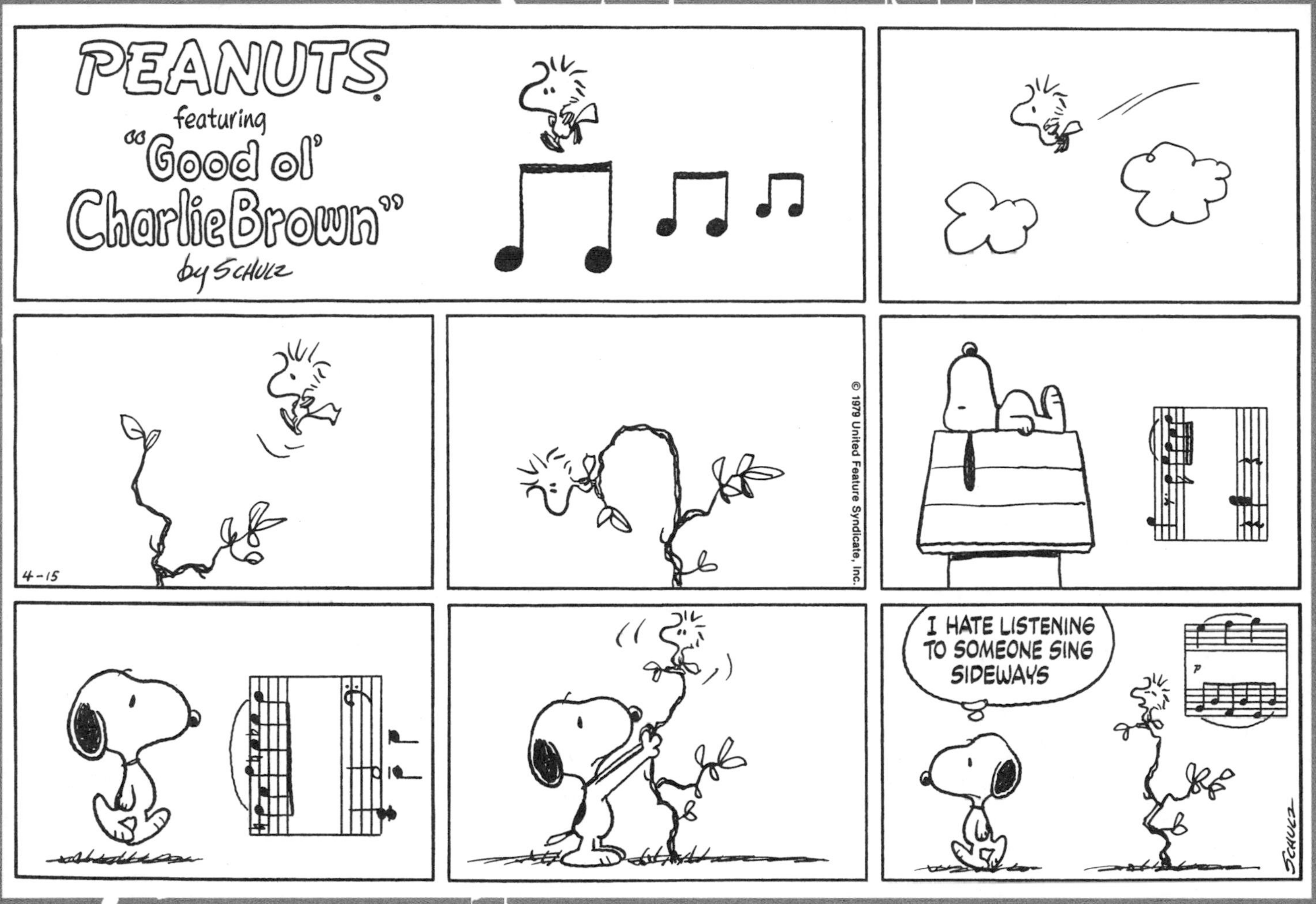
PEANUTS
featuring
"Good ol' CharlieBrown"
by SCHULZ
4-15
© 1979 United Feature Syndicate, Inc.
I HATE LISTENING TO SOMEONE SING SIDEWAYS
SCHULZ

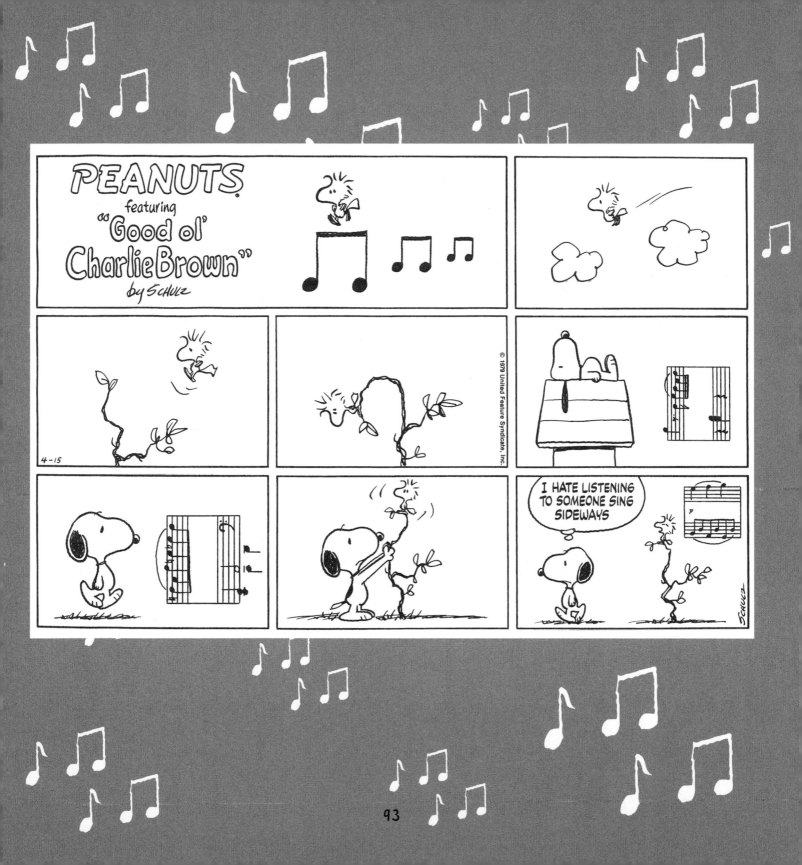

MAYBE YOUR SONGS AREN'T HAPPY ENOUGH
AFTER ALL, IT'S SPRING!
5-7
© 1979 United Feature Syndicate, Inc.
SING SOMETHING THAT MAKES PEOPLE HAPPY...
SCHULZ

CHURP!
HMM..
TRY IT WITH AN UMLAUT
5-8
© 1979 United Feature Syndicate, Inc.
CHÜRP
FORGET THE UMLAUT!
SCHULZ

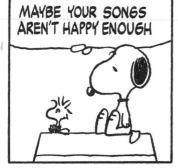

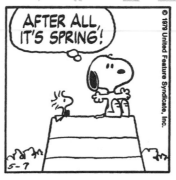

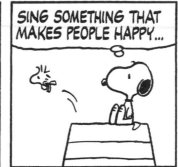

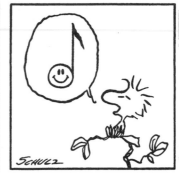

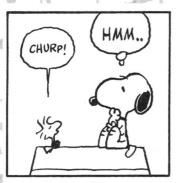

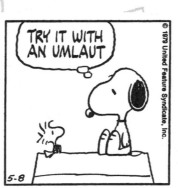

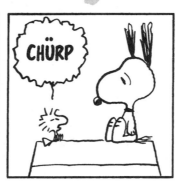

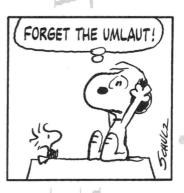

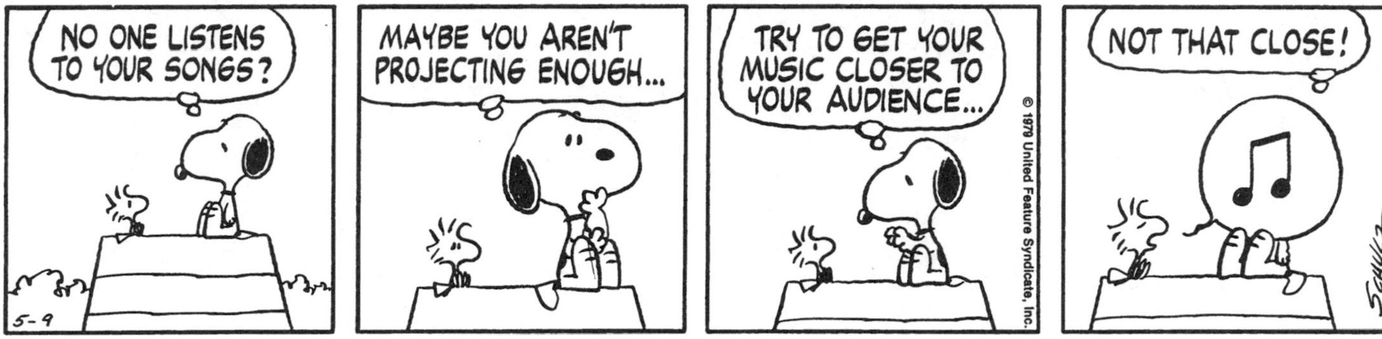
NO ONE LISTENS TO YOUR SONGS?
5-9
MAYBE YOU AREN'T PROJECTING ENOUGH...
TRY TO GET YOUR MUSIC CLOSER TO YOUR AUDIENCE...
© 1979 United Feature Syndicate, Inc.
NOT THAT CLOSE!
SCHULZ

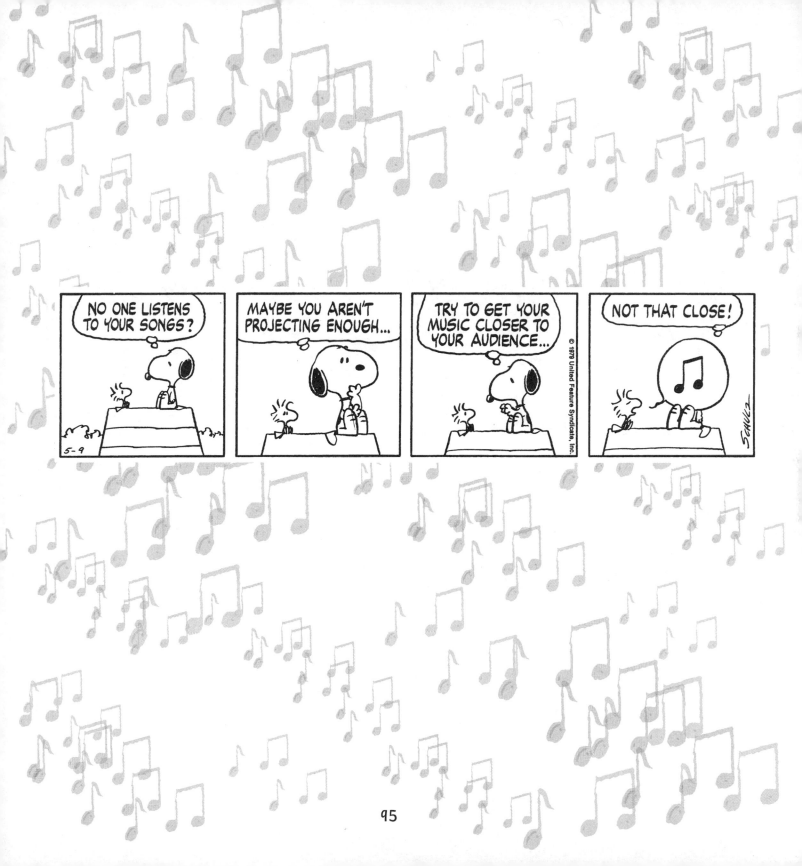

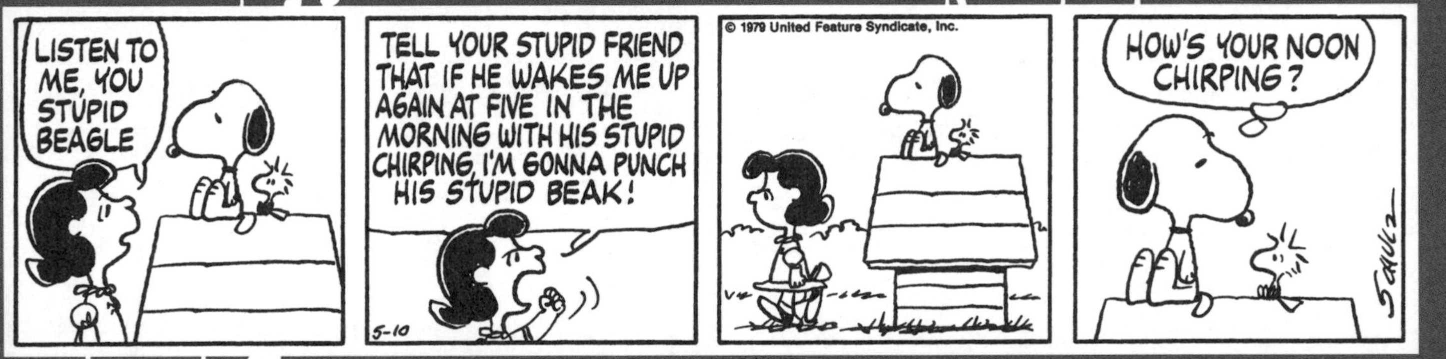
LISTEN TO ME, YOU STUPID BEAGLE
TELL YOUR STUPID FRIEND THAT IF HE WAKES ME UP AGAIN AT FIVE IN THE MORNING WITH HIS STUPID CHIRPING, I'M GONNA PUNCH HIS STUPID BEAK!
5-10
© 1979 United Feature Syndicate, Inc.
HOW'S YOUR NOON CHIRPING?
SCHULZ

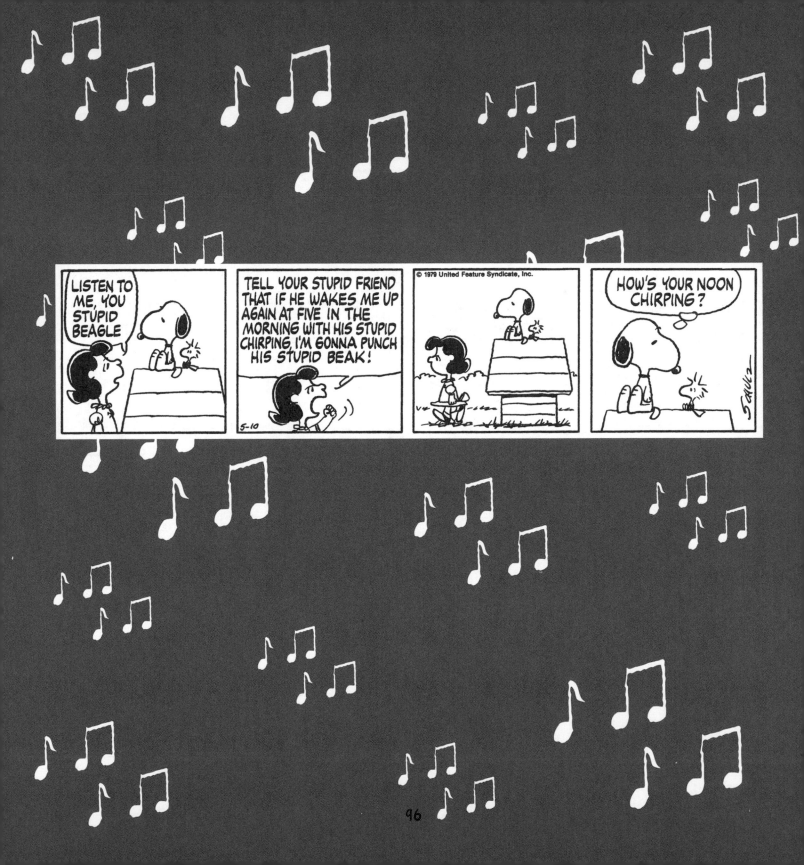

PEANUTS
featuring
"Good ol' Charlie Brown"
by SCHULZ
WHAT DID I DO?
HAPPY BIRTHDAY, AMY
© 1979 United Feature Syndicate, Inc.
8-5
SCHULZ

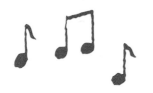

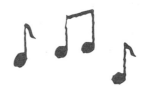

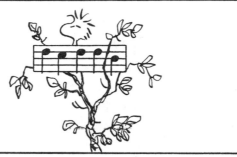

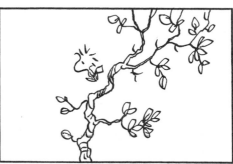

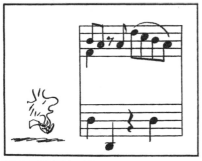

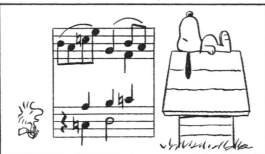

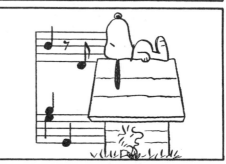

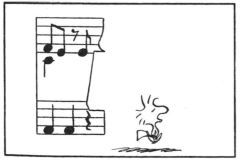

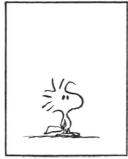

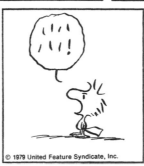

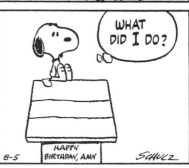

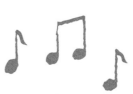

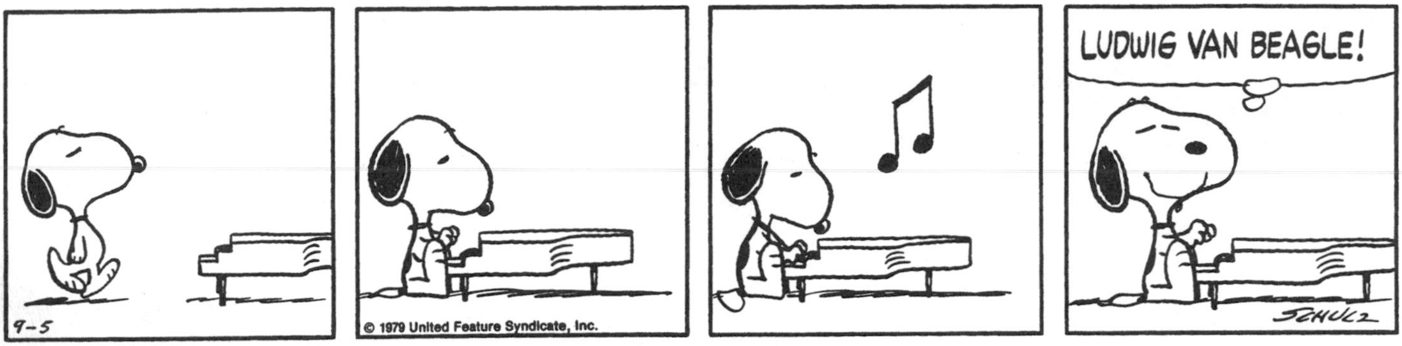
9-5
© 1979 United Feature Syndicate, Inc.
LUDWIG VAN BEAGLE!
SCHULZ

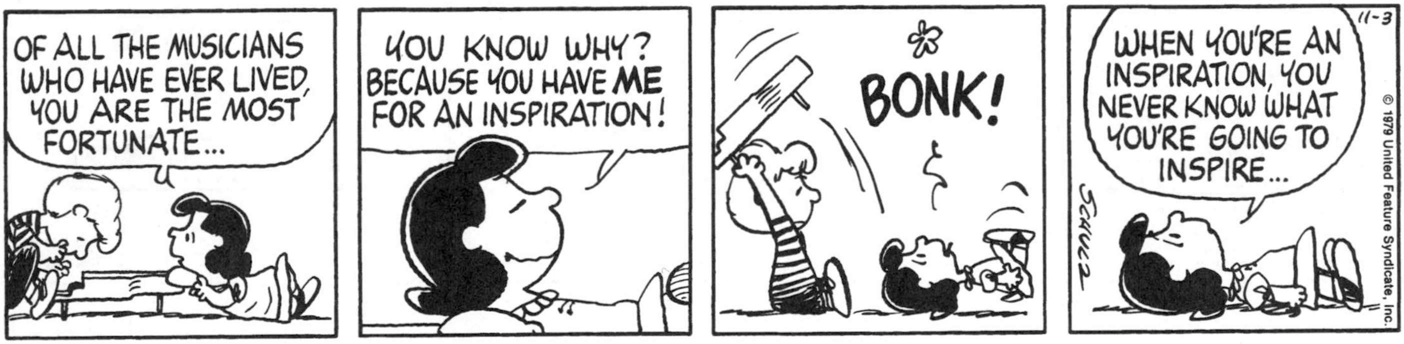
OF ALL THE MUSICIANS WHO HAVE EVER LIVED, YOU ARE THE MOST FORTUNATE...
YOU KNOW WHY? BECAUSE YOU HAVE **ME** FOR AN INSPIRATION!
BONK!
SCHULZ
11-3
WHEN YOU'RE AN INSPIRATION, YOU NEVER KNOW WHAT YOU'RE GOING TO INSPIRE...
© 1979 United Feature Syndicate, Inc.

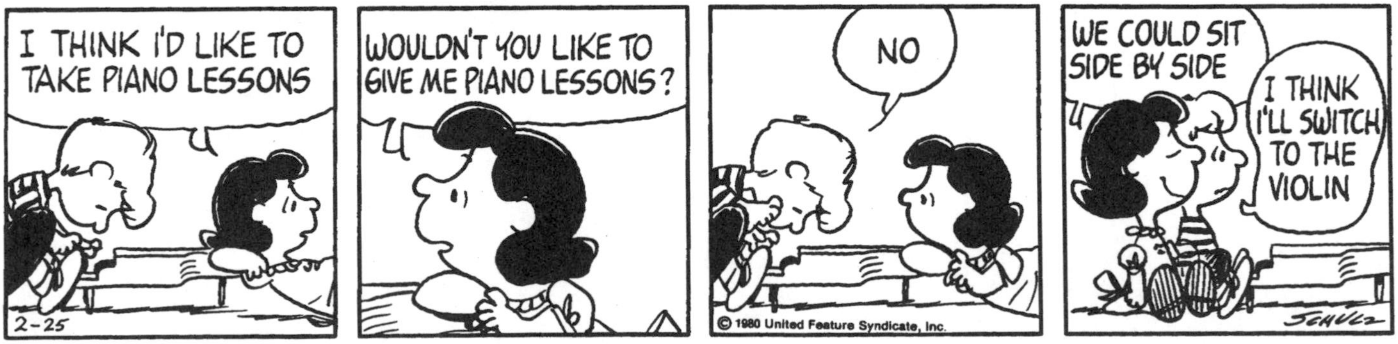
I THINK I'D LIKE TO TAKE PIANO LESSONS
2-25
WOULDN'T YOU LIKE TO GIVE ME PIANO LESSONS?
NO
© 1980 United Feature Syndicate, Inc.
WE COULD SIT SIDE BY SIDE
I THINK I'LL SWITCH TO THE VIOLIN
SCHULZ

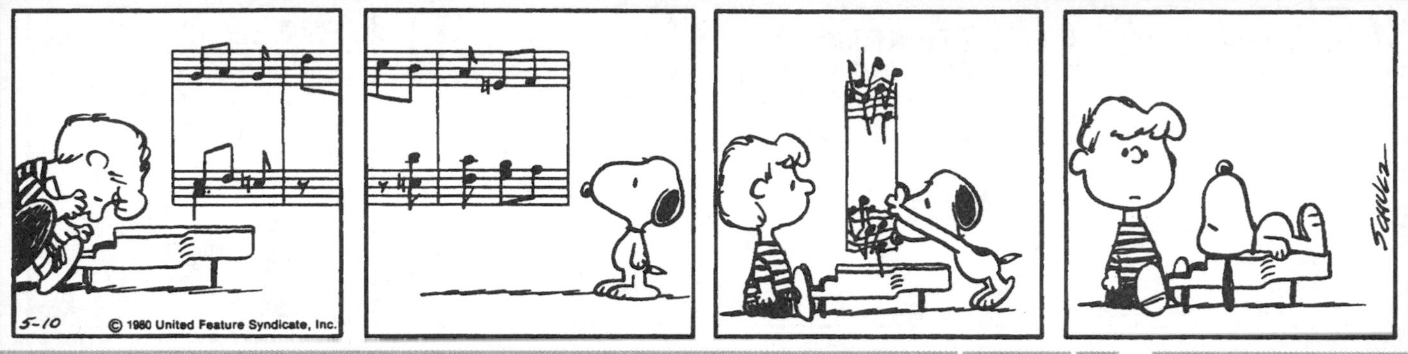
5-10
© 1980 United Feature Syndicate, Inc.

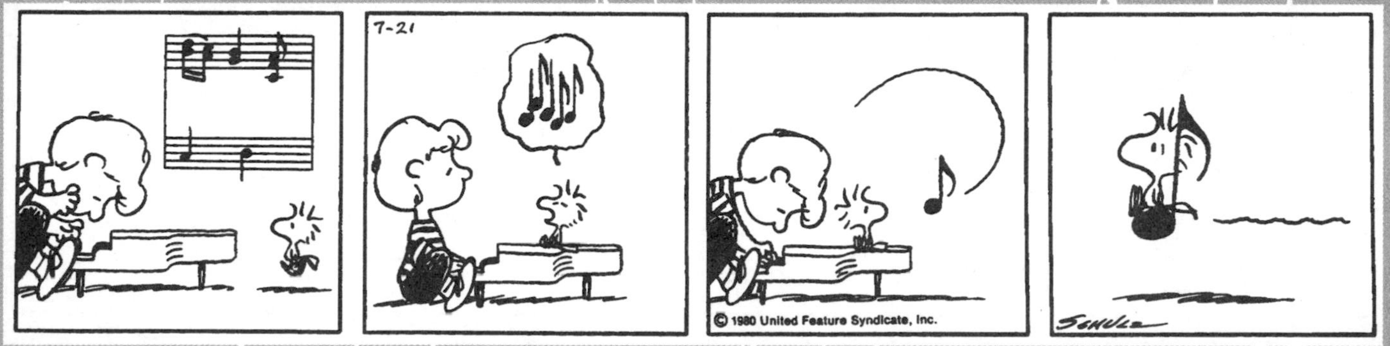
7-21
© 1980 United Feature Syndicate, Inc.

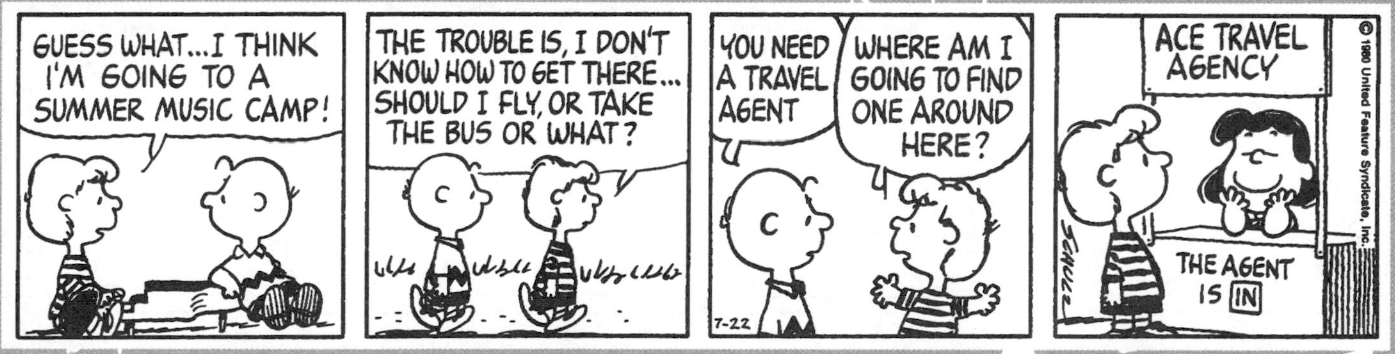
GUESS WHAT...I THINK I'M GOING TO A SUMMER MUSIC CAMP!
THE TROUBLE IS, I DON'T KNOW HOW TO GET THERE... SHOULD I FLY, OR TAKE THE BUS OR WHAT?
YOU NEED A TRAVEL AGENT
WHERE AM I GOING TO FIND ONE AROUND HERE?
7-22
ACE TRAVEL AGENCY
THE AGENT IS IN
© 1980 United Feature Syndicate, Inc.

HEY! THIS IS WHERE WE STARTED!
© 1980 United Feature Syndicate, Inc.
WE'VE BEEN FLYING ALL DAY AND GOING NO PLACE! I'M SUPPOSED TO BE AT MUSIC CAMP!
8-6
WHAT HAPPENED?
SORRY, SIR..THIS SECTION OF THE AIRPORT TERMINAL IS CLOSED FOR REPAIRS!
SCHULZ

8-20
© 1980 United Feature Syndicate, Inc.
SCHULZ

TOMORROW IS BEETHOVEN'S BIRTHDAY
SOME OF THE GREATEST MUSIC IN ALL THE WORLD WAS WRITTEN BY BEETHOVEN!
© 1980 United Feature Syndicate, Inc.
12-15
?
NO, HE WASN'T A BIRD!
SCHULZ

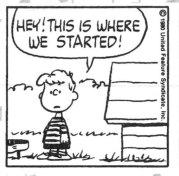

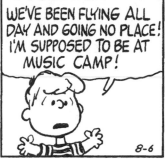

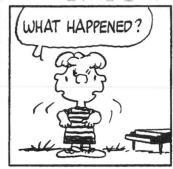

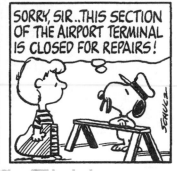

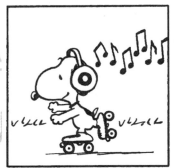

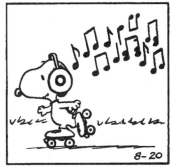

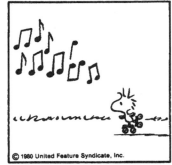

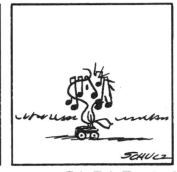

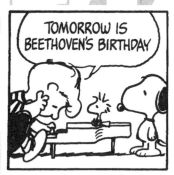

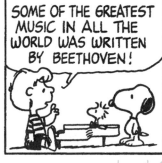

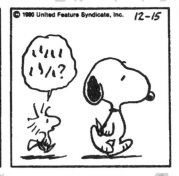

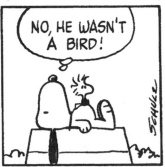

12-26
© 1980 United Feature Syndicate, Inc.
SCHULZ

4-4
© 1981 United Feature Syndicate, Inc.
WHAT CAN I SAY? WHEN YOU SING IN THE RAIN, YOU GET A MOUTH FULL OF WATER!
SCHULZ

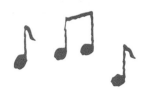

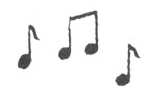

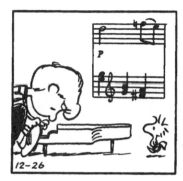

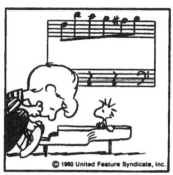

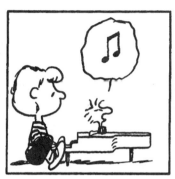

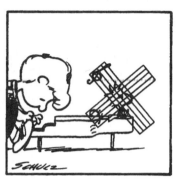

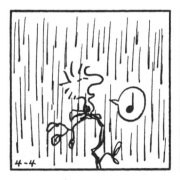

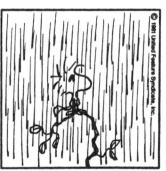

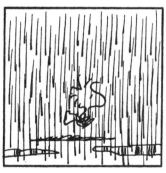

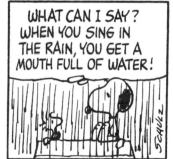

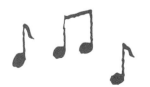

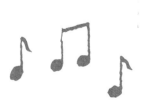

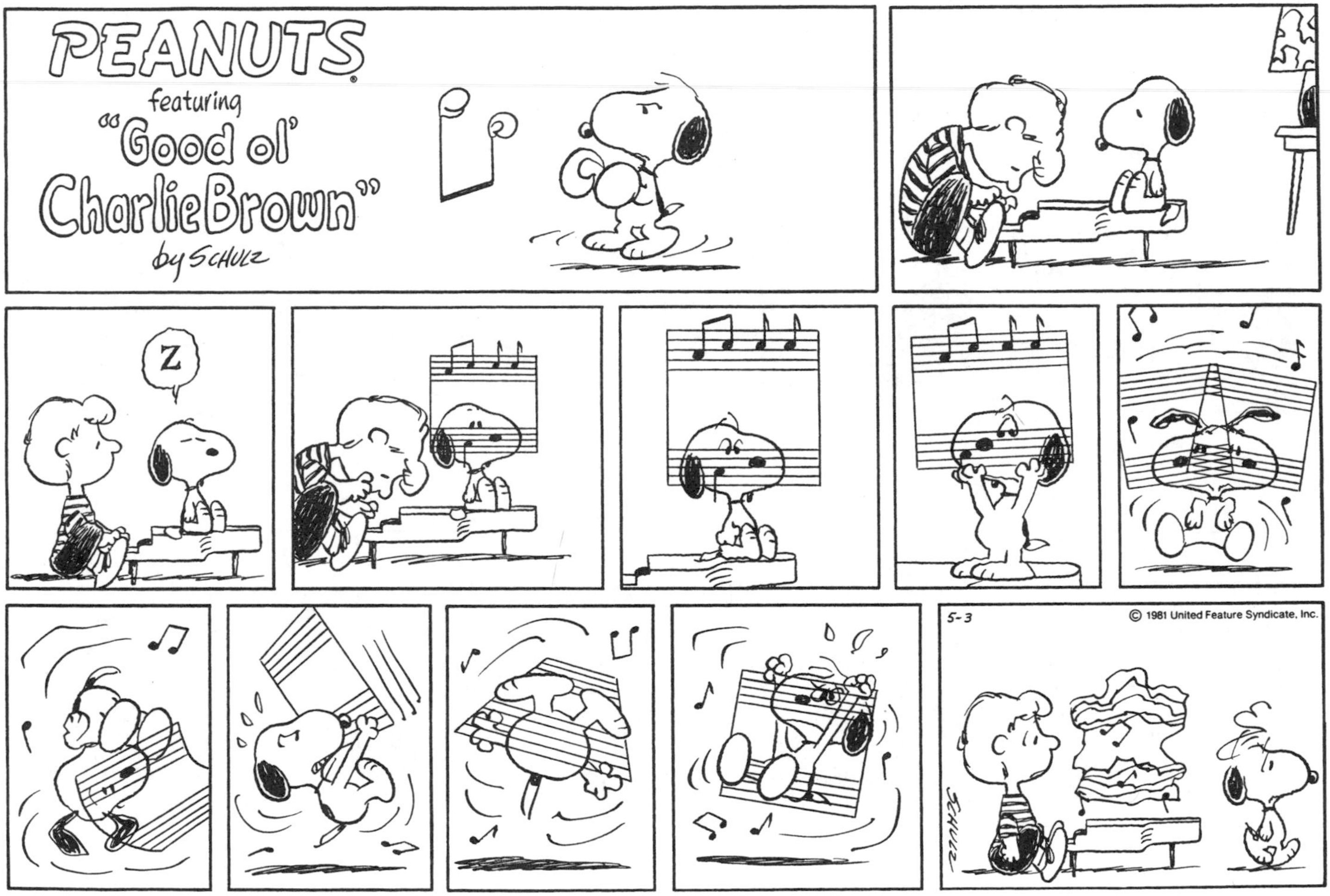
PEANUTS
featuring
"Good ol' Charlie Brown"
by SCHULZ
Z
5-3
© 1981 United Feature Syndicate, Inc.
SCHULZ

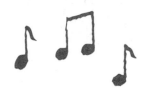

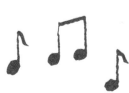

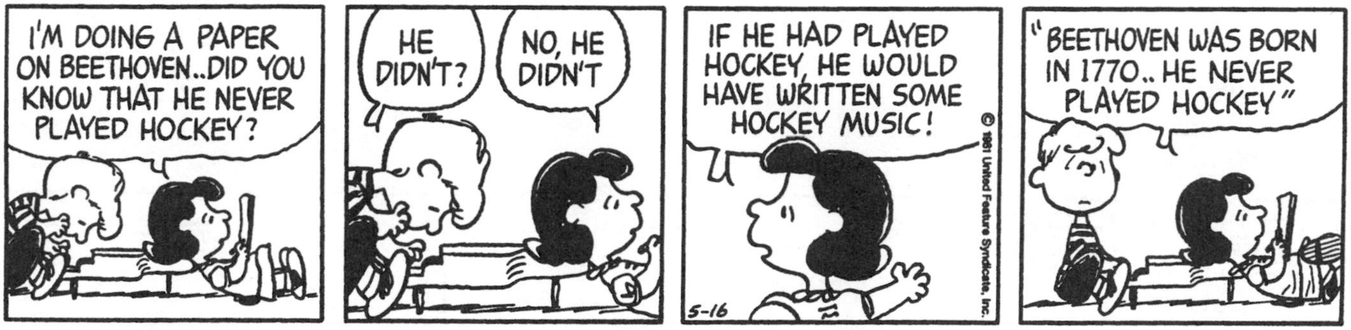
I'M DOING A PAPER ON BEETHOVEN..DID YOU KNOW THAT HE NEVER PLAYED HOCKEY?
HE DIDN'T?
NO, HE DIDN'T
IF HE HAD PLAYED HOCKEY, HE WOULD HAVE WRITTEN SOME HOCKEY MUSIC!
5-16
© 1981 United Feature Syndicate, Inc.
"BEETHOVEN WAS BORN IN 1770.. HE NEVER PLAYED HOCKEY"

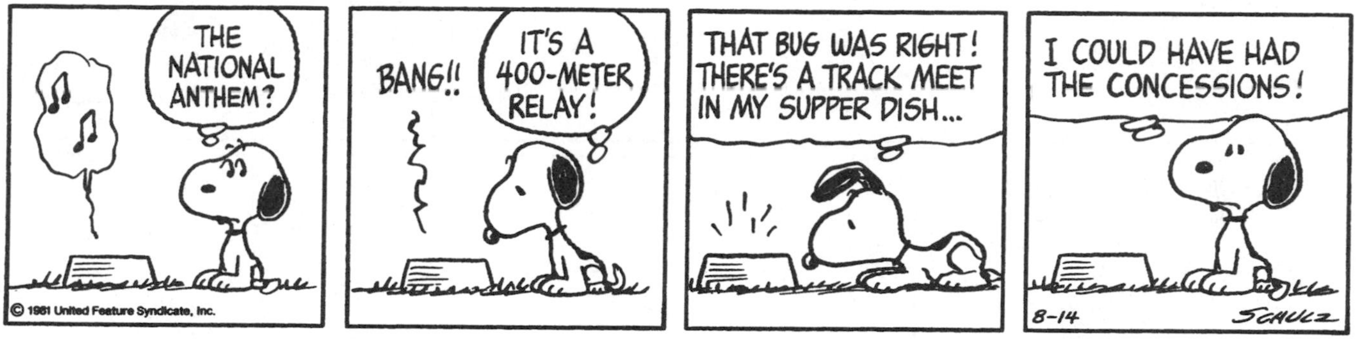
THE NATIONAL ANTHEM?
© 1981 United Feature Syndicate, Inc.
BANG!!
IT'S A 400-METER RELAY!
THAT BUG WAS RIGHT! THERE'S A TRACK MEET IN MY SUPPER DISH...
I COULD HAVE HAD THE CONCESSIONS!
8-14
SCHULZ

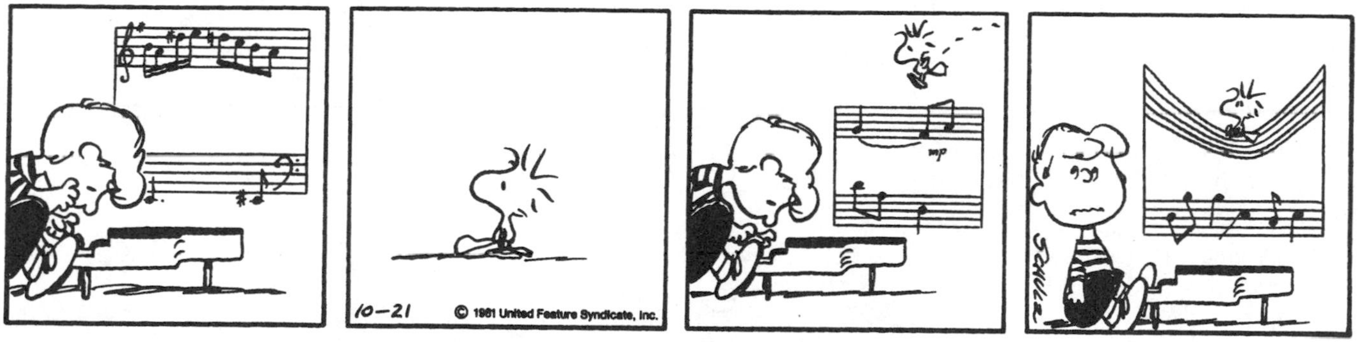
10-21
© 1981 United Feature Syndicate, Inc.
mp
SCHULZ

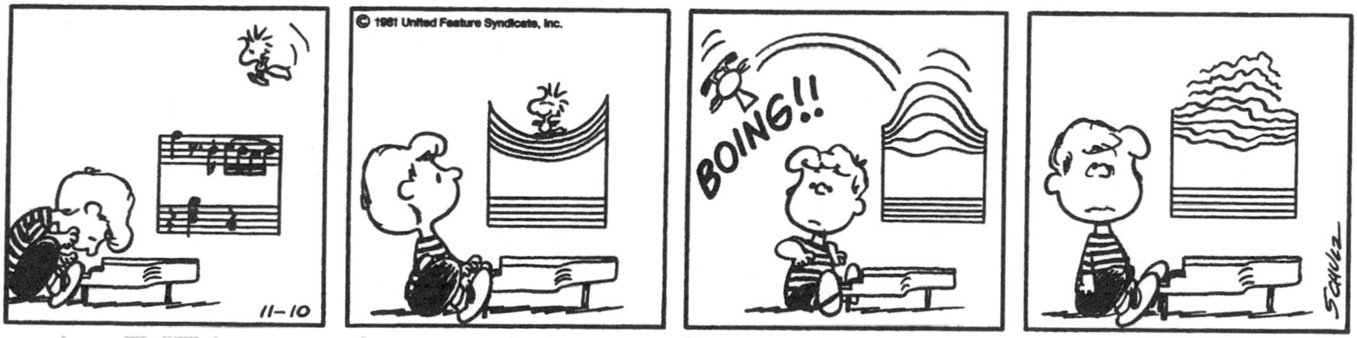
11-10
© 1981 United Feature Syndicate, Inc.
BOING!!
SCHULZ

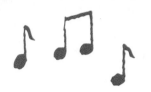

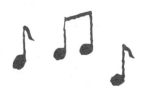

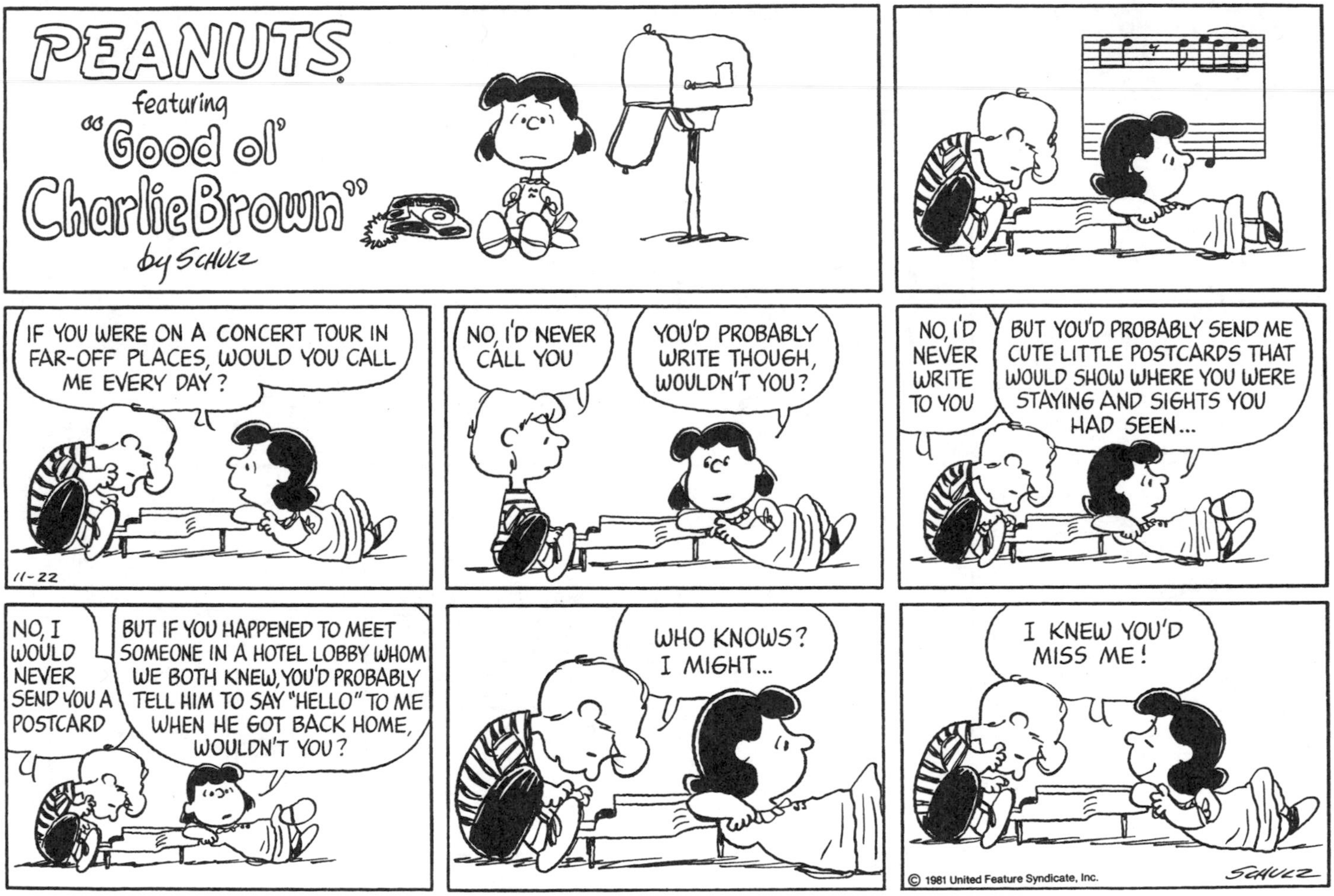
PEANUTS
featuring
"Good ol' CharlieBrown"
by SCHULZ
IF YOU WERE ON A CONCERT TOUR IN FAR-OFF PLACES, WOULD YOU CALL ME EVERY DAY?
11-22
NO, I'D NEVER CALL YOU
YOU'D PROBABLY WRITE THOUGH, WOULDN'T YOU?
NO, I'D NEVER WRITE TO YOU
BUT YOU'D PROBABLY SEND ME CUTE LITTLE POSTCARDS THAT WOULD SHOW WHERE YOU WERE STAYING AND SIGHTS YOU HAD SEEN...
NO, I WOULD NEVER SEND YOU A POSTCARD
BUT IF YOU HAPPENED TO MEET SOMEONE IN A HOTEL LOBBY WHOM WE BOTH KNEW, YOU'D PROBABLY TELL HIM TO SAY "HELLO" TO ME WHEN HE GOT BACK HOME, WOULDN'T YOU?
WHO KNOWS? I MIGHT...
I KNEW YOU'D MISS ME!
© 1981 United Feature Syndicate, Inc.
SCHULZ

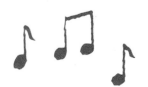

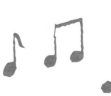

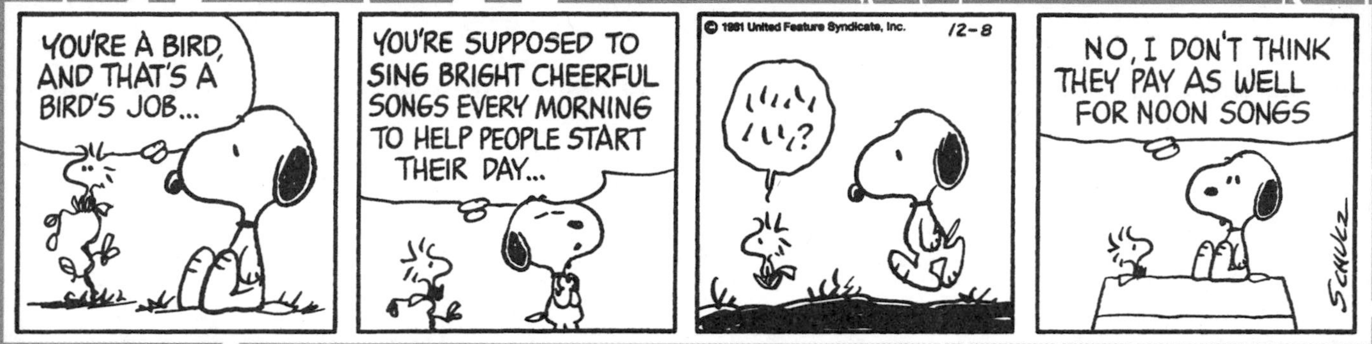
YOU'RE A BIRD, AND THAT'S A BIRD'S JOB...
YOU'RE SUPPOSED TO SING BRIGHT CHEERFUL SONGS EVERY MORNING TO HELP PEOPLE START THEIR DAY...
© 1981 United Feature Syndicate, Inc.
12-8
NO, I DON'T THINK THEY PAY AS WELL FOR NOON SONGS
SCHULZ

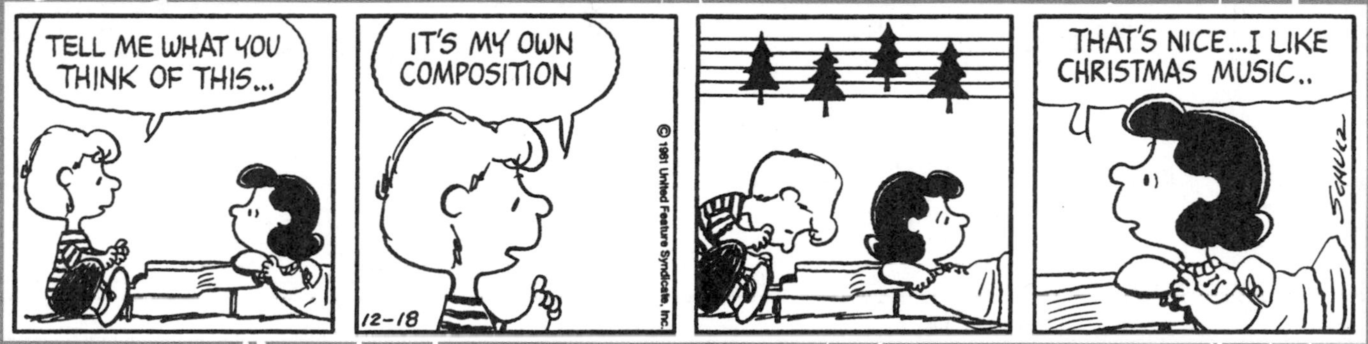
TELL ME WHAT YOU THINK OF THIS...
IT'S MY OWN COMPOSITION
12-18
© 1981 United Feature Syndicate, Inc.
THAT'S NICE...I LIKE CHRISTMAS MUSIC..
SCHULZ

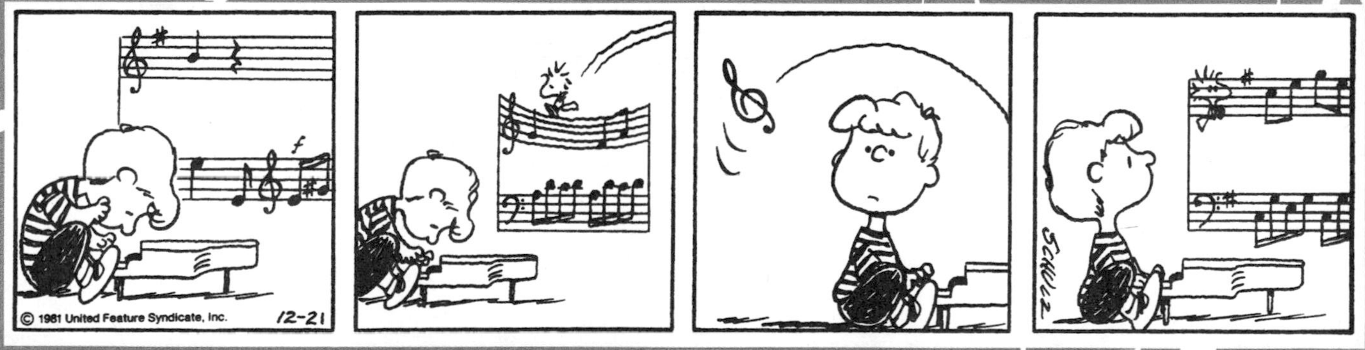
© 1981 United Feature Syndicate, Inc.
12-21
SCHULZ

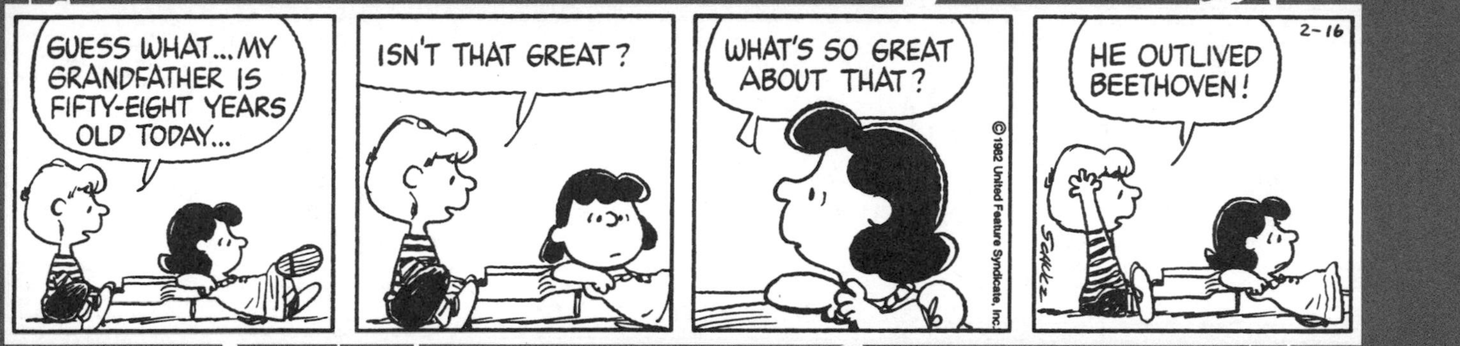
GUESS WHAT... MY GRANDFATHER IS FIFTY-EIGHT YEARS OLD TODAY...
ISN'T THAT GREAT?
WHAT'S SO GREAT ABOUT THAT?
© 1982 United Feature Syndicate, Inc.
2-16
HE OUTLIVED BEETHOVEN!
SCHULZ

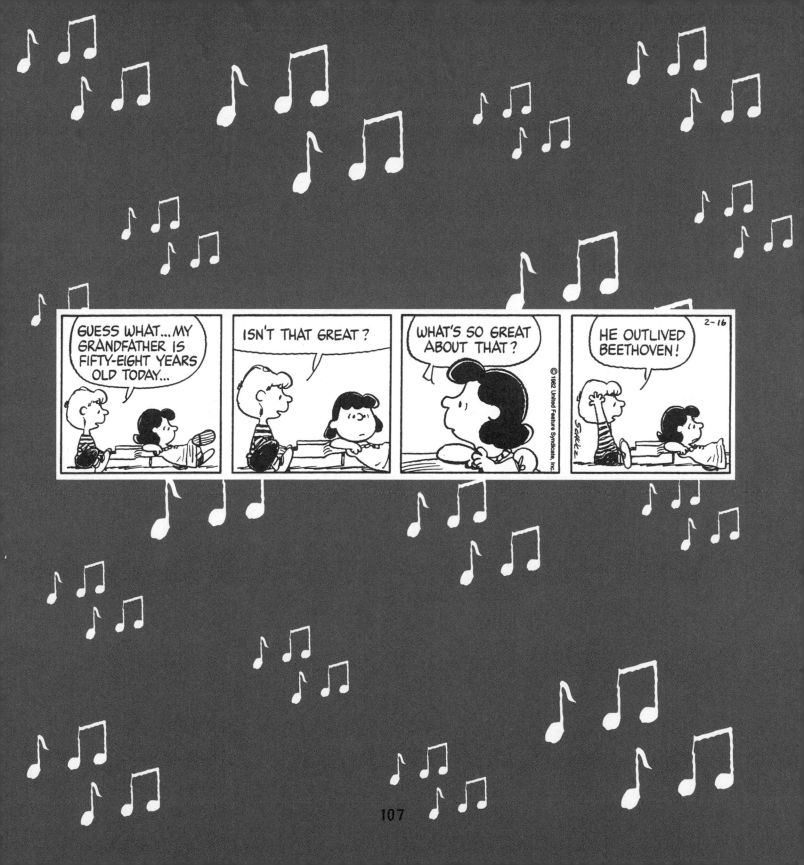

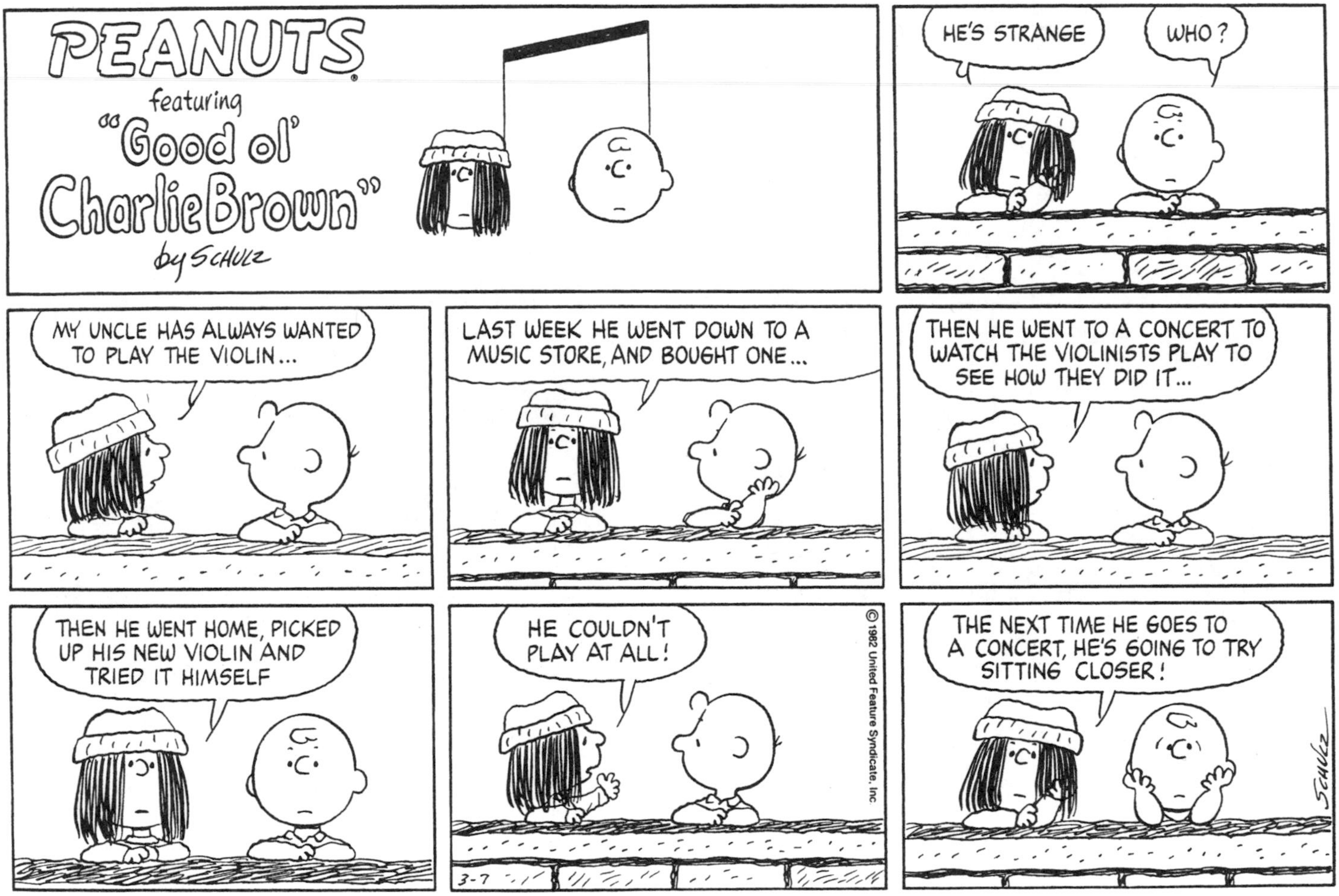
PEANUTS®
featuring
"Good ol' CharlieBrown"
by SCHULZ
HE'S STRANGE
WHO?
MY UNCLE HAS ALWAYS WANTED TO PLAY THE VIOLIN...
LAST WEEK HE WENT DOWN TO A MUSIC STORE, AND BOUGHT ONE...
THEN HE WENT TO A CONCERT TO WATCH THE VIOLINISTS PLAY TO SEE HOW THEY DID IT...
THEN HE WENT HOME, PICKED UP HIS NEW VIOLIN AND TRIED IT HIMSELF
HE COULDN'T PLAY AT ALL!
© 1982 United Feature Syndicate, Inc.
3-7
THE NEXT TIME HE GOES TO A CONCERT, HE'S GOING TO TRY SITTING CLOSER!
SCHULZ

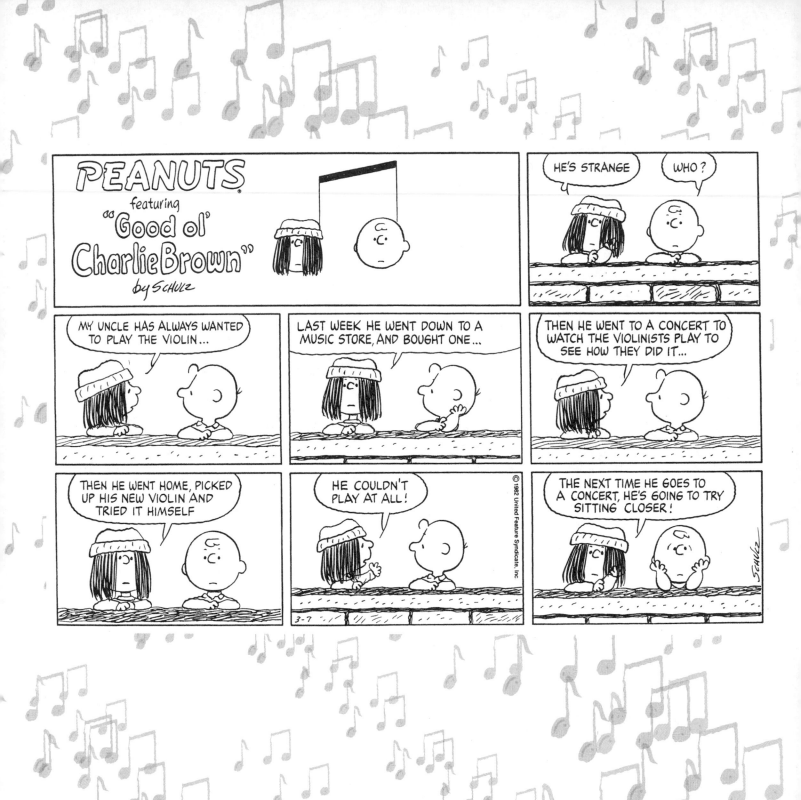

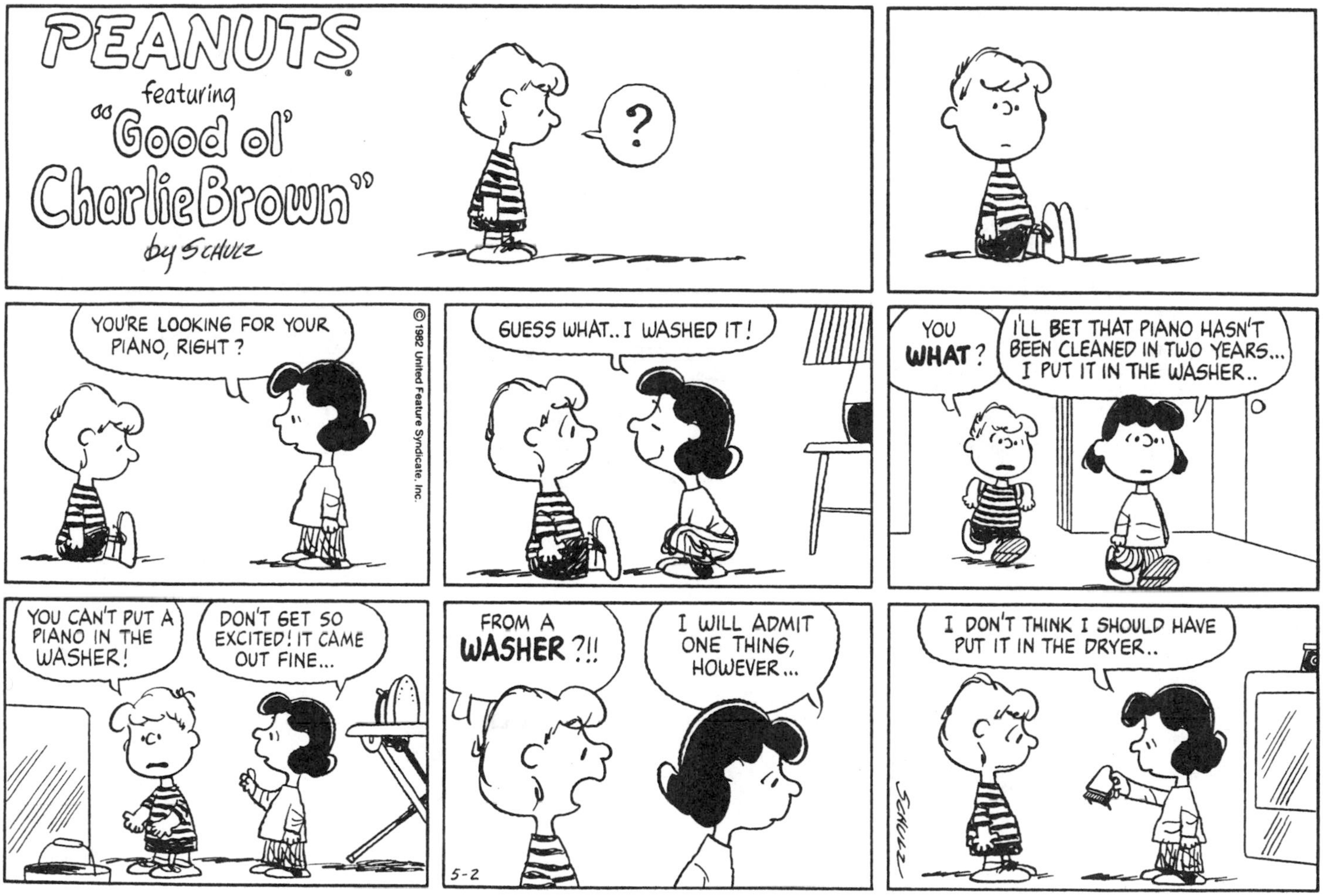
PEANUTS
featuring
"Good ol' Charlie Brown"
by SCHULZ
?
© 1982 United Feature Syndicate, Inc.
YOU'RE LOOKING FOR YOUR PIANO, RIGHT?
GUESS WHAT.. I WASHED IT!
YOU WHAT?
I'LL BET THAT PIANO HASN'T BEEN CLEANED IN TWO YEARS... I PUT IT IN THE WASHER..
YOU CAN'T PUT A PIANO IN THE WASHER!
DON'T GET SO EXCITED! IT CAME OUT FINE...
FROM A WASHER ?!!
I WILL ADMIT ONE THING, HOWEVER...
5-2
I DON'T THINK I SHOULD HAVE PUT IT IN THE DRYER..
SCHULZ

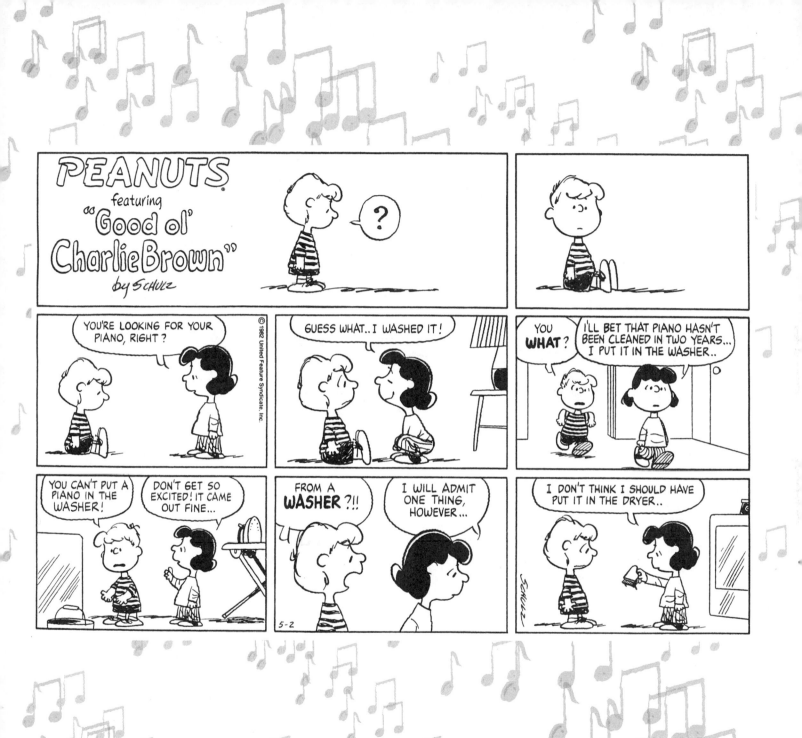

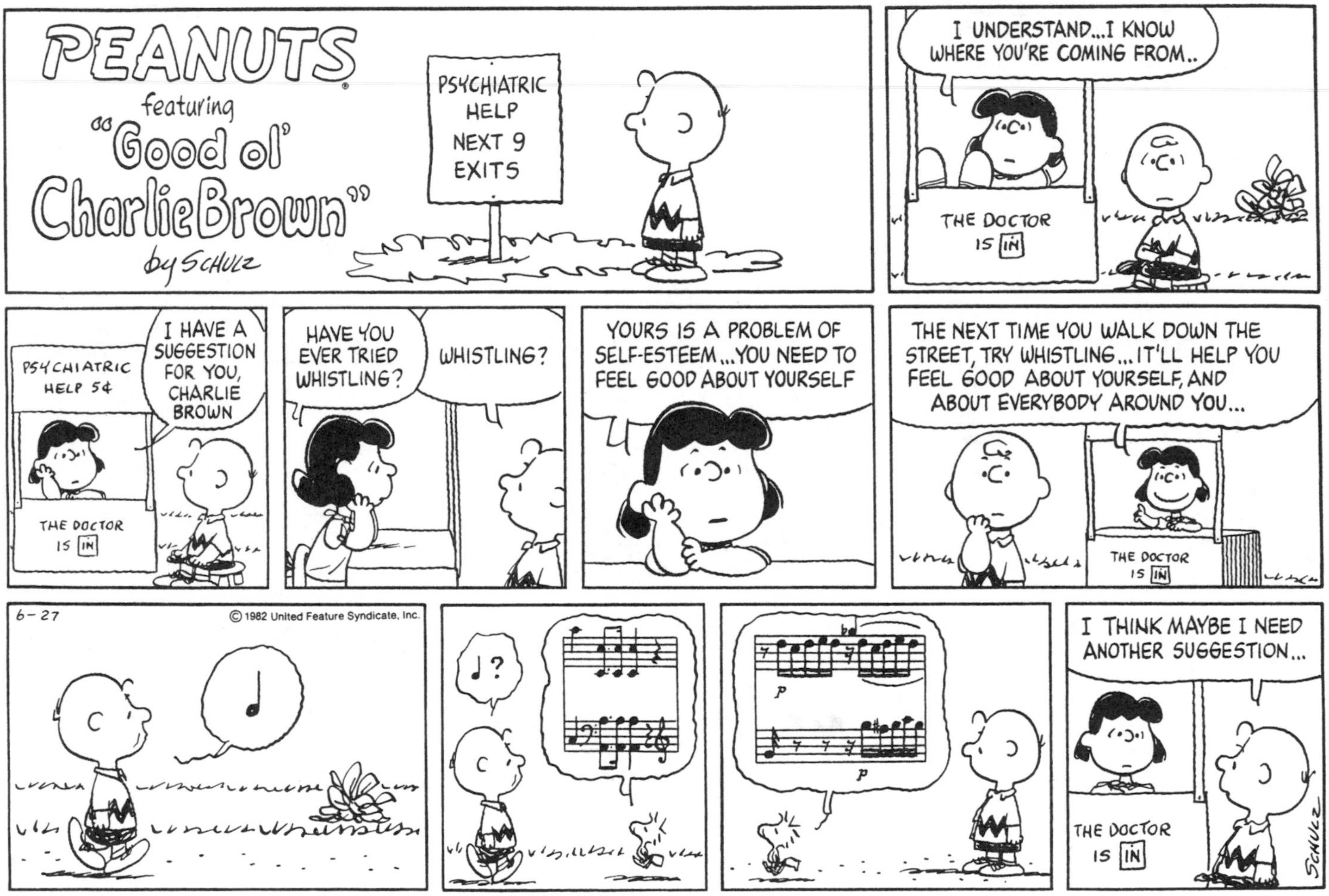
PEANUTS
featuring "Good ol' Charlie Brown"
by SCHULZ
PSYCHIATRIC HELP NEXT 9 EXITS
I UNDERSTAND...I KNOW WHERE YOU'RE COMING FROM..
THE DOCTOR IS IN
PSYCHIATRIC HELP 5¢
I HAVE A SUGGESTION FOR YOU, CHARLIE BROWN
THE DOCTOR IS IN
HAVE YOU EVER TRIED WHISTLING?
WHISTLING?
YOURS IS A PROBLEM OF SELF-ESTEEM...YOU NEED TO FEEL GOOD ABOUT YOURSELF
THE NEXT TIME YOU WALK DOWN THE STREET, TRY WHISTLING... IT'LL HELP YOU FEEL GOOD ABOUT YOURSELF, AND ABOUT EVERYBODY AROUND YOU...
THE DOCTOR IS IN
6-27
© 1982 United Feature Syndicate, Inc.
I THINK MAYBE I NEED ANOTHER SUGGESTION...
THE DOCTOR IS IN
SCHULZ

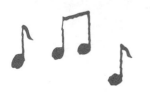

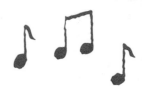

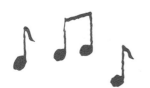

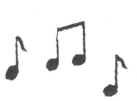

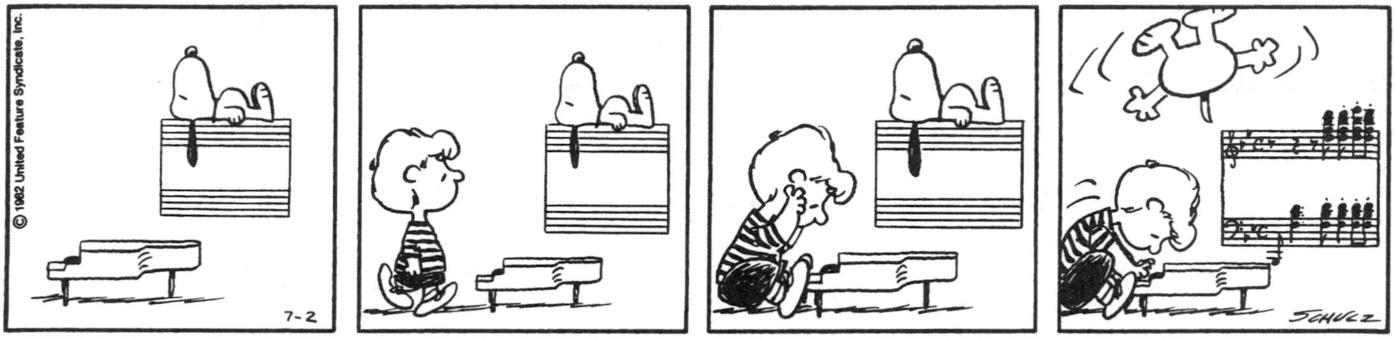
© 1982 United Feature Syndicate, Inc.
7-2
SCHULZ

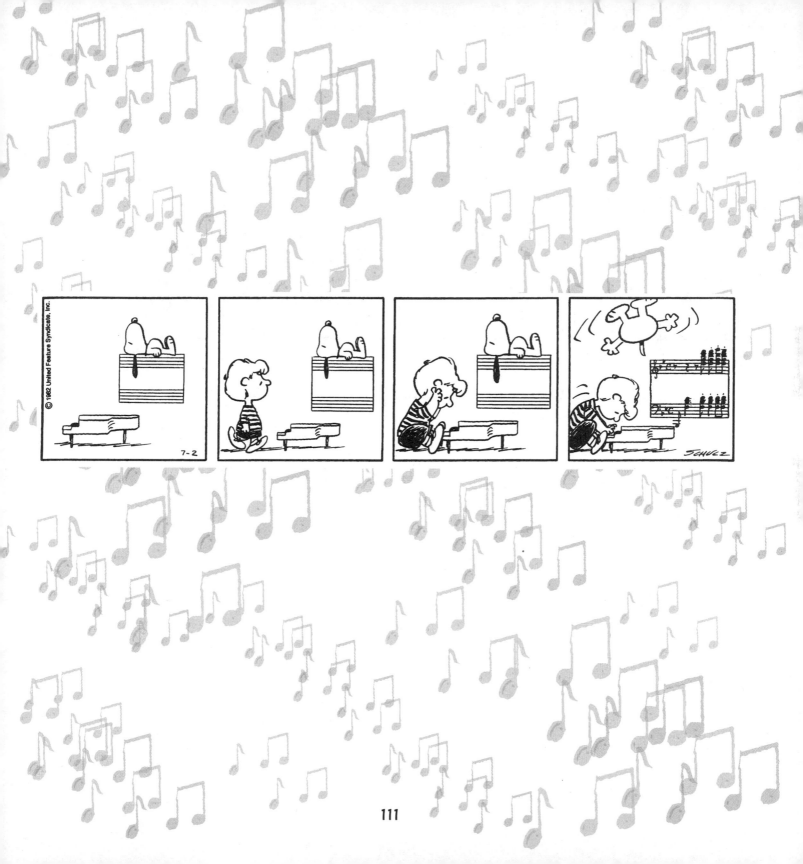

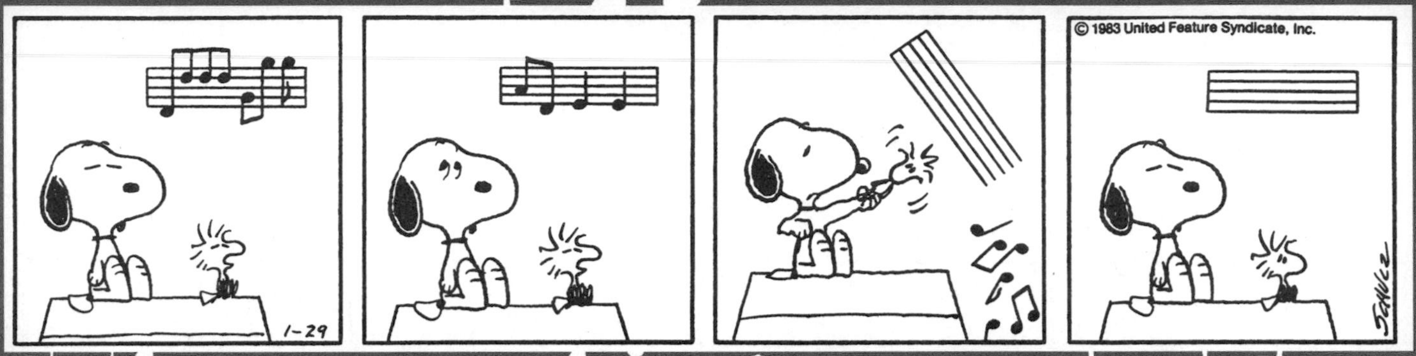
1-29
© 1983 United Feature Syndicate, Inc.
SCHULZ

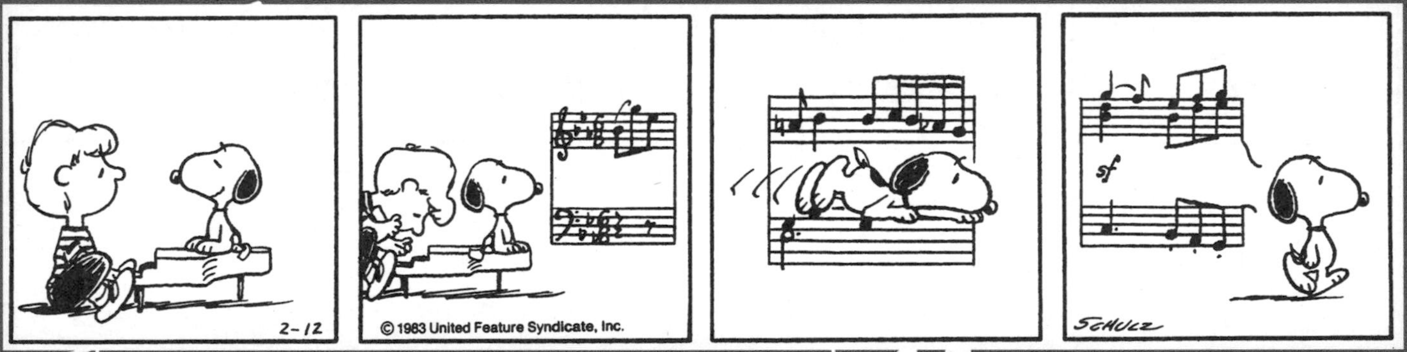
2-12
© 1983 United Feature Syndicate, Inc.
sf
SCHULZ

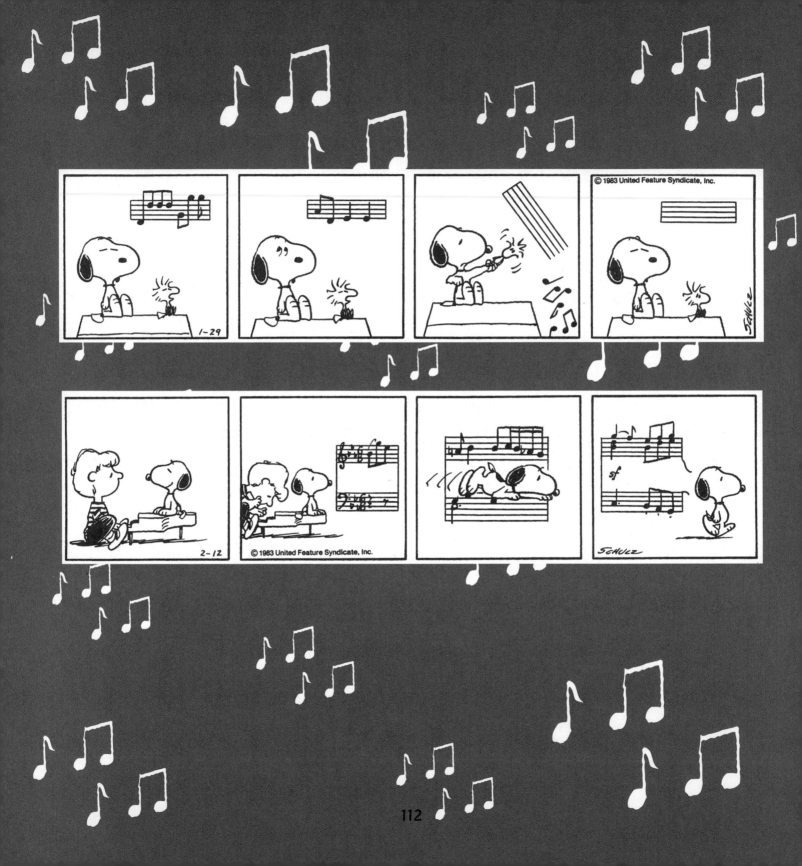

5-21
SCHULZ
© 1983 United Feature Syndicate, Inc.

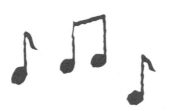

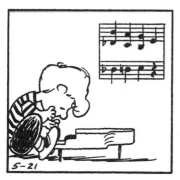

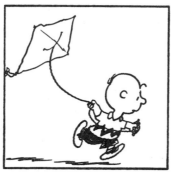

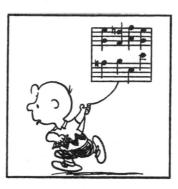

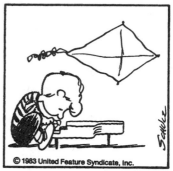

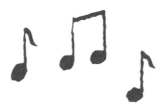

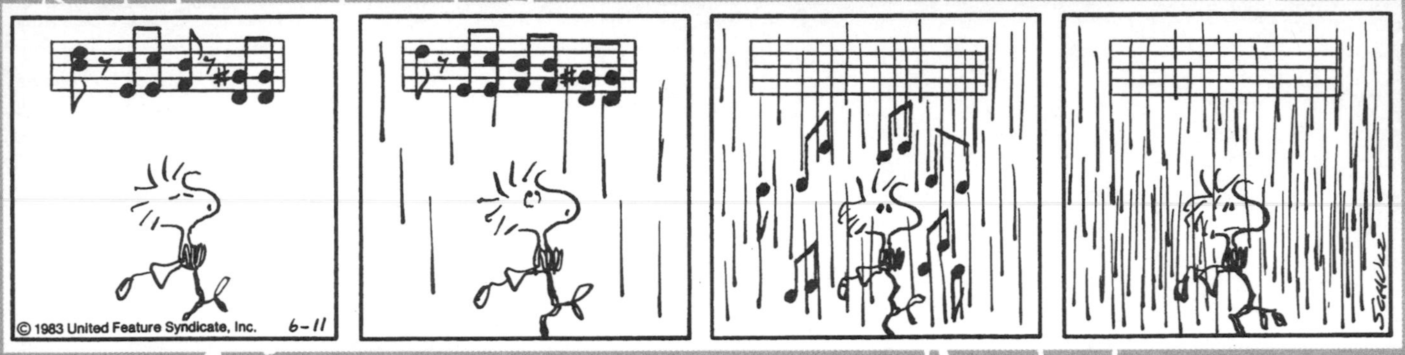
© 1983 United Feature Syndicate, Inc.
6-11
SCHULZ

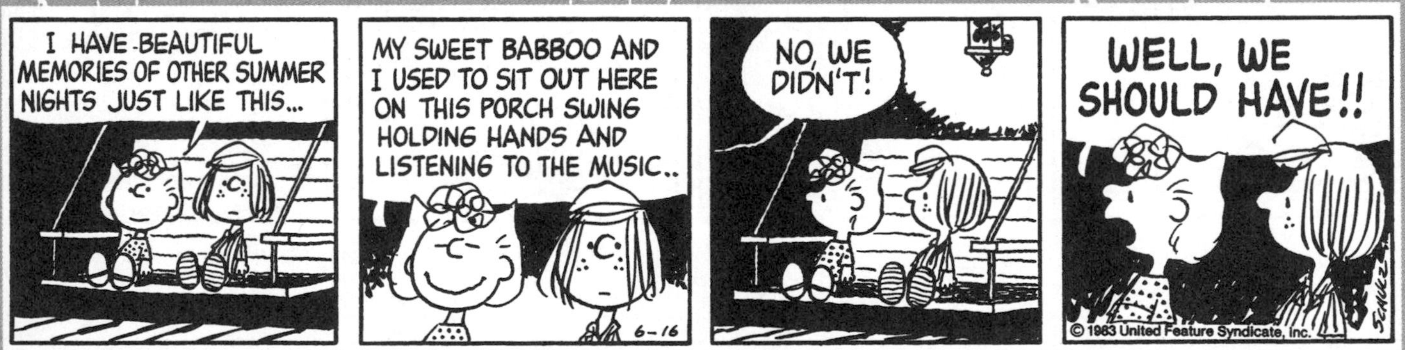
I HAVE BEAUTIFUL MEMORIES OF OTHER SUMMER NIGHTS JUST LIKE THIS...
MY SWEET BABBOO AND I USED TO SIT OUT HERE ON THIS PORCH SWING HOLDING HANDS AND LISTENING TO THE MUSIC..
6-16
NO, WE DIDN'T!
WELL, WE SHOULD HAVE!!
© 1983 United Feature Syndicate, Inc.
SCHULZ

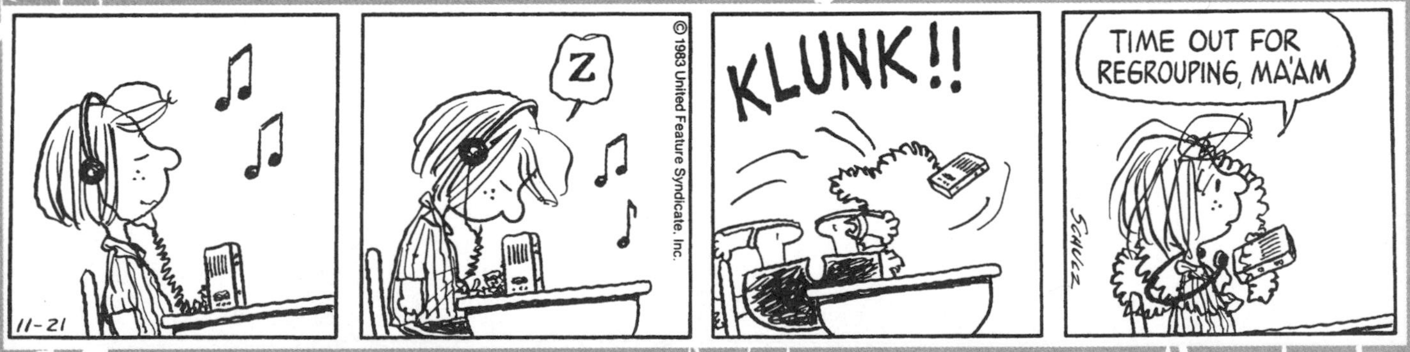
11-21
Z
© 1983 United Feature Syndicate, Inc.
KLUNK!!
SCHULZ
TIME OUT FOR REGROUPING, MA'AM

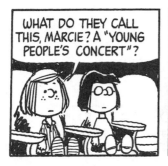

WHAT DO THEY CALL THIS, MARCIE? A "YOUNG PEOPLE'S CONCERT"?
HOW DO I KNOW I'M GOING TO LIKE THIS KIND OF MUSIC?
© 1984 United Feature Syndicate, Inc.
SHH...THE CONDUCTOR IS COMING OUT...WE'RE SUPPOSED TO APPLAUD...
2-27
WHY? HE HASN'T DONE ANYTHING YET
SCHULZ

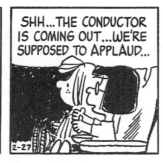

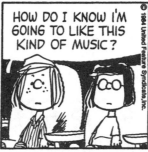

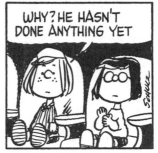

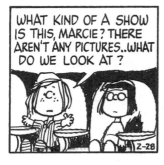

WHAT KIND OF A SHOW IS THIS, MARCIE? THERE AREN'T ANY PICTURES..WHAT DO WE LOOK AT?
2-28
THIS IS A CONCERT, SIR..JUST LISTEN TO THE MUSIC...
© 1984 United Feature Syndicate, Inc.
I DON'T BELIEVE THIS... AN AUDITORIUM FULL OF PEOPLE JUST SITTING HERE LISTENING TO MUSIC..
SOMEONE THOUGHT HE HAD A GOOD IDEA, BUT IT'LL NEVER GO...
SCHULZ

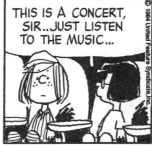

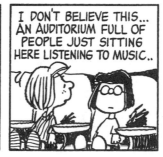

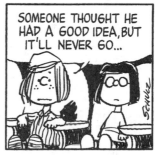

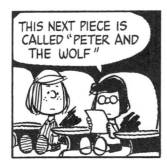

THIS NEXT PIECE IS CALLED "PETER AND THE WOLF"
DON'T SNAP YOUR FINGERS, SIR... IT ISN'T DONE AT CONCERTS LIKE THIS..
WHAT AM I SUPPOSED TO DO?
JUST SIT STILL AND LISTEN TO THE MUSIC
© 1984 United Feature Syndicate, Inc.
WEIRD!
SCHULZ
2-29

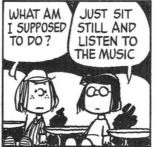

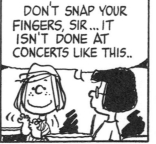

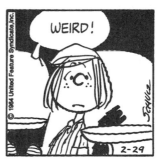

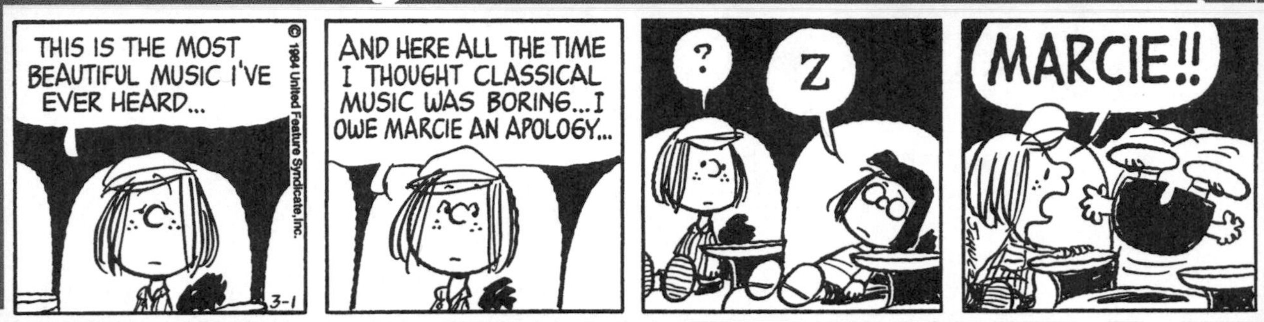
THIS IS THE MOST BEAUTIFUL MUSIC I'VE EVER HEARD...
© 1984 United Feature Syndicate, Inc.
AND HERE ALL THE TIME I THOUGHT CLASSICAL MUSIC WAS BORING...I OWE MARCIE AN APOLOGY...
?
Z
MARCIE!!

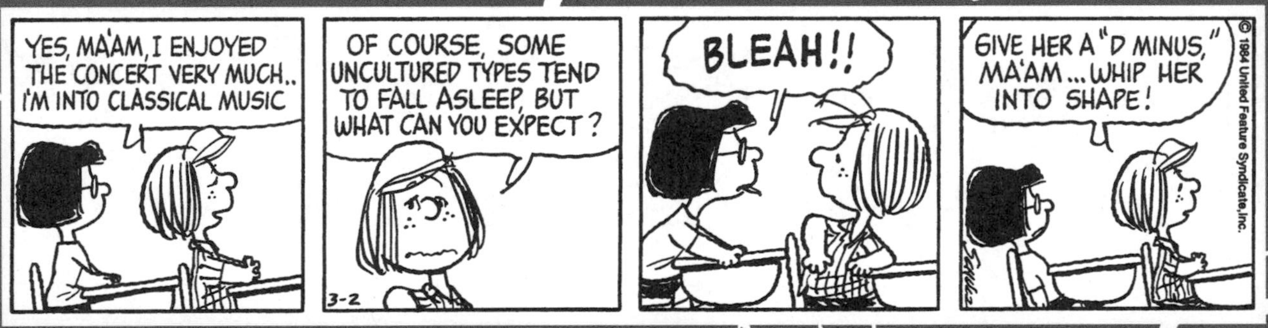
YES, MA'AM, I ENJOYED THE CONCERT VERY MUCH.. I'M INTO CLASSICAL MUSIC
OF COURSE, SOME UNCULTURED TYPES TEND TO FALL ASLEEP, BUT WHAT CAN YOU EXPECT?
BLEAH!!
GIVE HER A "D MINUS," MA'AM...WHIP HER INTO SHAPE!
© 1984 United Feature Syndicate, Inc.

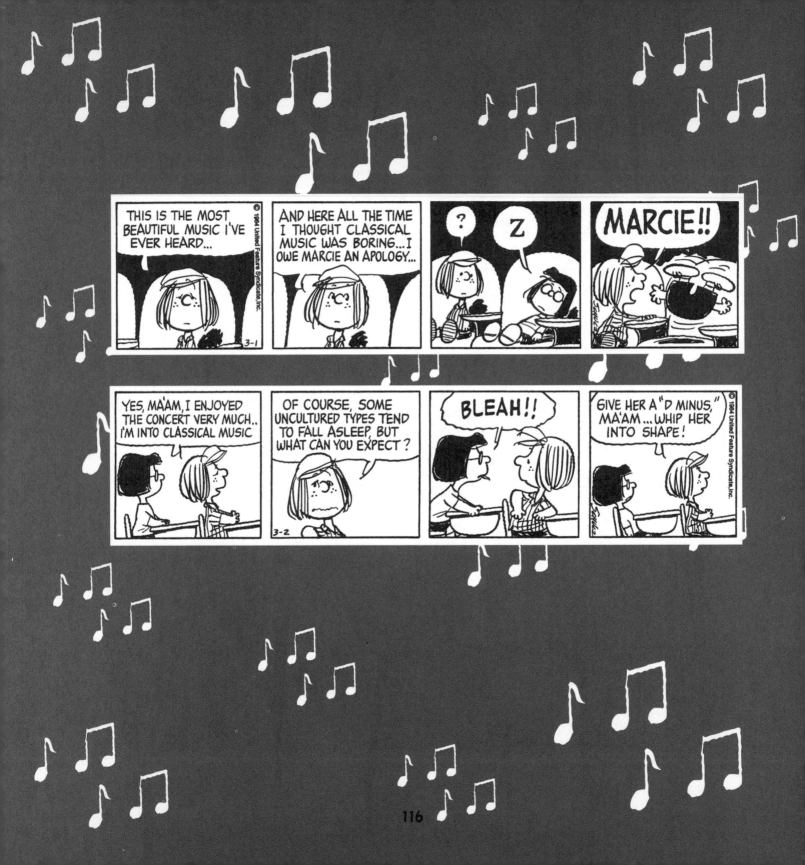

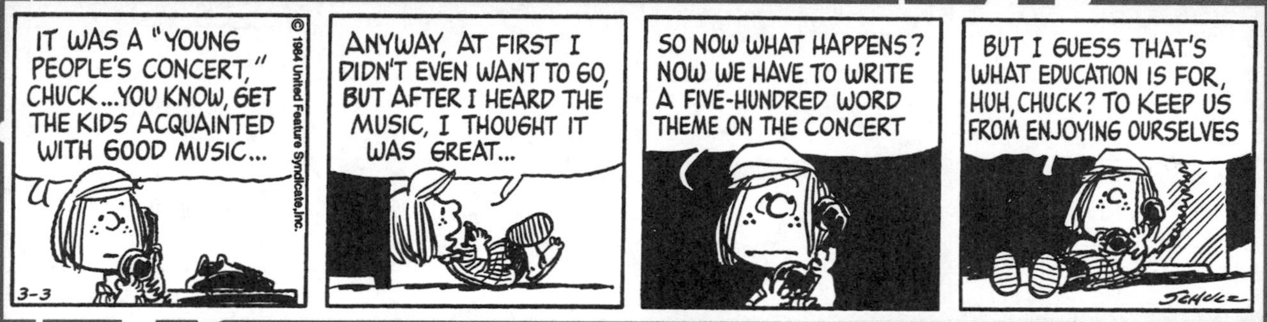
IT WAS A "YOUNG PEOPLE'S CONCERT," CHUCK...YOU KNOW, GET THE KIDS ACQUAINTED WITH GOOD MUSIC...
© 1984 United Feature Syndicate,Inc.
3-3
ANYWAY, AT FIRST I DIDN'T EVEN WANT TO GO, BUT AFTER I HEARD THE MUSIC, I THOUGHT IT WAS GREAT...
SO NOW WHAT HAPPENS? NOW WE HAVE TO WRITE A FIVE-HUNDRED WORD THEME ON THE CONCERT
BUT I GUESS THAT'S WHAT EDUCATION IS FOR, HUH, CHUCK? TO KEEP US FROM ENJOYING OURSELVES
SCHULZ

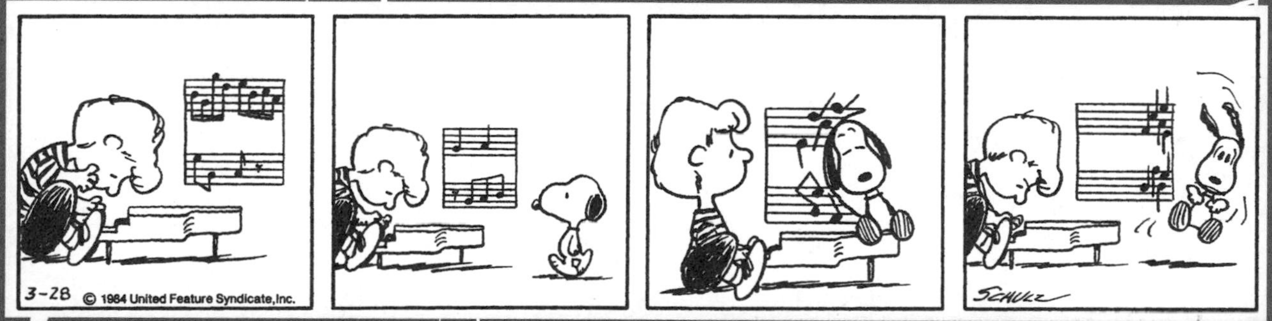
3-28 © 1984 United Feature Syndicate,Inc.
SCHULZ

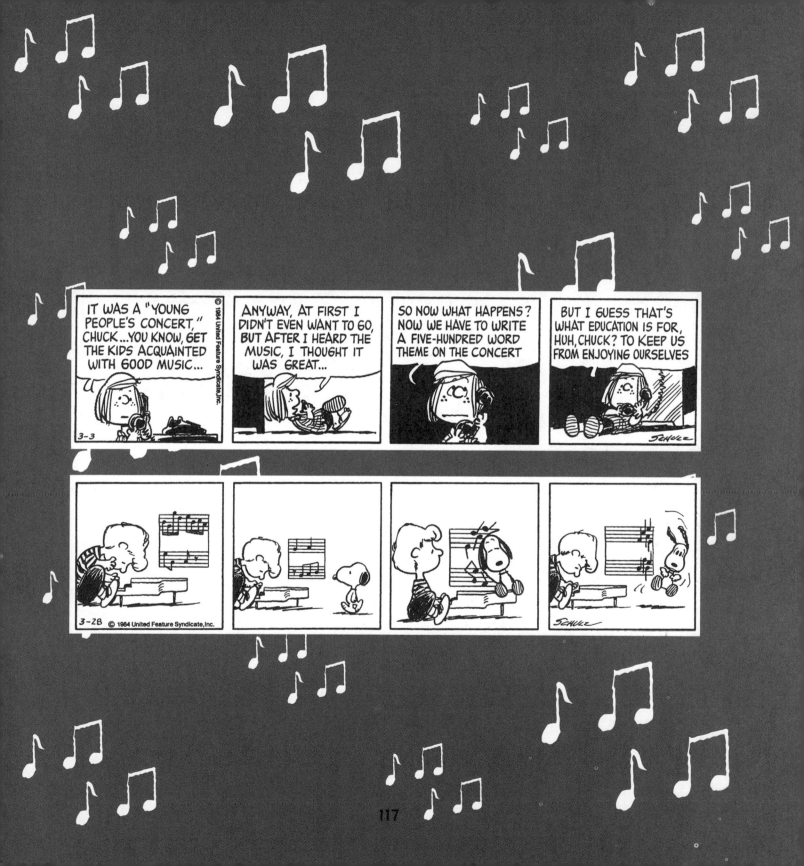

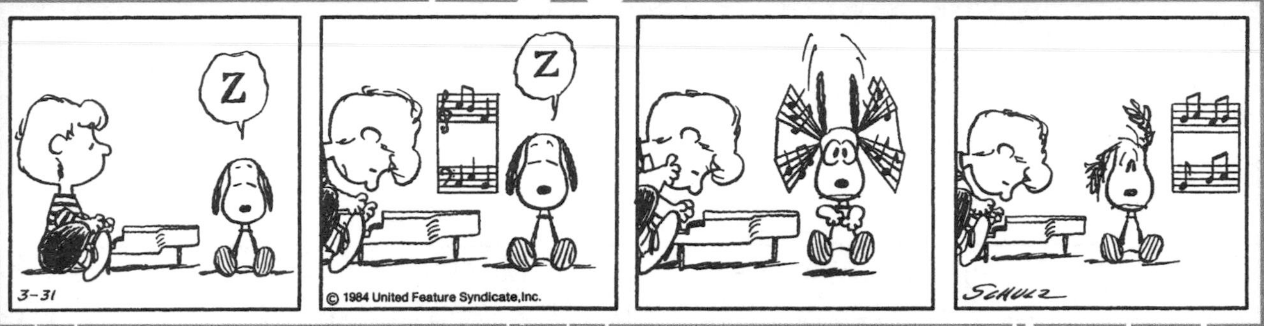
Z
Z
3-31
© 1984 United Feature Syndicate, Inc.
SCHULZ

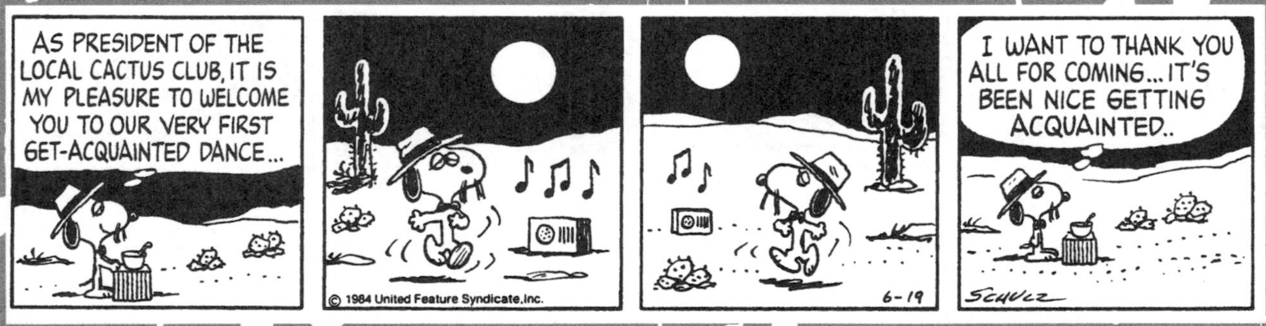
AS PRESIDENT OF THE LOCAL CACTUS CLUB, IT IS MY PLEASURE TO WELCOME YOU TO OUR VERY FIRST GET-ACQUAINTED DANCE...
© 1984 United Feature Syndicate, Inc.
6-19
I WANT TO THANK YOU ALL FOR COMING... IT'S BEEN NICE GETTING ACQUAINTED..
SCHULZ

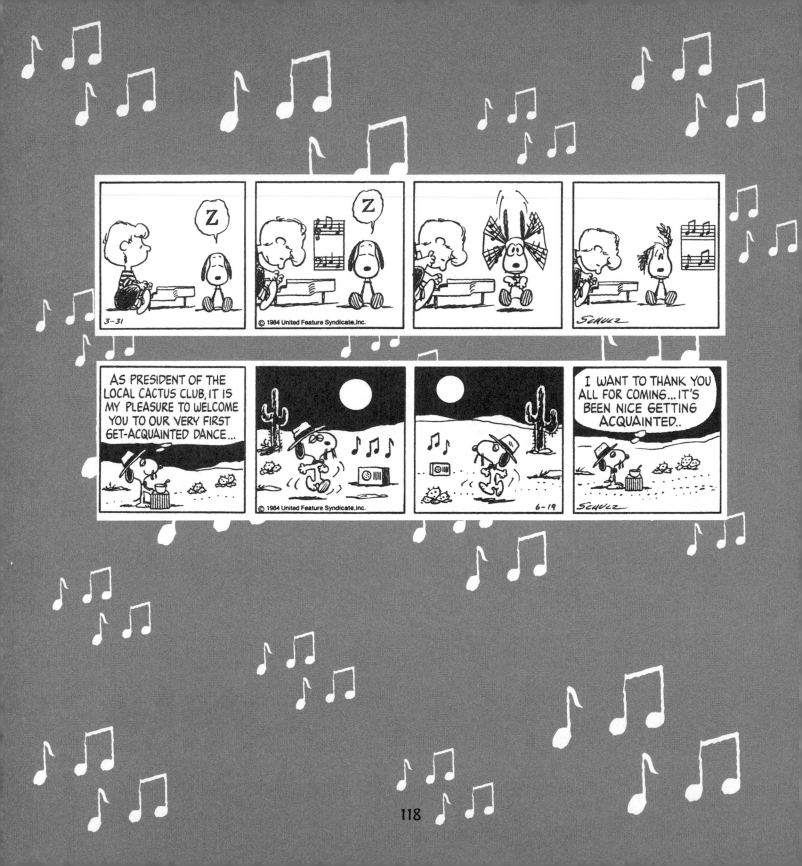

© 1984 United Feature Syndicate, Inc.
7-12
WELL, DON'T TRY TO WHISTLE IN THE WIND..
SCHULZ

© 1984 United Feature Syndicate, Inc
8-7
I BROUGHT SOME OF MY VACATION PICTURES FOR YOU TO SEE, SCHROEDER, BUT I GUESS YOU'RE BUSY...
WHY DON'T I JUST LEAVE THEM HERE, AND YOU CAN LOOK AT THEM LATER?
SCHULZ

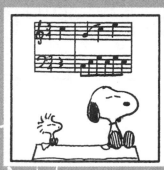

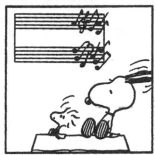

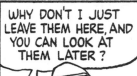

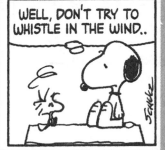

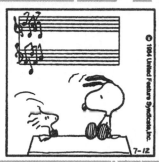

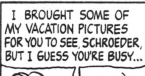

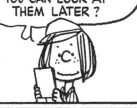

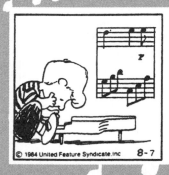

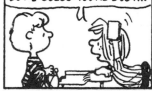

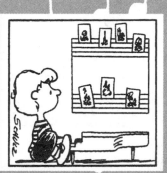

© 1984 United Feature Syndicate, Inc.
11-27
SCHULZ

EVERY TIME WE COME TO ONE OF THESE CONCERTS, THEY PLAY "PETER AND THE WOLF"
THEY MUST THINK WE DON'T UNDERSTAND ANYTHING ELSE
© 1985 United Feature Syndicate, Inc.
3/5
DON'T YOU LIKE "PETER AND THE WOLF"?
I DON'T KNOW.. I'VE NEVER UNDERSTOOD IT!
SCHULZ

WHY DOES THE CONDUCTOR HAVE THAT STICK, MARCIE?
THAT'S A BATON, SIR... HE USES IT TO LEAD THE ORCHESTRA...
© 1985 United Feature Syndicate, Inc.
3-6
I DON'T THINK HE NEEDS IT...
THEY ALL SEEM PRETTY WELL-BEHAVED TO ME..
SCHULZ

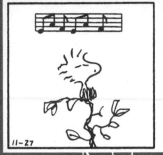

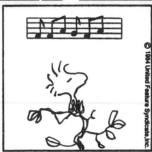

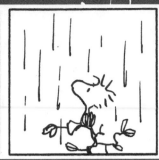

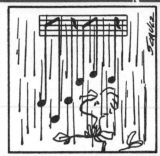

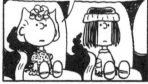

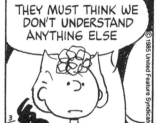

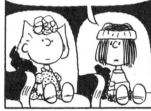

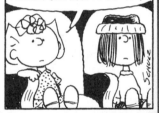

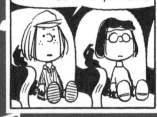

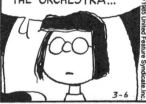

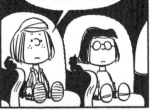

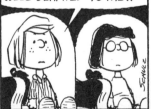

THAT WAS BEAUTIFUL, WASN'T IT?
IT WAS GREAT, SIR!
A STANDING OVATION...
WHOOP!!!
© 1985 United Feature Syndicate, Inc.
EVERY PLACE WE GO, MARCIE, YOU EMBARRASS ME!

IT'S RAINING... WE'RE GOING TO CAMP, AND IT'S RAINING!
I HATE GOING TO CAMP! I ESPECIALLY HATE GOING TO CAMP WHEN IT'S RAINING!
THE FARMERS NEED RAIN
WHAT FOR?
© 1985 United Feature Syndicate, Inc.
THEIR COWS ARE GOING TO GET ALL WET!

IT'S STILL RAINING SO WE'RE SUPPOSED TO GO OVER TO THE REC HALL FOR A SING-A-LONG...
WHAT'S A SING-A-LONG?
A COUNSELOR LEADS THE SINGING..SHE'LL SAY, "OH, COME ON, YOU CAN SING LOUDER THAN THAT!" THEN SHE'LL WANT US TO CLAP OUR HANDS...
© 1985 United Feature Syndicate, Inc.
THEN SHE'LL SAY, "C'MON, BOYS, LET'S SEE IF YOU CAN SING LOUDER THAN THE GIRLS! C'MON, GIRLS.. SHOW THE BOYS HOW LOUD YOU CAN SING!"
I THINK I'LL JUST STAND OUT HERE IN THE RAIN..

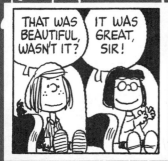

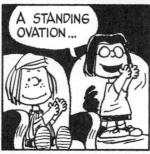

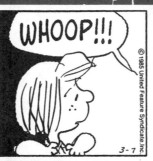

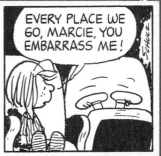

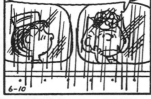

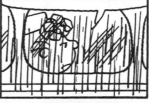

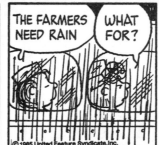

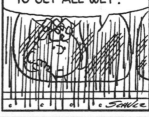

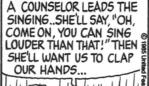

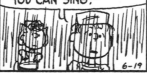

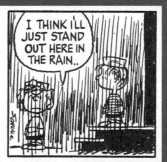

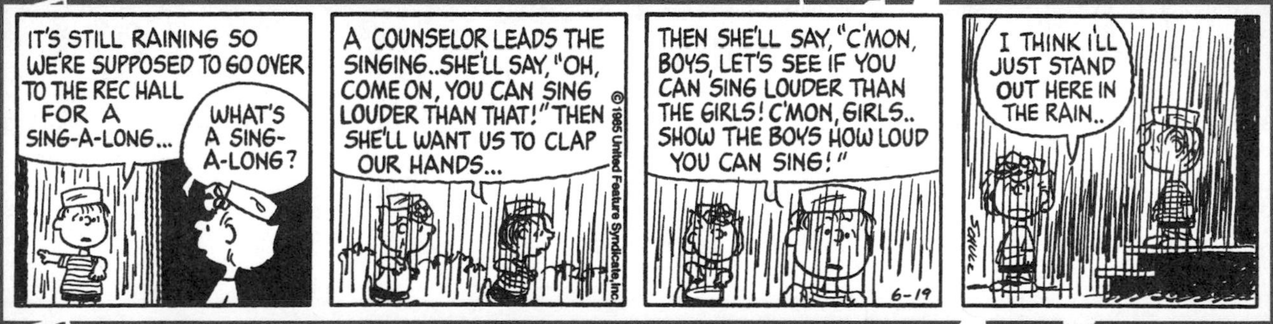

PEANUTS featuring "Good ol' Charlie Brown" by Schulz

Row R.. Seat 3

THESE ARE GOOD SEATS

I SEE THEY'RE PLAYING "PETER AND THE WOLF" AGAIN...EVERY TIME WE GO TO A "TINY TOTS" CONCERT, THEY PLAY "PETER AND THE WOLF"!

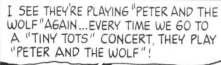

WHERE'S YOUR TICKET STUB, MARCIE?

I THREW IT AWAY

YOU SHOULD ALWAYS SAVE YOUR TICKET STUB, MARCIE

I DON'T NEED IT..I'M ALREADY IN MY SEAT...

I ALWAYS SAVE MY TICKET STUB IN CASE THEY HAVE A DRAWING FOR A BIG PRIZE...

© 1985 United Feature Syndicate, Inc.

6-30

AT A CONCERT?

I'M THINKING MAYBE THEY'LL GIVE AWAY A VIOLIN..THEY SEEM TO HAVE MORE THAN THEY NEED..

YOU'RE WEIRD, SIR!

ANOTHER TINY TOTS CONCERT, AND LOOK WHAT THEY'RE PLAYING...
"PETER AND THE WOLF"
AGAIN?
MAYBE THIS TIME WE'LL BE LUCKY...
MAYBE THIS TIME THE WOLF WILL GET HIM!
© 1985 United Feature Syndicate, Inc.
7-10

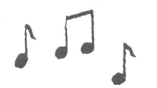

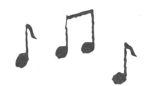

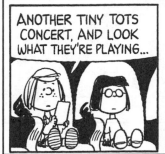

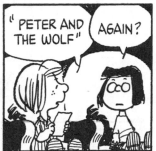

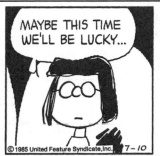

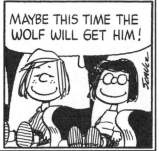

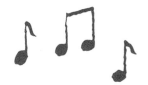

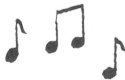

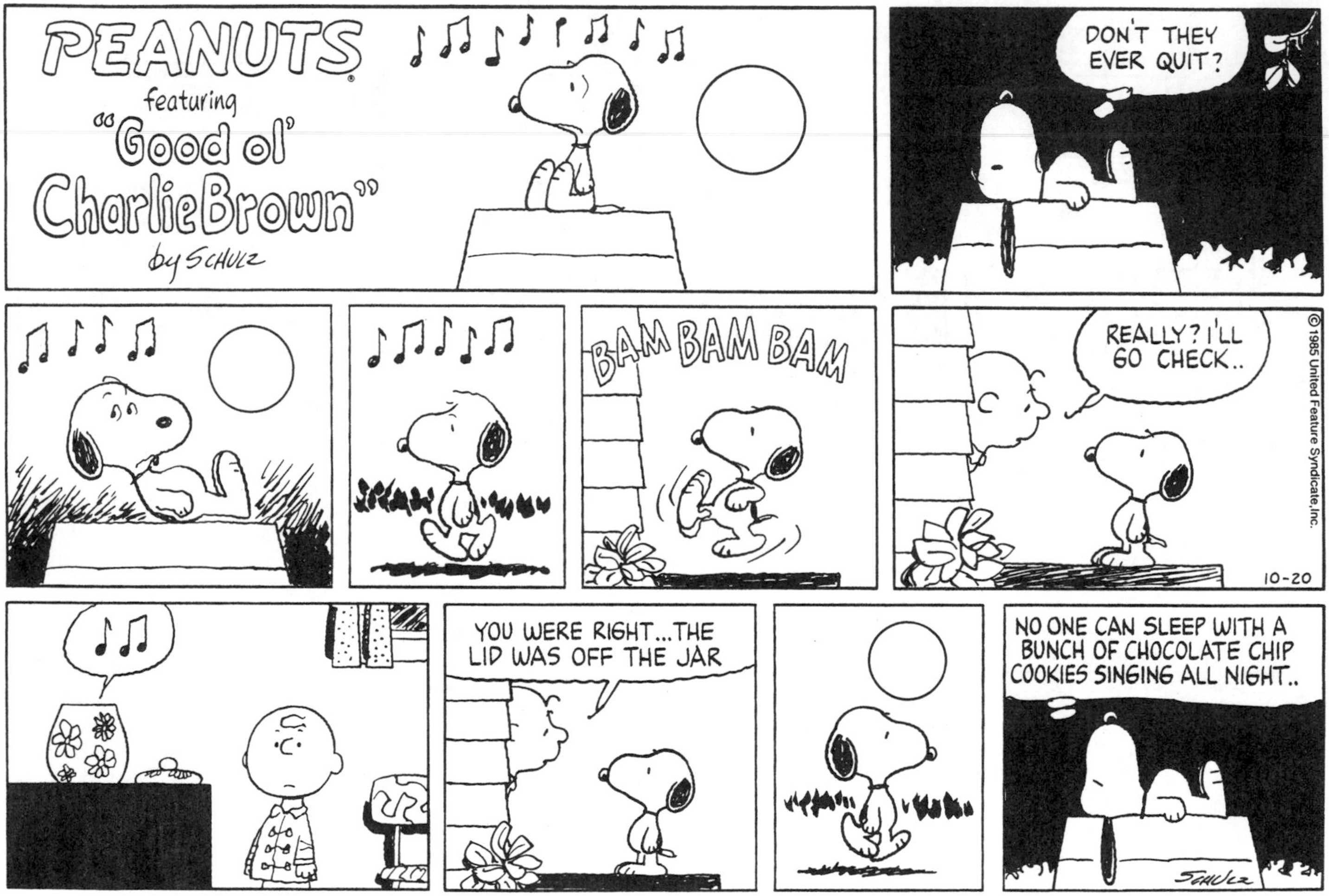
PEANUTS
featuring "Good ol' Charlie Brown"
by SCHULZ
DON'T THEY EVER QUIT?
BAM BAM BAM
REALLY? I'LL GO CHECK..
© 1985 United Feature Syndicate, Inc.
10-20
YOU WERE RIGHT...THE LID WAS OFF THE JAR
NO ONE CAN SLEEP WITH A BUNCH OF CHOCOLATE CHIP COOKIES SINGING ALL NIGHT..
SCHULZ

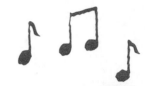

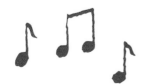

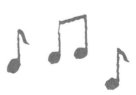

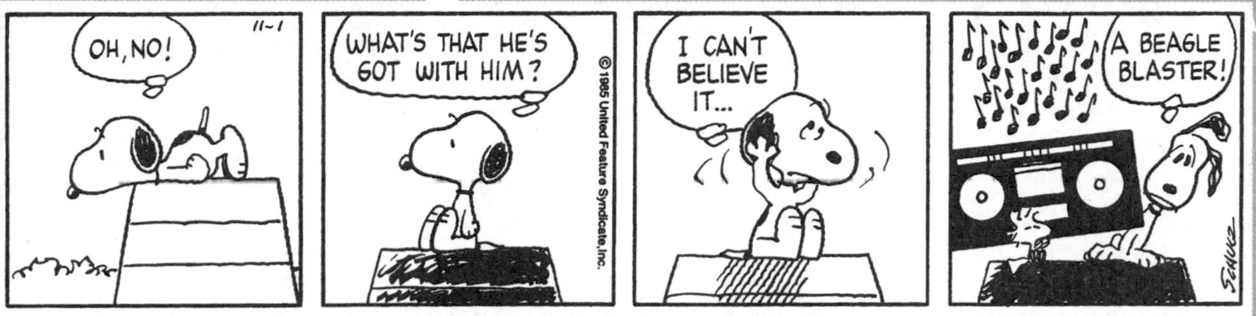
11-1
OH, NO!
WHAT'S THAT HE'S GOT WITH HIM?
© 1985 United Feature Syndicate, Inc.
I CAN'T BELIEVE IT...
A BEAGLE BLASTER!
SCHULZ

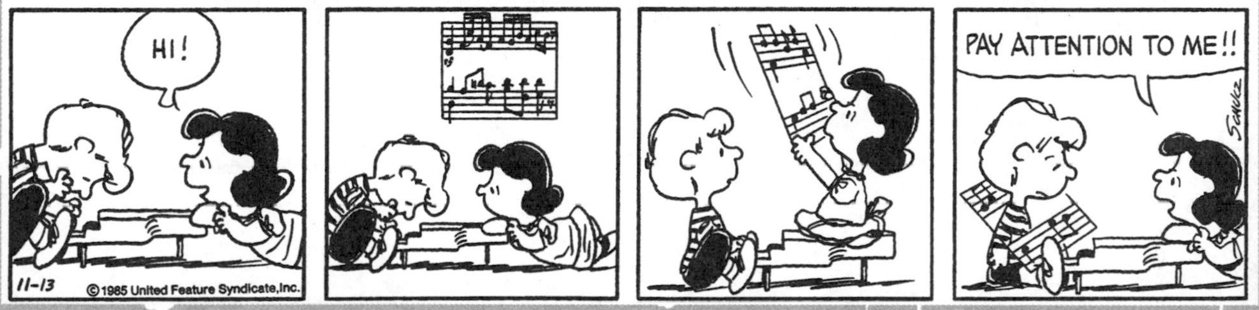
HI!
11-13
© 1985 United Feature Syndicate, Inc.
PAY ATTENTION TO ME!!
SCHULZ

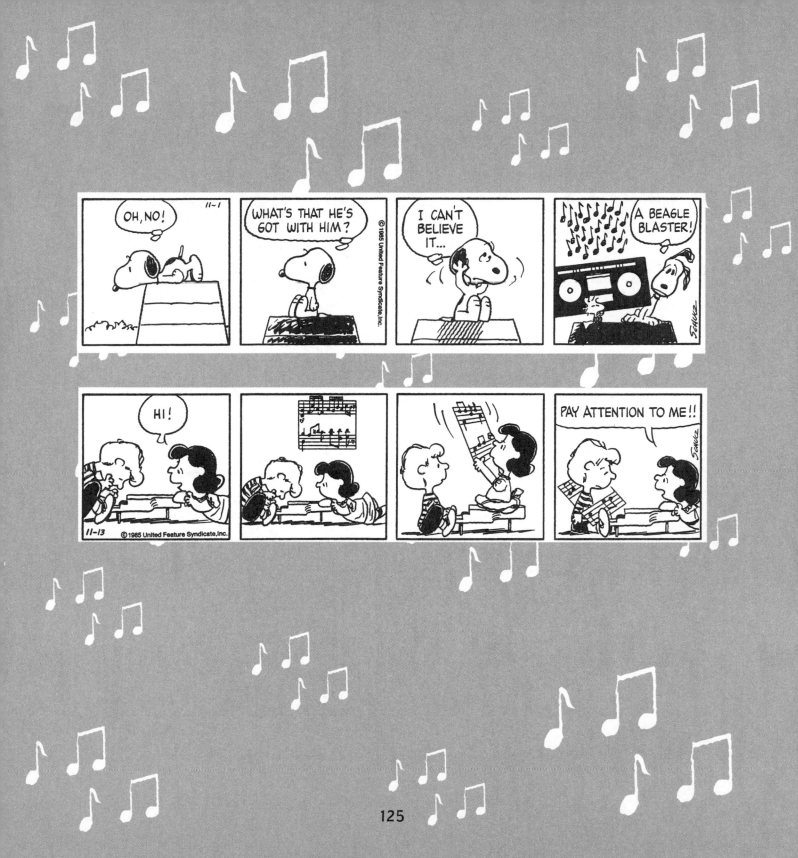

WHAT ARE WE GOING TO HEAR TODAY, MARCIE?
HANDEL'S "MESSIAH"
THE MOST EXCITING PART IS WHEN THEY GET TO THE "HALLELUJAH CHORUS," AND EVERYONE STANDS...
STANDING IS EXCITING?
12-18
© 1985 United Feature Syndicate, Inc.

IT'S THE "HALLELUJAH CHORUS," SIR.. EVERYONE IS STANDING UP...
THEY'RE WHAT?
STANDING UP...
YIPE!!
EVERYWHERE WE GO, MARCIE, YOU EMBARRASS ME!
© 1985 United Feature Syndicate, Inc.
12-19
SCHULZ

Yesterday we heard a beautiful performance of the Messiah.
12-20
WHAT WAS HANDEL'S FIRST NAME, MARCIE?
I'M ASHAMED TO ADMIT I DON'T KNOW
I'LL JUST HAVE TO GUESS..
SCHULZ
It was written by Joe Handel.
© 1985 United Feature Syndicate, Inc.

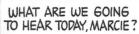

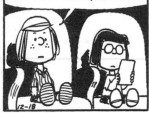

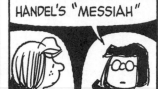

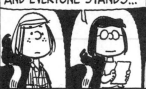

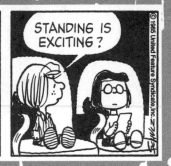

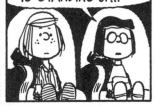

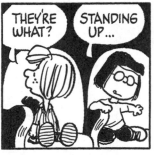

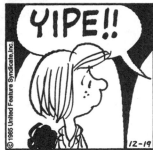

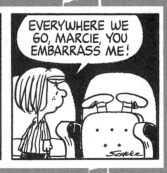

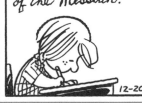

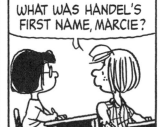

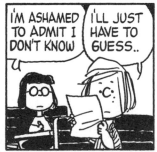

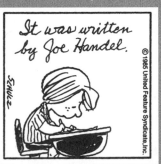

Panel 1: ARE YOU ENJOYING THE CONCERT, SIR?

Panel 2: SORT OF...THIS IS A LONG PIECE, ISN'T IT?

© 1986 United Feature Syndicate, Inc.

2-4

Panel 3: YOU HAVE TO CONCENTRATE ON THE MUSIC, AND NOT LET YOUR MIND WANDER..

Panel 4: I THINK MAYBE I'LL HAVE FRENCH TOAST FOR BREAKFAST TOMORROW...

Panel 1: THIS IS MY REPORT ON THE CONCERT WE WENT TO YESTERDAY..

Panel 2: THE MUSIC WAS NICE, AND WE ALL HAD A GOOD TIME..

© 1986 United Feature Syndicate, Inc.

Panel 3: ACTUALLY, THE BEST PART WAS WHEN MARCIE WENT FOR A DRINK, AND THE WATER FROM THE FOUNTAIN HIT HER IN THE FACE!

2-5

Panel 4: YOU'RE WEIRD, SIR!

Panel 1: LOOK AT THIS LIST OF PEOPLE WHO SUPPORT THE SYMPHONY, SIR...

Panel 2: SEE? THEY HAVE GUARANTORS, BENEFACTORS, SUSTAINERS, SPONSORS, DONORS AND FRIENDS..

2-27

Panel 3: WHERE DO WE FIT IN?

© 1986 United Feature Syndicate, Inc.

Panel 4: WE'RE THE LISTENERS!

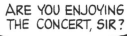

I HOPE THIS CONCERT DOESN'T LAST TOO LONG
WHEN DO YOU THINK IT'LL BE OVER?
© 1986 United Feature Syndicate, Inc.
2-28
WHEN THEY PLAY THE LAST NOTE
THANKS, MARCIE!
SCHULZ

DID BEETHOVEN EVER TEACH KINDERGARTEN? PROBABLY NOT...
© 1986 United Feature Syndicate, Inc.
PROBABLY DIDN'T LIKE KIDS...PROBABLY HATED KIDS..PROBABLY FORGOT THAT HE WAS A KID ONCE HIMSELF...
BONK!
WAS BEETHOVEN EVER A KID?
SCHULZ
6-7

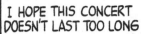

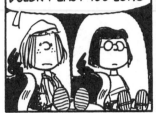

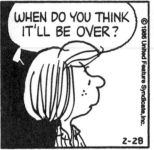

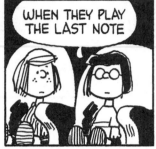

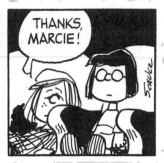

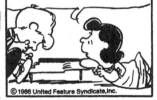

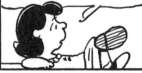

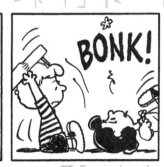

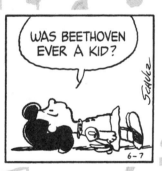

LOOK, MARCIE..TWELVE OF THE CHAIRS IN THE ORCHESTRA ARE EMPTY
THIS FIRST PIECE IS FOR A SMALL ORCHESTRA, SIR..
THEY DON'T NEED ALL OF THE PLAYERS
© 1986 United Feature Syndicate, Inc.
I THOUGHT MAYBE THEY HAD THE FLU..

© 1986 United Feature Syndicate, Inc.
HOW OLD WERE WE WHEN THEY STARTED PLAYING?

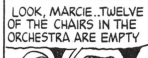

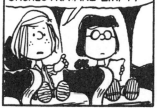

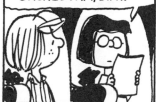

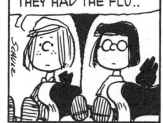

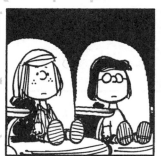

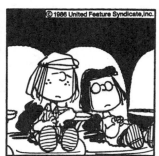

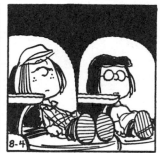

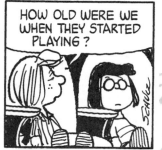

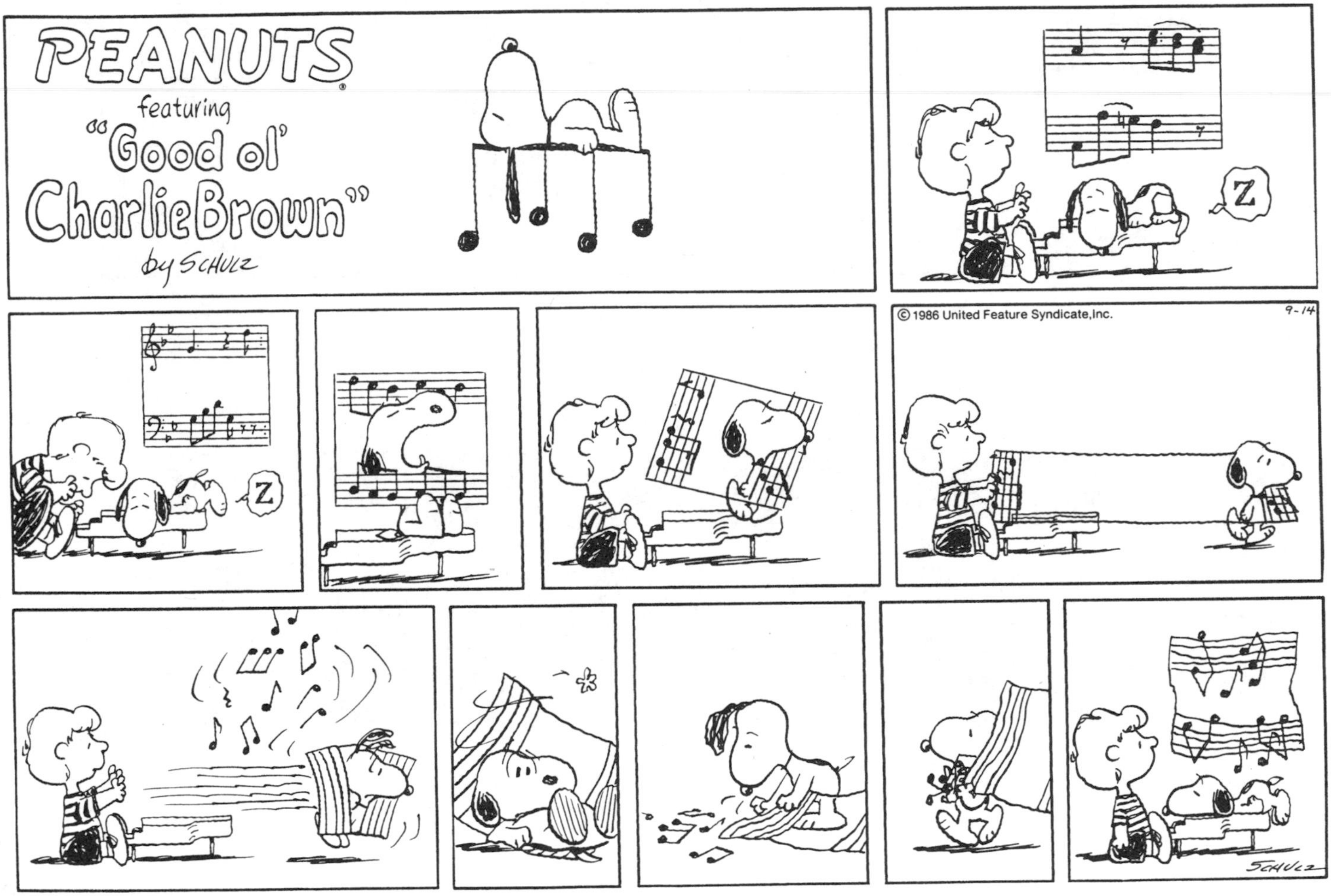
PEANUTS
featuring
"Good ol' Charlie Brown"
by SCHULZ
Z
Z
© 1986 United Feature Syndicate, Inc.
9-14
SCHULZ

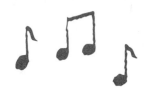

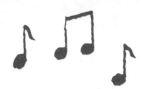

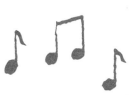

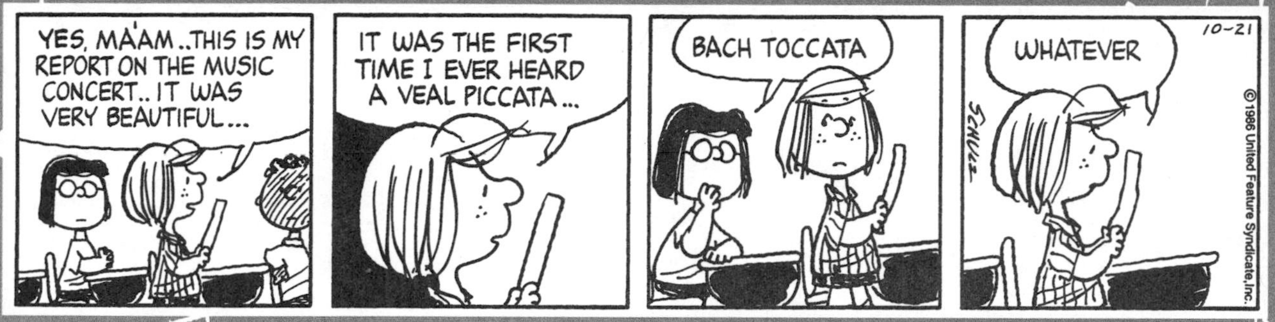
YES, MA'AM..THIS IS MY REPORT ON THE MUSIC CONCERT.. IT WAS VERY BEAUTIFUL...
IT WAS THE FIRST TIME I EVER HEARD A VEAL PICCATA...
BACH TOCCATA
WHATEVER
10-21
© 1986 United Feature Syndicate, Inc.

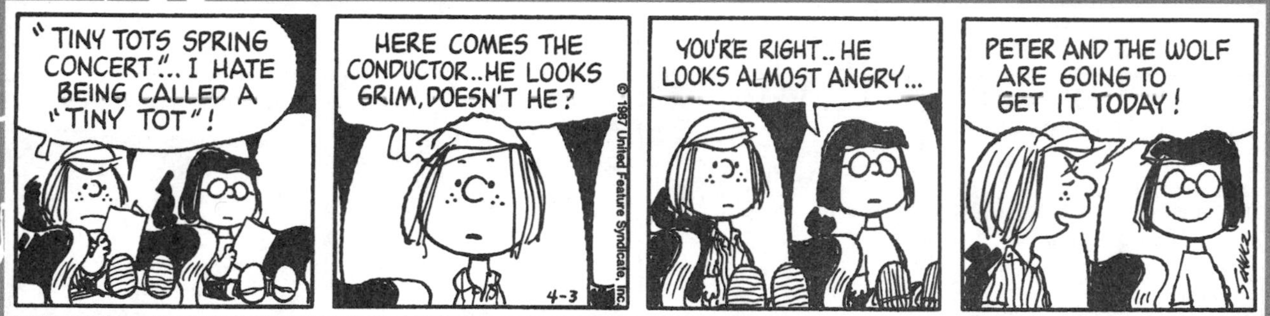
"TINY TOTS SPRING CONCERT"... I HATE BEING CALLED A "TINY TOT"!
HERE COMES THE CONDUCTOR..HE LOOKS GRIM, DOESN'T HE?
4-3
© 1987 United Feature Syndicate, Inc.
YOU'RE RIGHT.. HE LOOKS ALMOST ANGRY...
PETER AND THE WOLF ARE GOING TO GET IT TODAY!

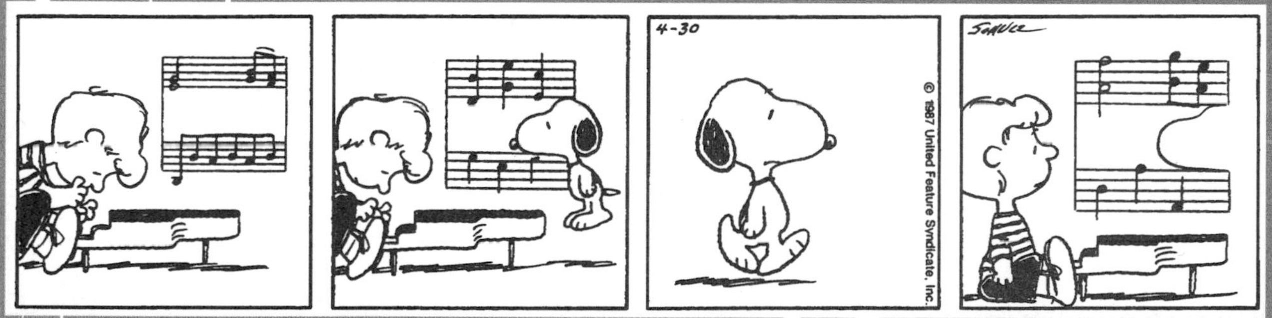
4-30
© 1987 United Feature Syndicate, Inc.

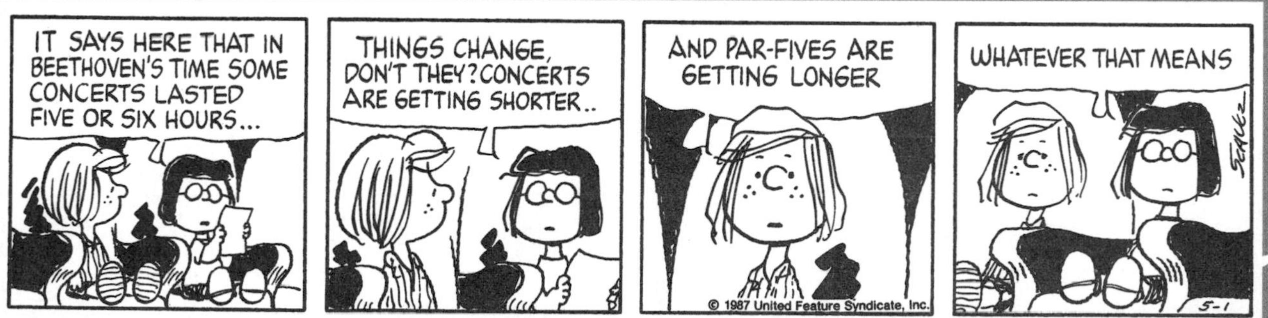
IT SAYS HERE THAT IN BEETHOVEN'S TIME SOME CONCERTS LASTED FIVE OR SIX HOURS...
THINGS CHANGE, DON'T THEY? CONCERTS ARE GETTING SHORTER..
AND PAR-FIVES ARE GETTING LONGER
© 1987 United Feature Syndicate, Inc.
WHATEVER THAT MEANS
5-1

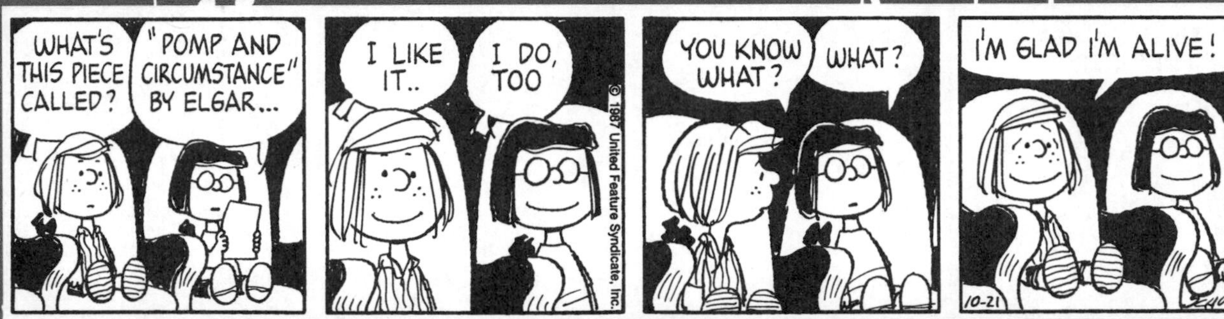
WHAT'S THIS PIECE CALLED?
"POMP AND CIRCUMSTANCE" BY ELGAR...
I LIKE IT..
I DO, TOO
© 1987 United Feature Syndicate, Inc.
YOU KNOW WHAT?
WHAT?
I'M GLAD I'M ALIVE!
10-21

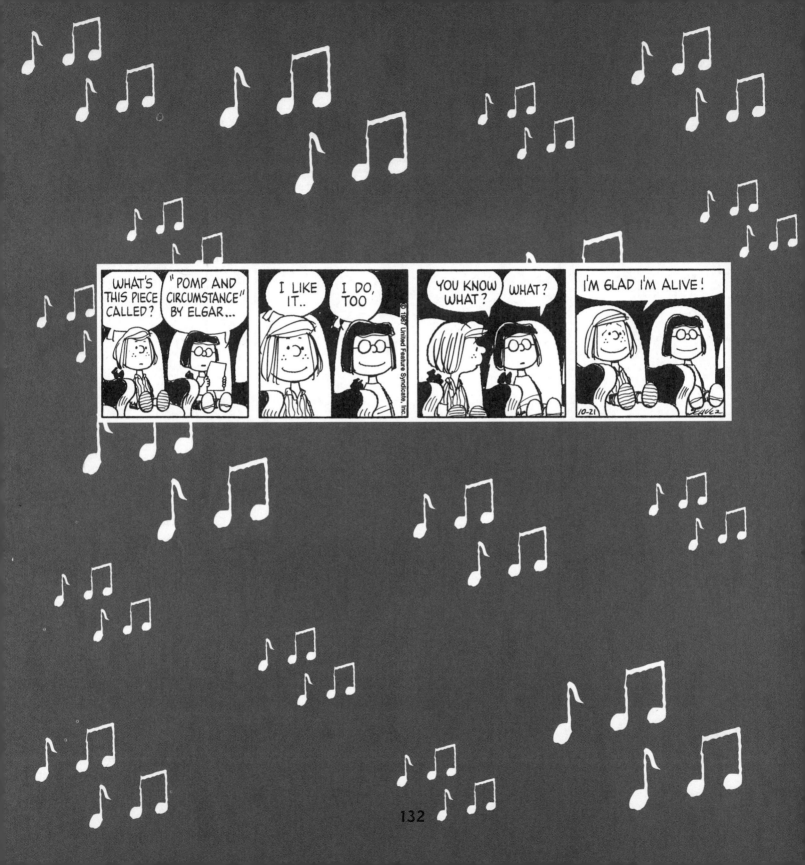

PEANUTS
by SCHULZ

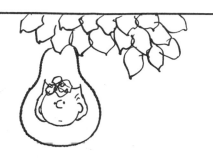

"FOUR CALLING BIRDS, AND A PARTRIDGE IN A PEAR TREE.."

THAT SONG DRIVES ME CRAZY!

WHAT IN THE WORLD IS A "CALLING BIRD"?

A CALLING BIRD IS A KIND OF PARTRIDGE..

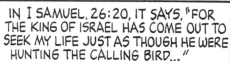

IN I SAMUEL, 26:20, IT SAYS, "FOR THE KING OF ISRAEL HAS COME OUT TO SEEK MY LIFE JUST AS THOUGH HE WERE HUNTING THE CALLING BIRD..."

THERE'S A PLAY ON WORDS HERE, YOU SEE.. DAVID WAS STANDING ON A MOUNTAIN CALLING, AND HE COMPARED HIMSELF TO A PARTRIDGE BEING HUNTED...

ISN'T THAT FASCINATING?

12-20

© 1987 United Feature Syndicate, Inc.

IF I GET SOCKS AGAIN FOR CHRISTMAS THIS YEAR, I'LL GO EVEN MORE CRAZY!

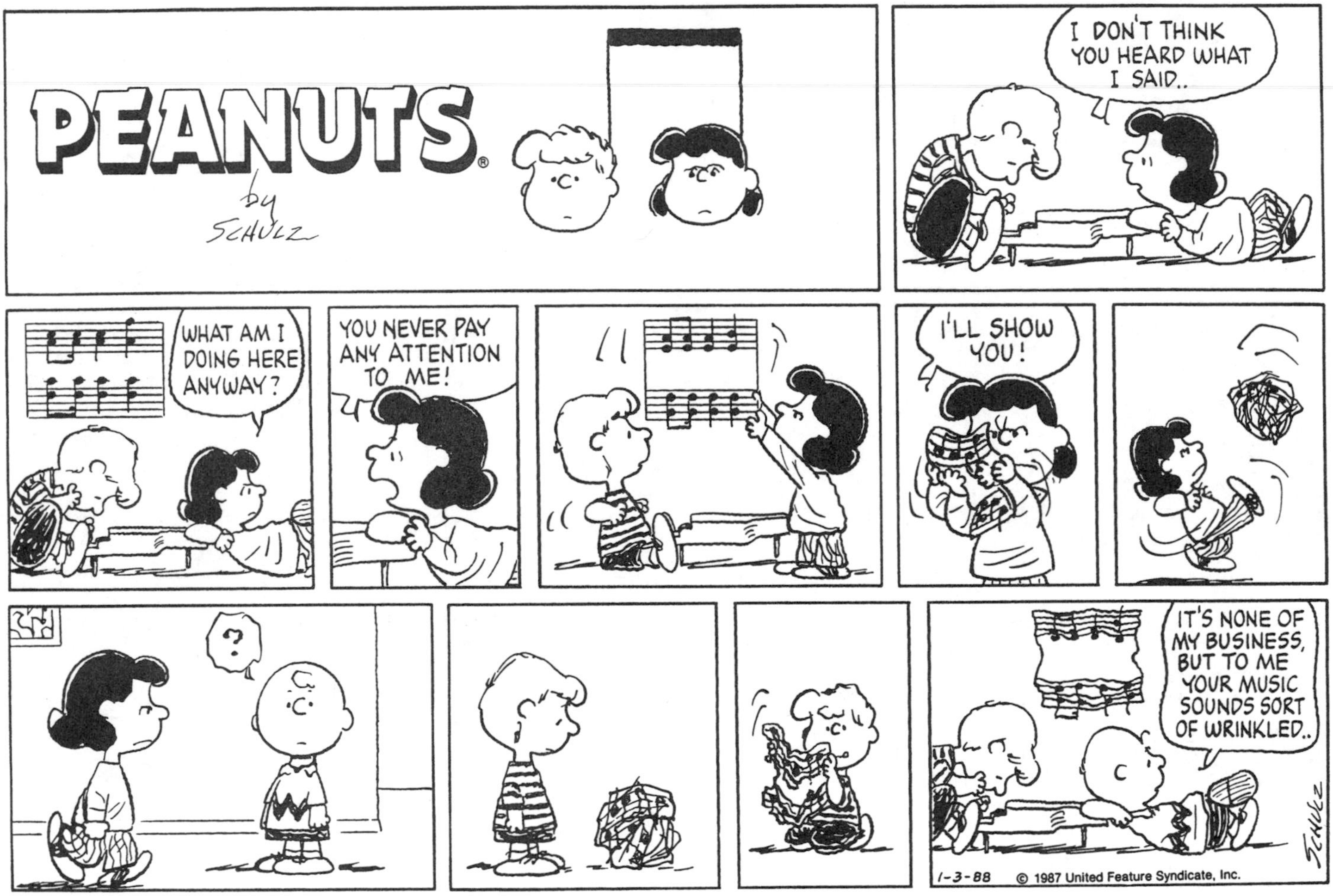
PEANUTS
by SCHULZ
I DON'T THINK YOU HEARD WHAT I SAID..
WHAT AM I DOING HERE ANYWAY?
YOU NEVER PAY ANY ATTENTION TO ME!
I'LL SHOW YOU!
?
IT'S NONE OF MY BUSINESS, BUT TO ME YOUR MUSIC SOUNDS SORT OF WRINKLED..
SCHULZ
1-3-88

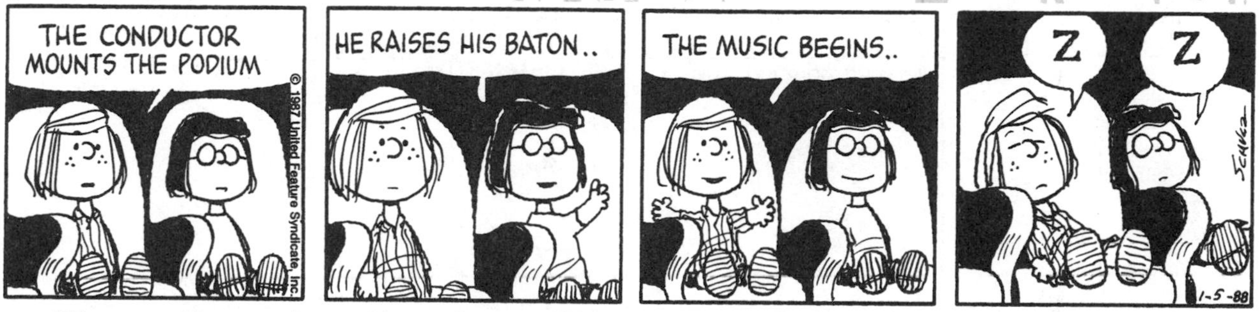
THE CONDUCTOR MOUNTS THE PODIUM
© 1987 United Feature Syndicate, Inc.
HE RAISES HIS BATON..
THE MUSIC BEGINS..
Z
Z
SCHULZ
1-5-88

THIS IS MY REPORT ON THE "TINY TOTS" CONCERT OUR CLASS WENT TO YESTERDAY..
THE ORCHESTRA PLAYED "PETER AND THE WOLF"
© 1987 United Feature Syndicate, Inc.
1-6-88
HOW DO I KNOW?
I'VE SLEPT THROUGH IT BEFORE..

YOU SHOULDN'T HAVE ADMITTED TO THE TEACHER THAT YOU FELL ASLEEP AT THE CONCERT, SIR..
CONCERTS ARE SUPPOSED TO BE EDUCATIONAL..
1-7-88
YOU'RE SUPPOSED TO LISTEN TO THE MUSIC AND RELAX
THAT'S WHAT I DID..
AND THEN I FELL ASLEEP..
© 1987 United Feature Syndicate, Inc.

I DECIDED TO COME TO THIS CONCERT PREPARED
© 1987 United Feature Syndicate, Inc.
I'VE READ ALL ABOUT THE COMPOSERS AND ALL ABOUT THE MUSIC WE'RE GOING TO HEAR..
1-8-88
GOOD FOR YOU, MARCIE
I CAME PREPARED, TOO!

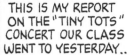

WHAT'S THIS NEW PIECE THEY'RE PLAYING? I'VE NEVER HEARD OF IT...
© 1988 United Feature Syndicate, Inc.
SOME CONDUCTORS LIKE TO PERFORM NEW MUSIC TO CHALLENGE THEIR LISTENERS..
3-26
BORING IS CHALLENGING ?
SCHULZ

IT SAYS HERE THEY'RE SERVING SHERBET AFTER THE CONCERT...
NO, IT SAYS THEY'RE PLAYING SCHUBERT DURING THE CONCERT..
© 1988 United Feature Syndicate, Inc.
3-31
FOR A MINUTE THERE I WAS GLAD I CAME
YOU'RE WEIRD, SIR!
SCHULZ

DOES HE HAVE TO PLAY THAT STUPID THING SO LOUD?
IT BRINGS TEARS TO MY EARS!
SCHULZ
5-30
© 1988 United Feature Syndicate, Inc.

mp
9-15
© 1968 United Feature Syndicate, Inc.
SCHULZ

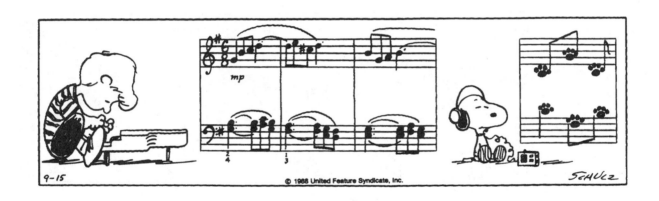

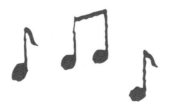

TODAY IS BEETHOVEN'S BIRTHDAY!
IT IS? WHAT DID YOU BUY ME?
© 1988 United Feature Syndicate, Inc.
12-16
YOU DON'T BUY PRESENTS FOR GIRLS ON BEETHOVEN'S BIRTHDAY
WHAT A WASTE!
SCHULZ

This is my report on the trip our class took to the "Sing-It-Yourself Messiah"
12-26
© 1988 United Feature Syndicate, Inc.
SCHULZ
I was the only one who was asked to leave the auditorium.

THAT WAS THE FIRST MOVEMENT OF THE SYMPHONY, SIR..NOW, THEY'RE PLAYING THE SLOW MOVEMENT..
© 1989 United Feature Syndicate, Inc.
JUST LIKE MY LIFE..I'M IN THE SLOW MOVEMENT..
SCHULZ
1-31

PEANUTS
by SCHULZ
FANTASTIC!
THAT WAS GREAT! WHAT A PIANO PLAYER! THAT'S WHAT I'D LIKE TO BE.. A CONCERT PIANIST!
© 1989 United Feature Syndicate, Inc.
I'M GOING TO ASK MY DAD TO BUY ME A PIANO, AND I'M GOING TO BE GREAT AND I'M GONNA TOUR THE WORLD!
5-28
HA HA HA HA HA HA
LET ME SEE THE PROGRAM AGAIN, WILL YOU, SIR? I FORGOT WHAT THEY'RE PLAYING NEXT...
WHAT DID YOU DO WITH THE PROGRAM?
SCHULZ

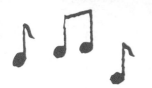

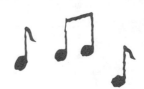

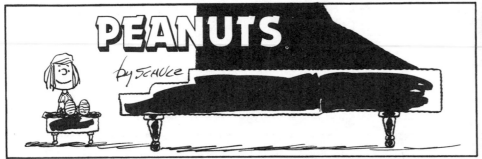

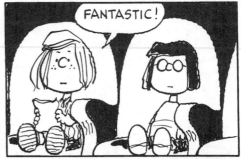

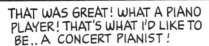

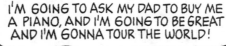

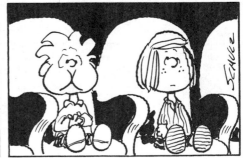

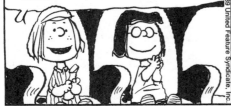

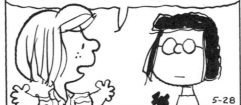

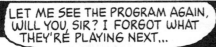

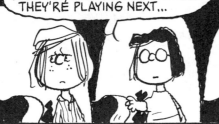

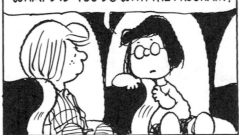

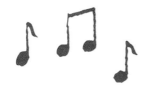

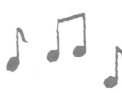

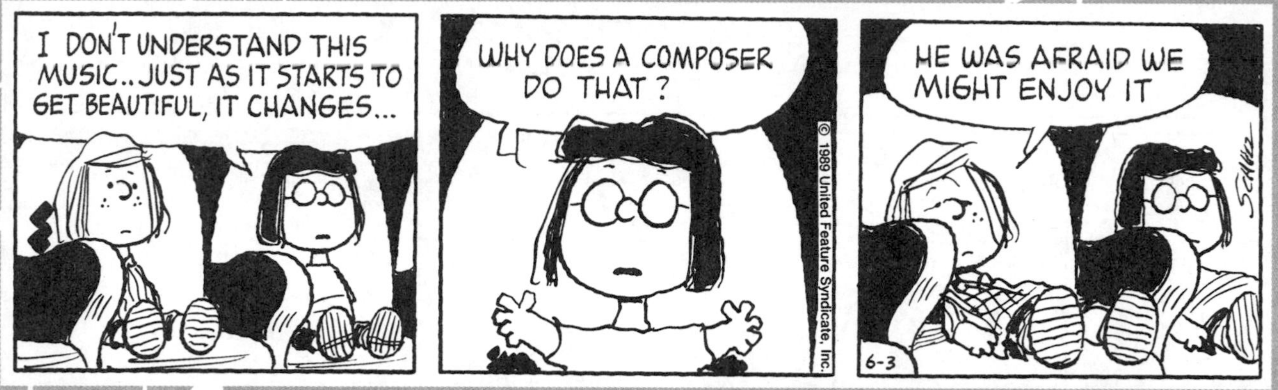
I DON'T UNDERSTAND THIS MUSIC..JUST AS IT STARTS TO GET BEAUTIFUL, IT CHANGES...
WHY DOES A COMPOSER DO THAT ?
© 1989 United Feature Syndicate, Inc.
HE WAS AFRAID WE MIGHT ENJOY IT
SCHULZ
6-3

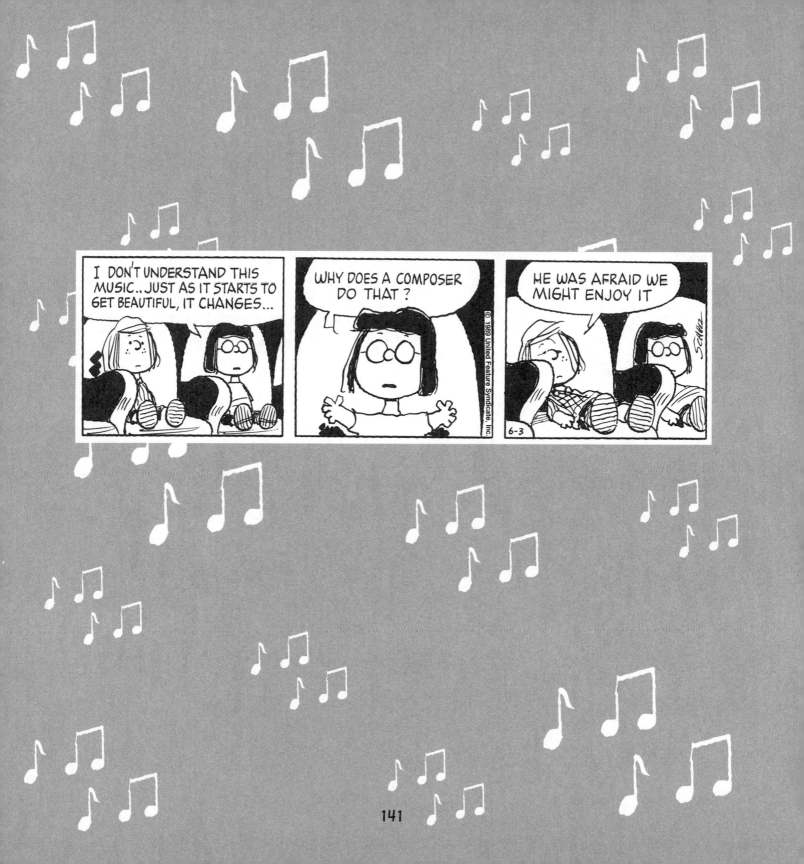

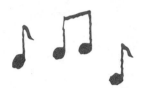

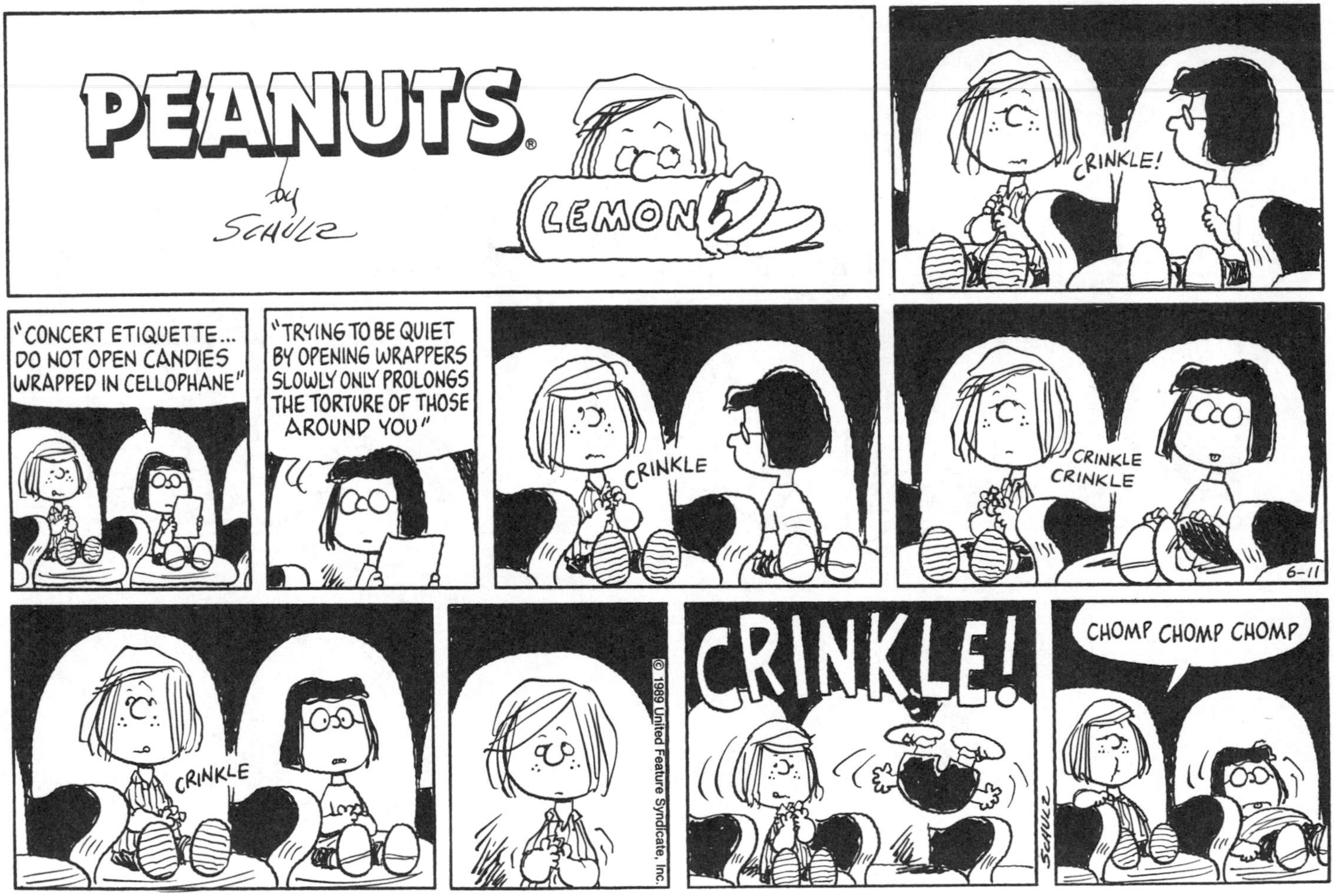
PEANUTS
by SCHULZ
LEMON
CRINKLE!
"CONCERT ETIQUETTE... DO NOT OPEN CANDIES WRAPPED IN CELLOPHANE"
"TRYING TO BE QUIET BY OPENING WRAPPERS SLOWLY ONLY PROLONGS THE TORTURE OF THOSE AROUND YOU"
CRINKLE
CRINKLE CRINKLE
6-11
CRINKLE
© 1989 United Feature Syndicate, Inc.
CRINKLE!
SCHULZ
CHOMP CHOMP CHOMP

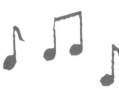

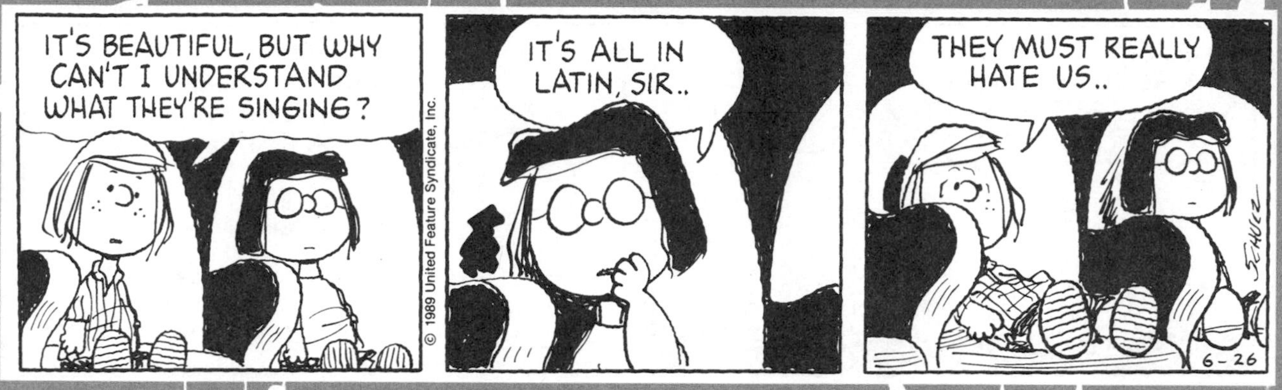
IT'S BEAUTIFUL, BUT WHY CAN'T I UNDERSTAND WHAT THEY'RE SINGING?
© 1989 United Feature Syndicate, Inc.
IT'S ALL IN LATIN, SIR..
THEY MUST REALLY HATE US..
SCHULZ
6-26

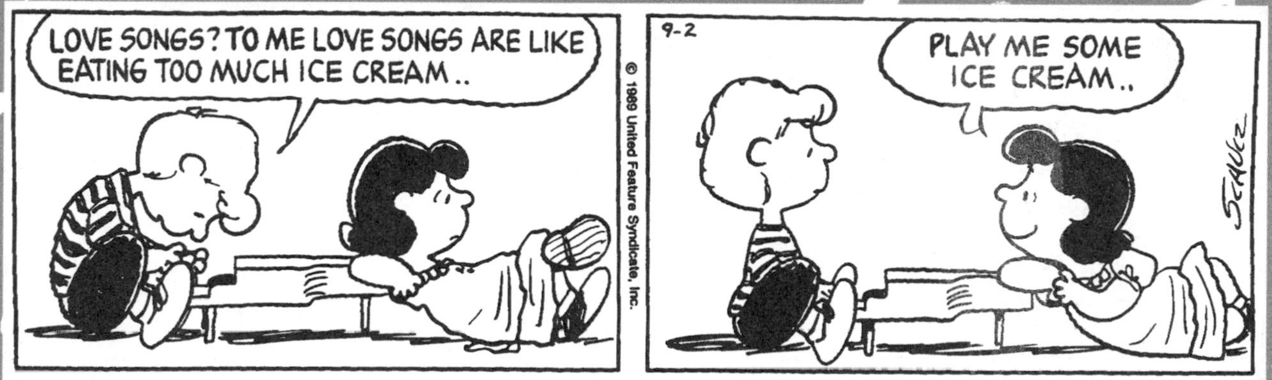
LOVE SONGS? TO ME LOVE SONGS ARE LIKE EATING TOO MUCH ICE CREAM..
© 1989 United Feature Syndicate, Inc.
9-2
PLAY ME SOME ICE CREAM..
SCHULZ

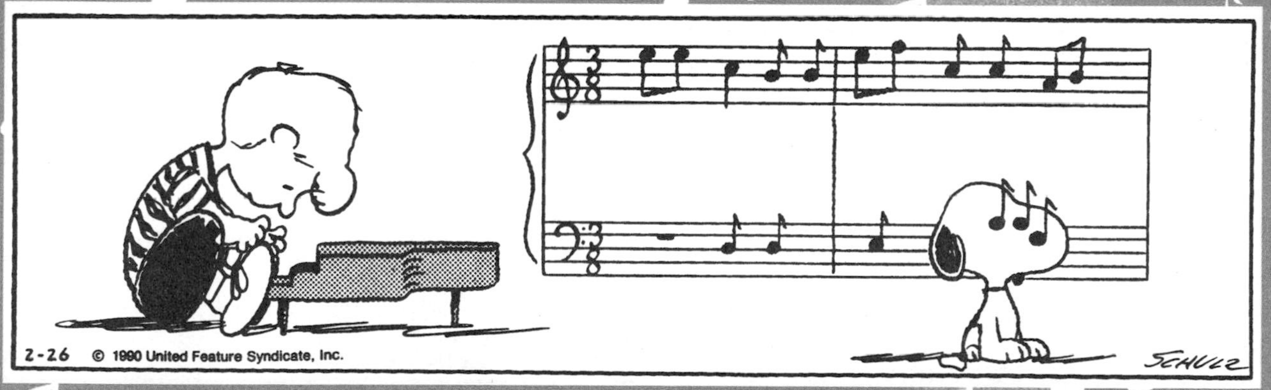
2-26
© 1990 United Feature Syndicate, Inc.
SCHULZ

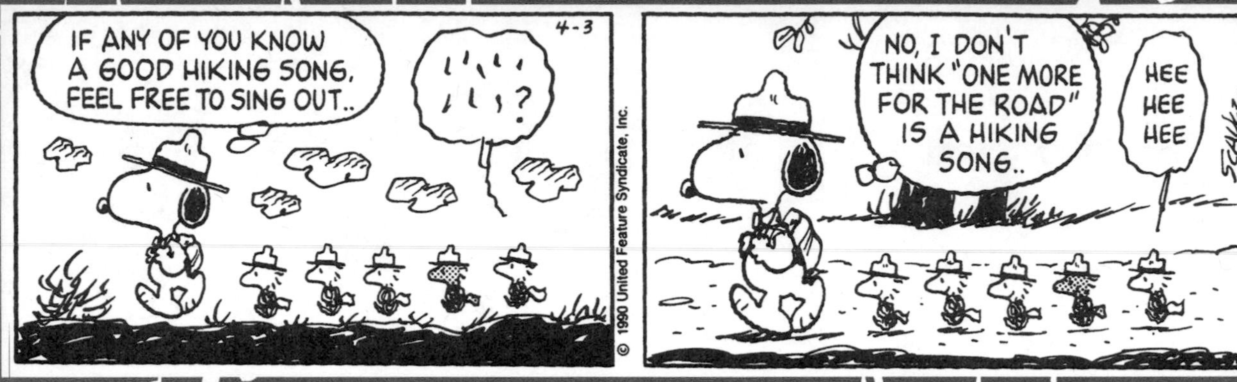
4-3
IF ANY OF YOU KNOW A GOOD HIKING SONG, FEEL FREE TO SING OUT..
?
© 1990 United Feature Syndicate, Inc.
NO, I DON'T THINK "ONE MORE FOR THE ROAD" IS A HIKING SONG..
HEE HEE HEE
SCHULZ

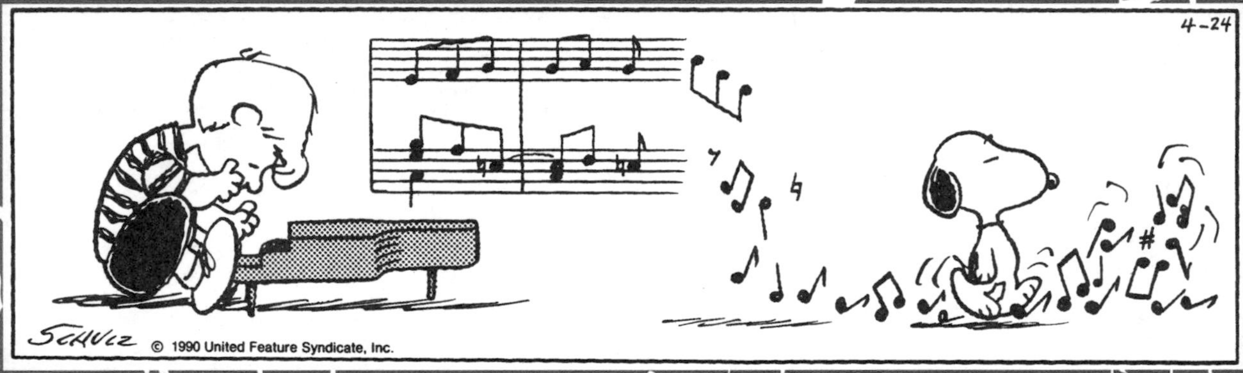
4-24
SCHULZ © 1990 United Feature Syndicate, Inc.

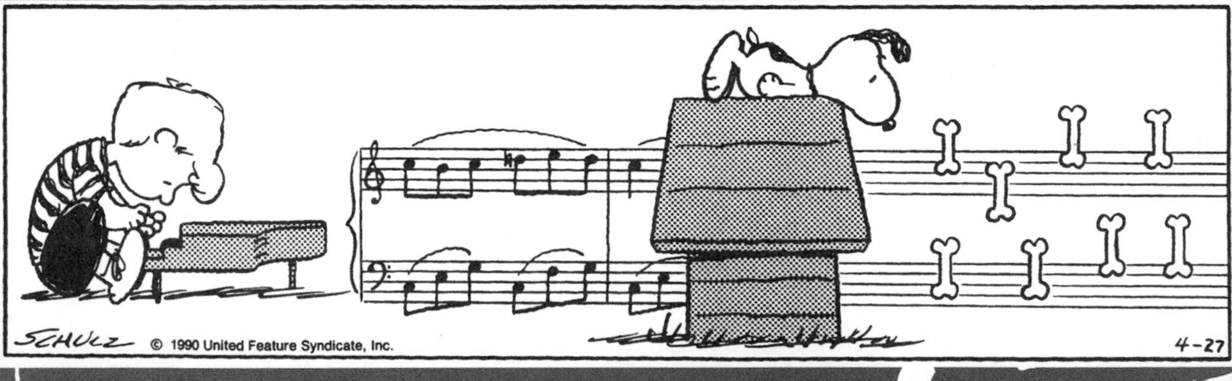
SCHULZ © 1990 United Feature Syndicate, Inc.
4-27

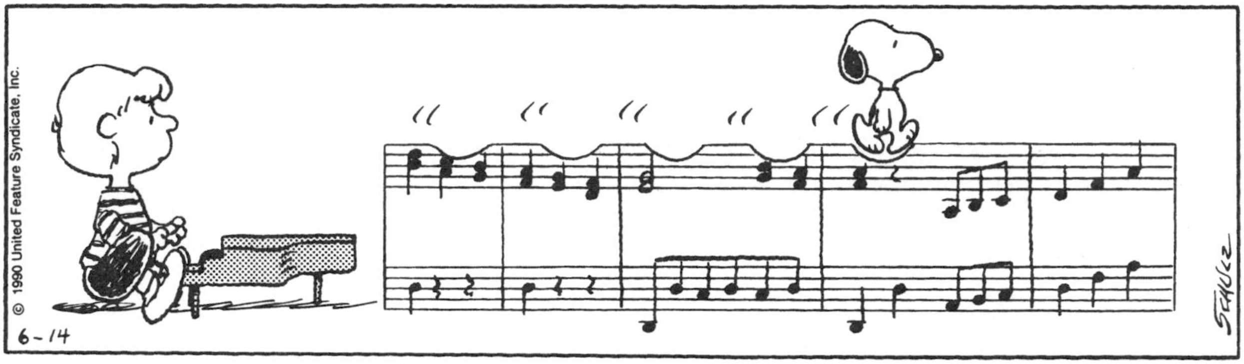
© 1990 United Feature Syndicate, Inc.
6-14
SCHULZ

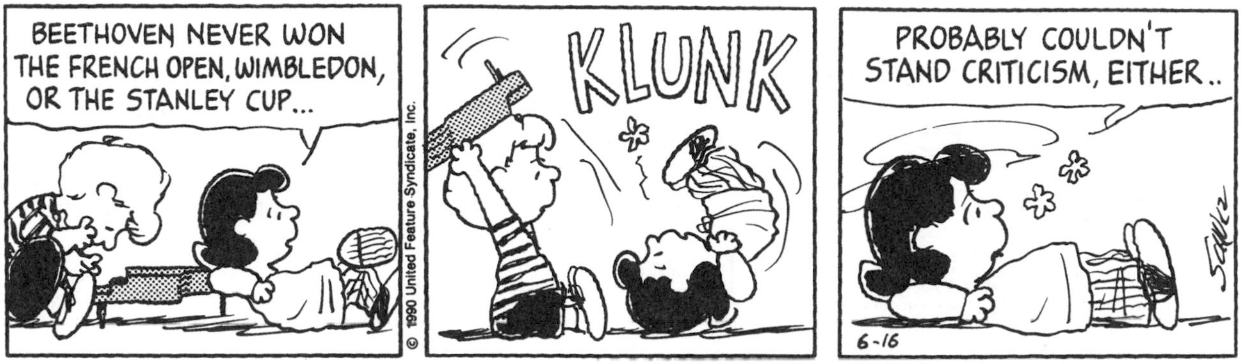
BEETHOVEN NEVER WON THE FRENCH OPEN, WIMBLEDON, OR THE STANLEY CUP...
© 1990 United Feature Syndicate, Inc.
KLUNK
PROBABLY COULDN'T STAND CRITICISM, EITHER..
6-16
SCHULZ

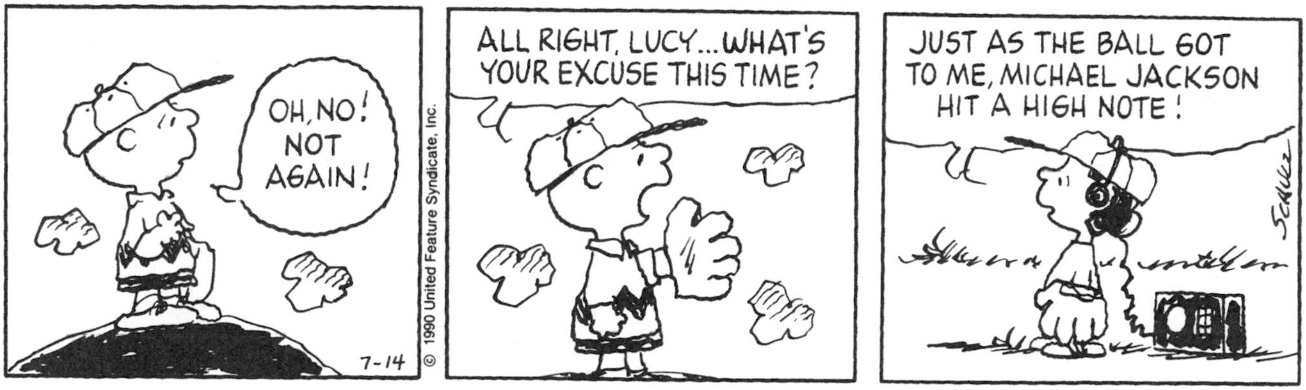
OH, NO! NOT AGAIN!
7-14
© 1990 United Feature Syndicate, Inc.
ALL RIGHT, LUCY... WHAT'S YOUR EXCUSE THIS TIME?
JUST AS THE BALL GOT TO ME, MICHAEL JACKSON HIT A HIGH NOTE!
SCHULZ

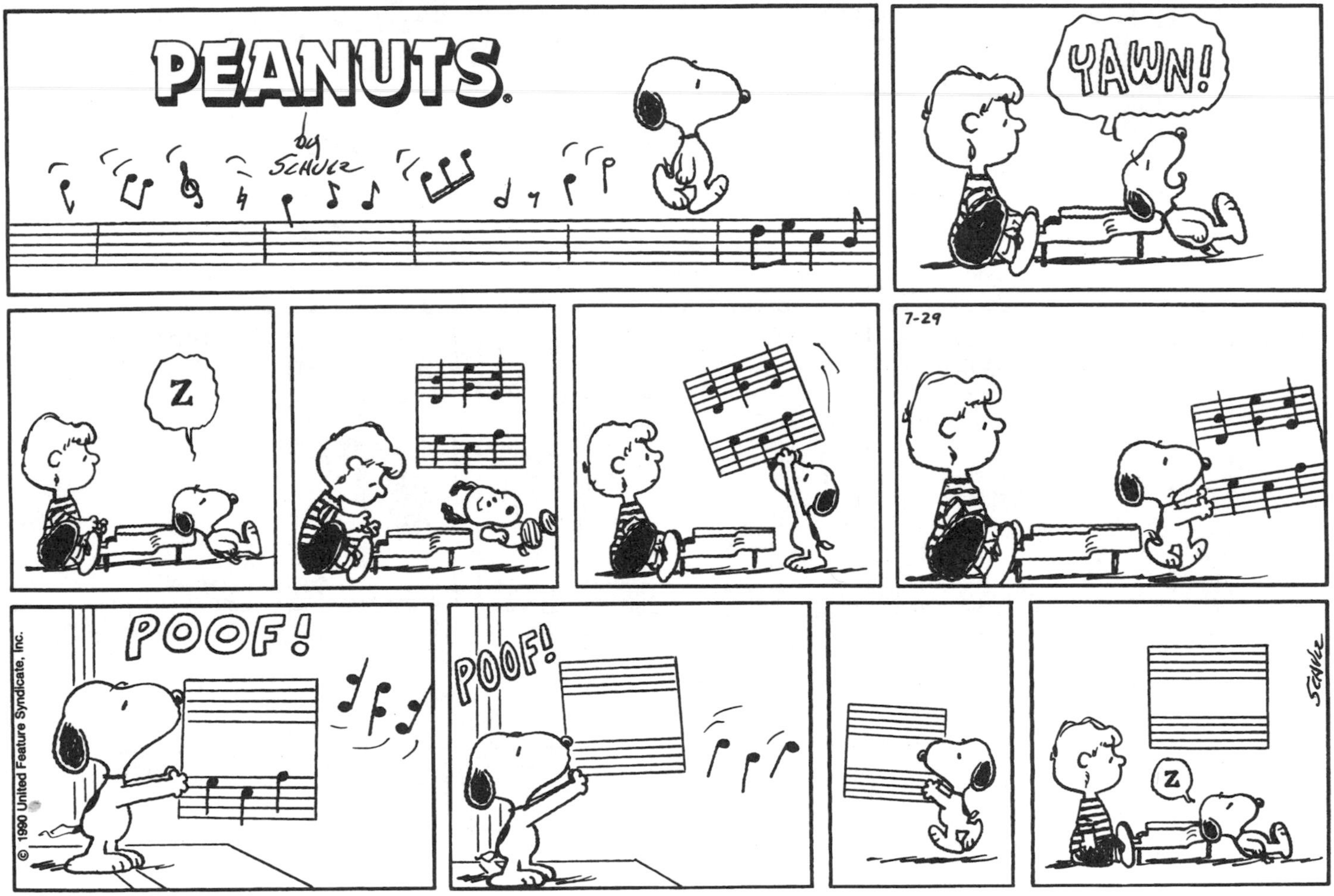
PEANUTS
by SCHULZ
YAWN!
Z
7-29
© 1990 United Feature Syndicate, Inc.
POOF!
POOF!
Z
SCHULZ

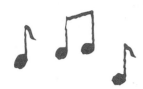

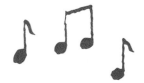

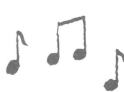

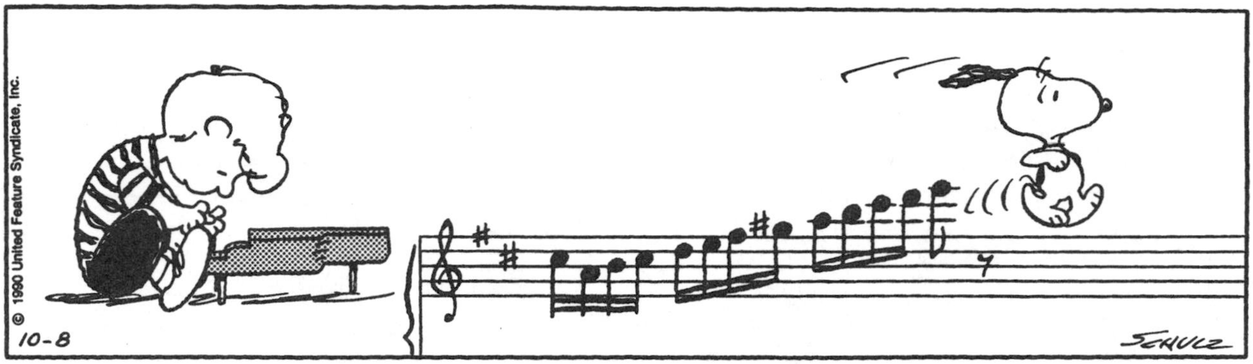
© 1990 United Feature Syndicate, Inc.
10-8
SCHULZ

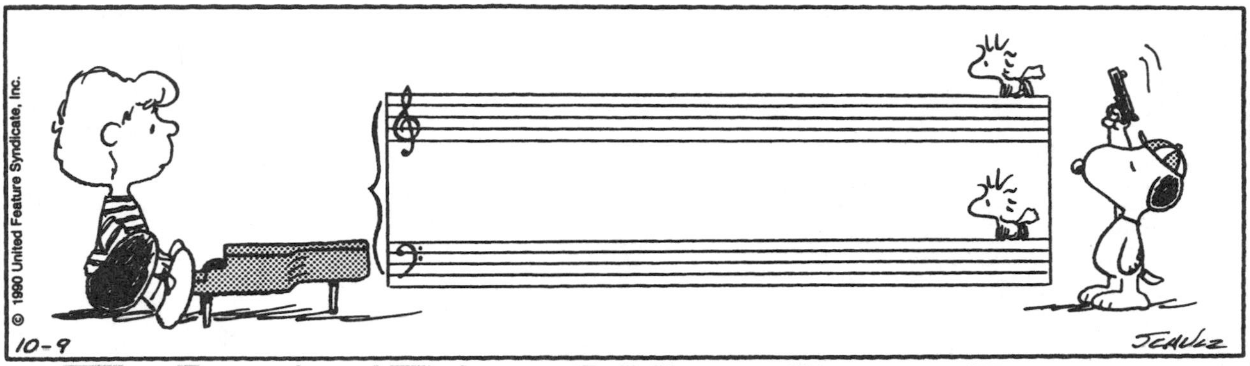
© 1990 United Feature Syndicate, Inc.
10-9
SCHULZ

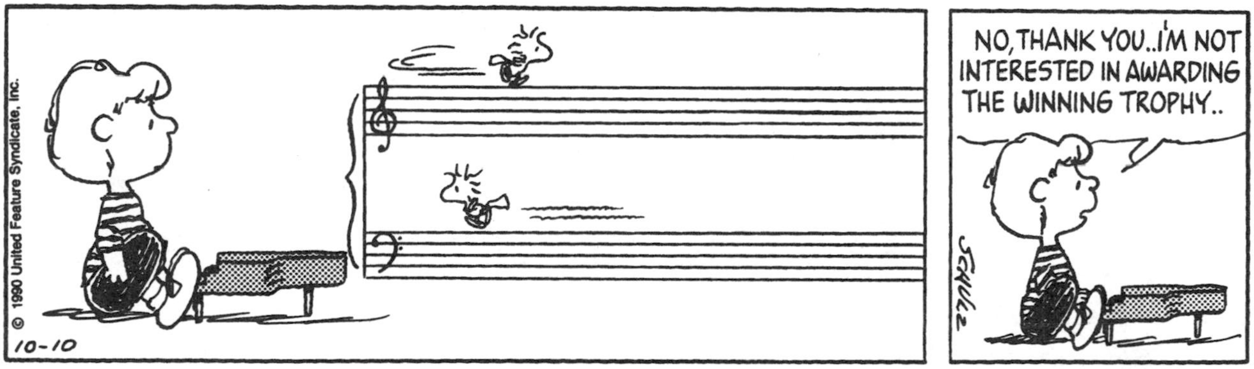
© 1990 United Feature Syndicate, Inc.
10-10
NO, THANK YOU..I'M NOT INTERESTED IN AWARDING THE WINNING TROPHY..
SCHULZ

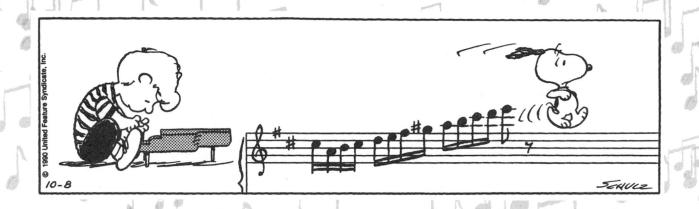

MUSICIANS PLAY A LOT OF LOVE SONGS, BUT THEY DON'T REALLY HEAR THEM, DO THEY?
10-12
© 1990 United Feature Syndicate, Inc.
ACTUALLY, THEY DON'T HEAR ANYTHING!
SCHULZ

THIS NEXT PIECE IS A CONCERTO FOR FLUTE AND ORCHESTRA...
© 1990 United Feature Syndicate, Inc.
IT WAS COMPOSED BY ELLEN ZWILICH WHO, INCIDENTALLY, JUST HAPPENS TO BE A WOMAN!
10-13
GOOD GOING, ELLEN
SCHULZ

11-12
© 1990 United Feature Syndicate, Inc.
SCHULZ

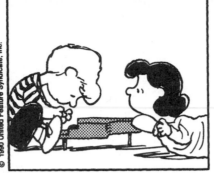

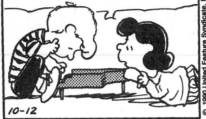

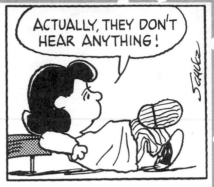

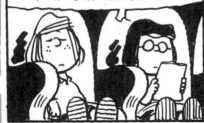

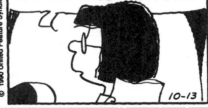

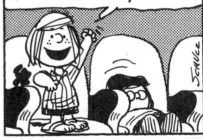

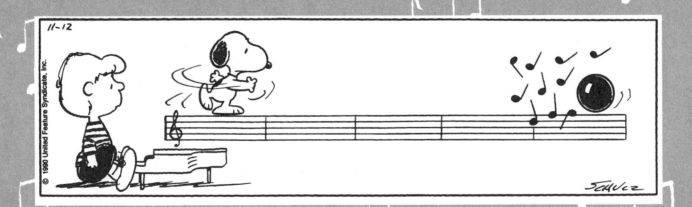

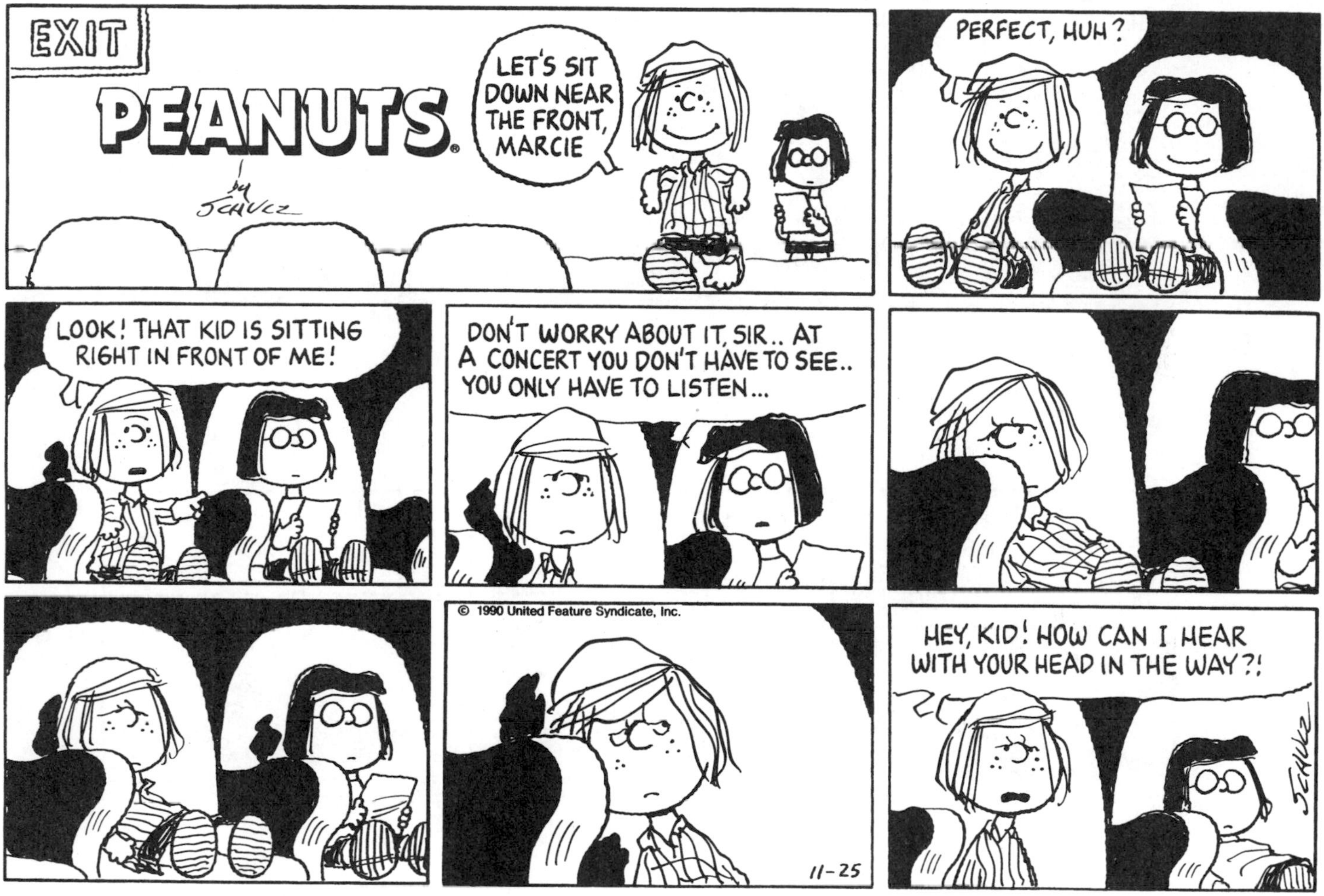
EXIT
PEANUTS
by SCHULZ
LET'S SIT DOWN NEAR THE FRONT, MARCIE
PERFECT, HUH?
LOOK! THAT KID IS SITTING RIGHT IN FRONT OF ME!
DON'T WORRY ABOUT IT, SIR.. AT A CONCERT YOU DON'T HAVE TO SEE.. YOU ONLY HAVE TO LISTEN...
© 1990 United Feature Syndicate, Inc.
11-25
HEY, KID! HOW CAN I HEAR WITH YOUR HEAD IN THE WAY?!
SCHULZ

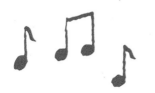

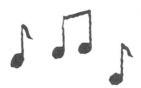

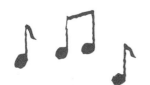

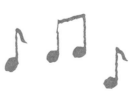

WHAT ARE WE DOING HERE?
IT'S ANOTHER "TINY TOTS" CONCERT
WHAT'S ON THE PROGRAM?
IF THEY PLAY "PETER AND THE WOLF" AGAIN, I'LL GO CRAZY..
THAT'S WHAT THEY'RE PLAYING, SIR..
I HOPE THE WOLF EATS HIM!
© 1991 United Feature Syndicate, Inc.
SCHULZ 1-15

YOU CAN'T HAVE A MEANINGFUL DISCUSSION WITH A BIRD BECAUSE BIRDS DON'T KNOW ANYTHING!
© 1991 United Feature Syndicate, Inc.
ALL THEY KNOW IS FLYING AND WORMS..
ALL RIGHT, AND MAYBE A COUPLE OF OLD SONGS
2-1
SCHULZ

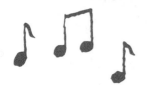

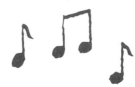

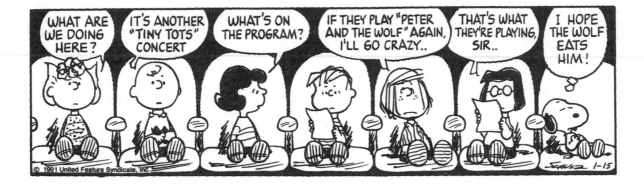

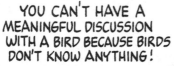

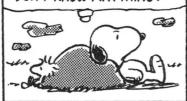

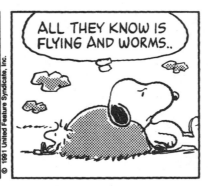

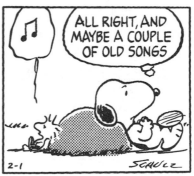

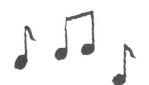

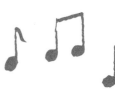

© 1991 United Feature Syndicate, Inc.
3-2
SCHULZ

© 1991 United Feature Syndicate, Inc.
4-27
SCHULZ

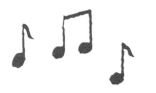

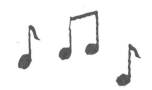

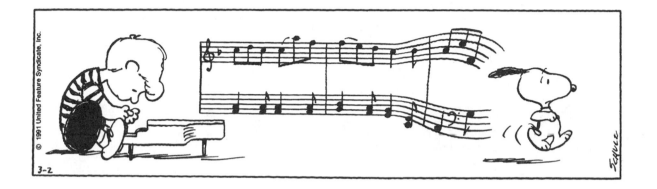

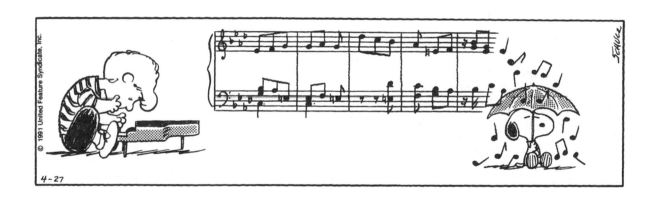

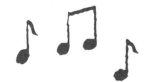

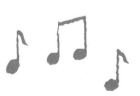

mf
Z Z Z Z
Z Z Z Z
© 1991 United Feature Syndicate, Inc.
8-2
SCHULZ

I HATE ELEVATOR MUSIC AND TELEPHONE MUSIC, BUT YOU KNOW WHAT I HATE THE MOST?
© 1991 United Feature Syndicate, Inc.
8-3
THUMB AND BLANKET MUSIC!
SCHULZ

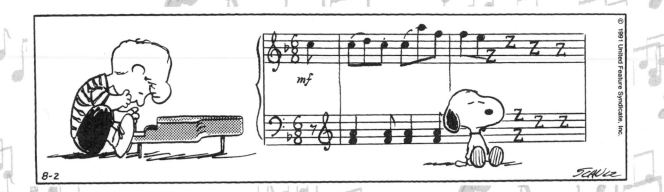

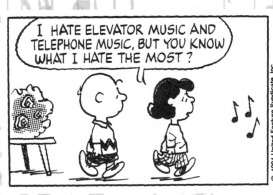

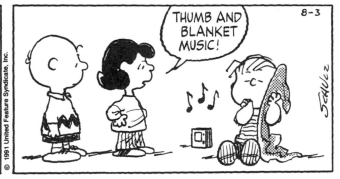

SCHULZ
9-23 © 1991 United Feature Syndicate, Inc.

DID YOU HEAR WHAT HE SAID HE WAS GOING TO PLAY? WOW, THIS SHOULD BE GOOD!
5/4
© 1992 United Feature Syndicate, Inc.
HE SAID HE WAS GOING TO PLAY AN "ETUDE"
RATS! I THOUGHT HE SAID, "HEY, DUDE"
SCHULZ

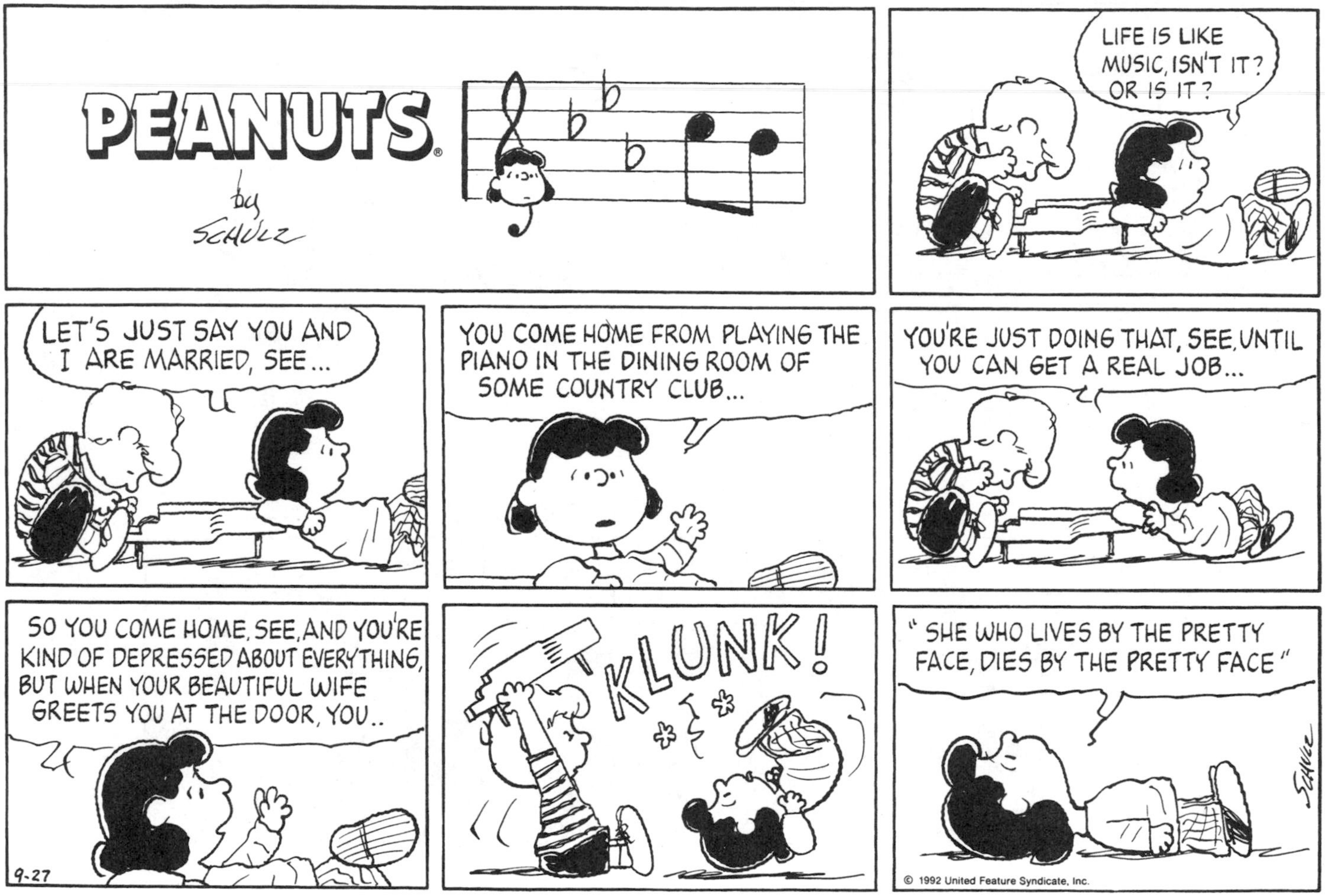
PEANUTS
by SCHULZ
LIFE IS LIKE MUSIC, ISN'T IT? OR IS IT?
LET'S JUST SAY YOU AND I ARE MARRIED, SEE...
YOU COME HOME FROM PLAYING THE PIANO IN THE DINING ROOM OF SOME COUNTRY CLUB...
YOU'RE JUST DOING THAT, SEE, UNTIL YOU CAN GET A REAL JOB...
SO YOU COME HOME, SEE, AND YOU'RE KIND OF DEPRESSED ABOUT EVERYTHING, BUT WHEN YOUR BEAUTIFUL WIFE GREETS YOU AT THE DOOR, YOU..
9-27
KLUNK!
" SHE WHO LIVES BY THE PRETTY FACE, DIES BY THE PRETTY FACE "
SCHULZ
© 1992 United Feature Syndicate, Inc.

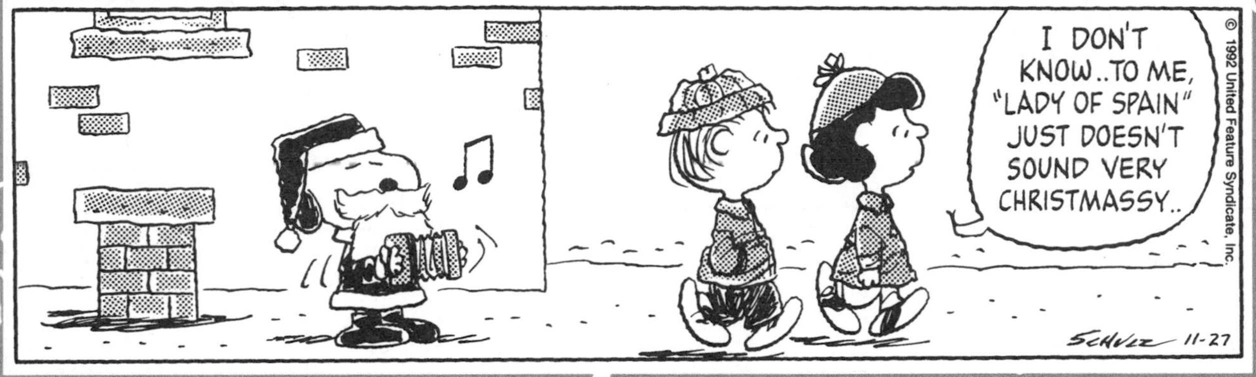
I DON'T KNOW..TO ME, "LADY OF SPAIN" JUST DOESN'T SOUND VERY CHRISTMASSY..
© 1992 United Feature Syndicate, Inc.
SCHULZ 11-27

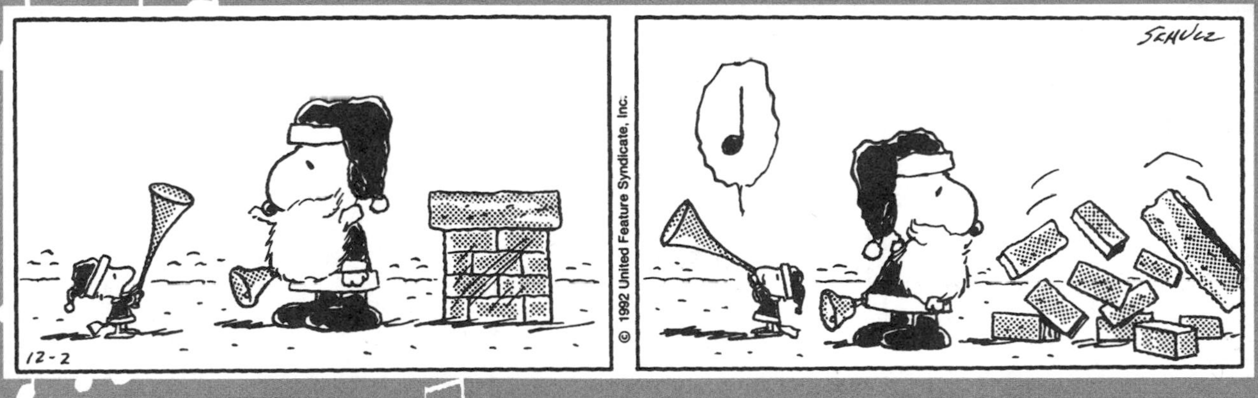
12-2
© 1992 United Feature Syndicate, Inc.
SCHULZ

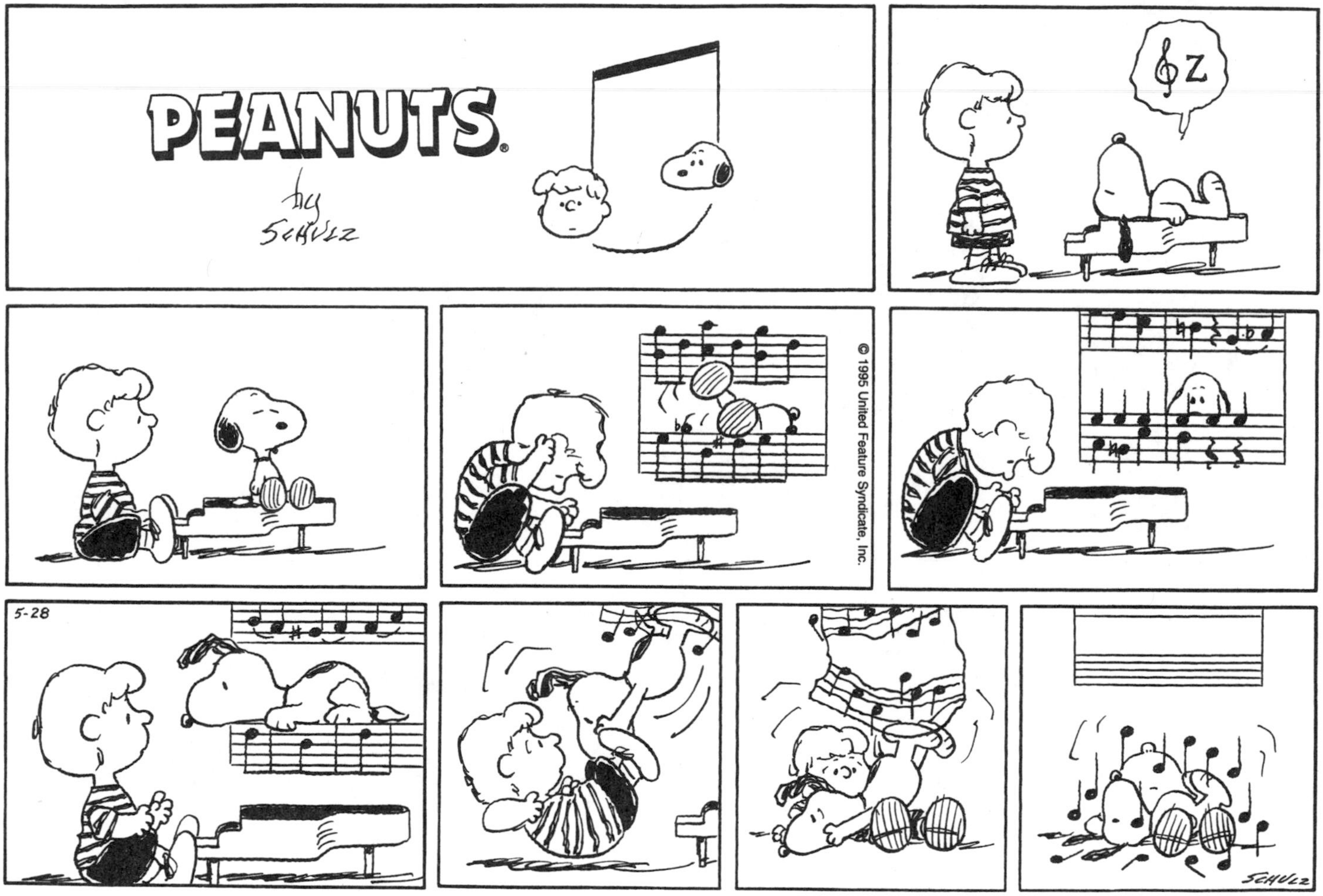
PEANUTS
by SCHULZ
𝄞Z
© 1995 United Feature Syndicate, Inc.
5-28
SCHULZ

PEANUTS
by SCHULZ
I CAN'T HEAR IT..
CAN'T HEAR WHAT?
I CAN'T HEAR THE HARP..
SHH..
WHEN WE GET HOME, I'M GOING TO HAVE SOME COLD CEREAL..
OR MAYBE SOME TOAST WITH GRAPE JELLY
LISTEN TO THE MUSIC, SIR..
HERE, HAVE A MINT..
THANK YOU
© 1995 United Feature Syndicate, Inc.
OH, SURE! TAKE THE BEST ONE!
I DIDN'T TAKE THE BEST ONE..
YOU TOOK AN ORANGE ONE! THE ORANGE ONES ARE MY FAVORITE!
I JUST TOOK WHATEVER WAS ON TOP!
BOOT!
6-4
THIS IS MY REPORT ON THE CONCERT THEY TOOK US TO YESTERDAY.. I NEVER HEARD THE HARP..
SCHULZ

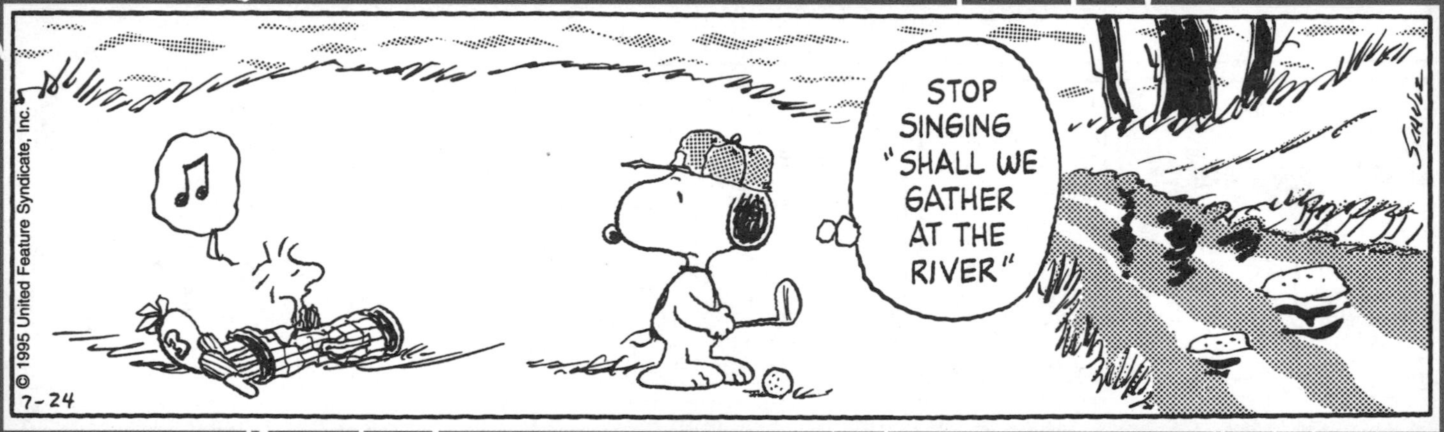
© 1995 United Feature Syndicate, Inc.
7-24
STOP SINGING "SHALL WE GATHER AT THE RIVER"
SCHULZ

PEANUTS
by Schulz

I'M AWAKE!

YES, MA'AM.. WE WENT TO THE CONCERT, AND HEARD "ADAGIO FOR STRINGS" BY SAMUEL THE BARBER..

7-30

NOT SAMUEL THE BARBER! SAMUEL BARBER! GOOD GRIEF!

CAN'T YOU EVER GET ANYTHING RIGHT?!.

© 1995 United Feature Syndicate, Inc.

WHAT'S WRONG WITH YOU? DON'T YOU EVER LISTEN? DON'T YOU EVER READ?!

SAMUEL THE BARBER! THAT'S NOT EVEN FUNNY! WHEN ARE YOU EVER GOING TO LEARN SOMETHING?!

DON'T YOU EVER THINK?

YES, MA'AM.. AND THEN THEY PLAYED "PETER AND THE FOX"

"WOLF," FRANKLIN.. "HAROLD AND THE WOLF"

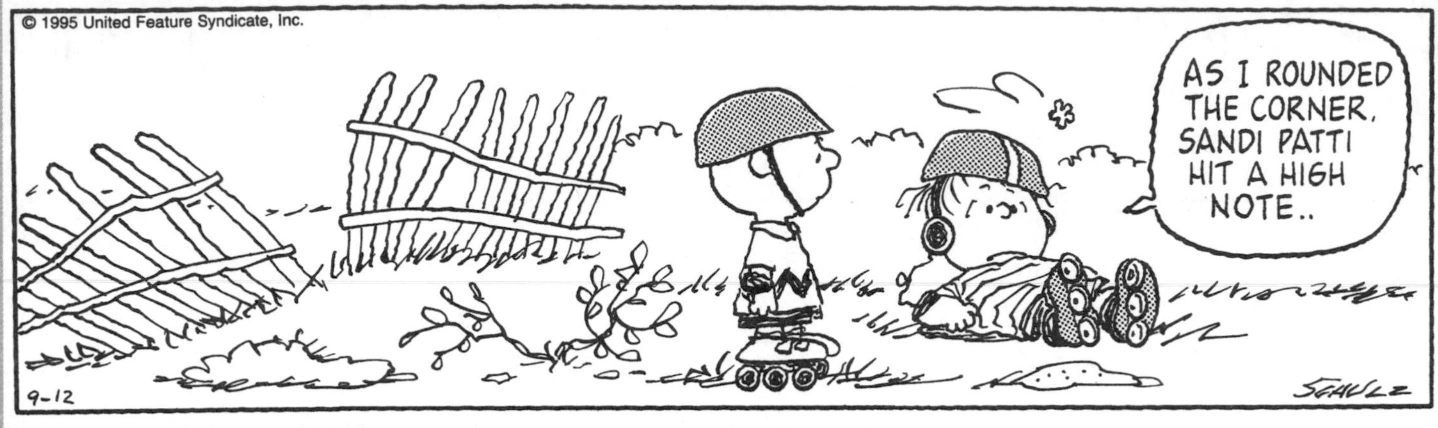
© 1995 United Feature Syndicate, Inc.
AS I ROUNDED THE CORNER, SANDI PATTI HIT A HIGH NOTE..
9-12
SCHULZ

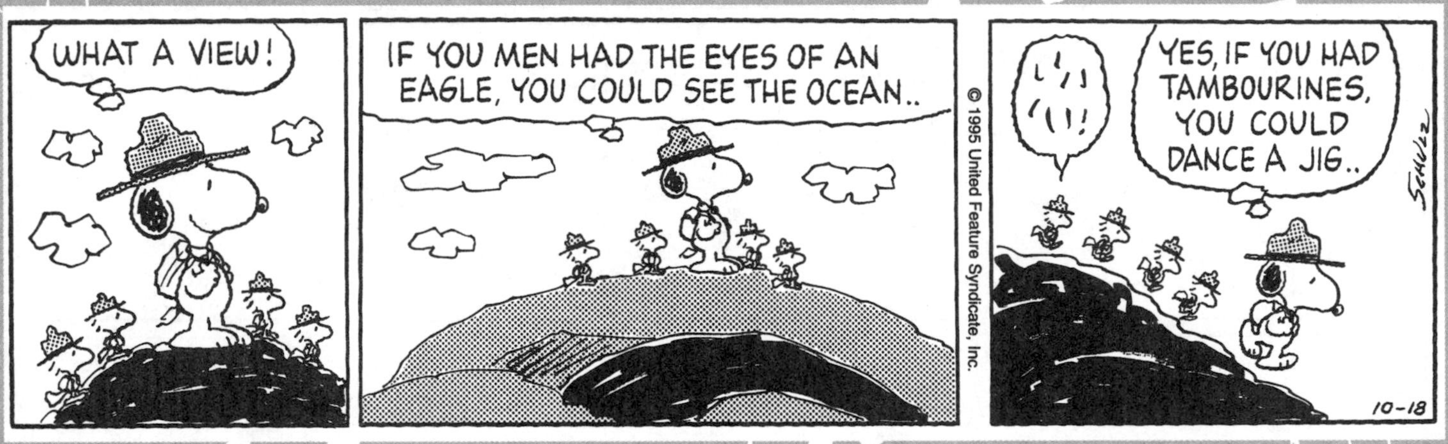
WHAT A VIEW!
IF YOU MEN HAD THE EYES OF AN EAGLE, YOU COULD SEE THE OCEAN..
© 1995 United Feature Syndicate, Inc.
YES, IF YOU HAD TAMBOURINES, YOU COULD DANCE A JIG..
SCHULZ
10-18

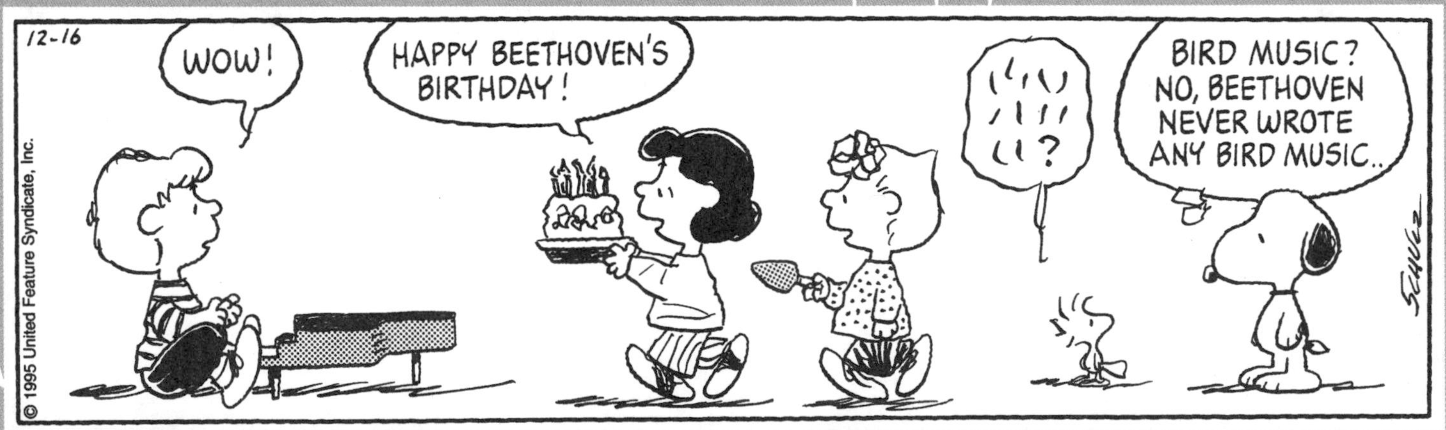
12-16
© 1995 United Feature Syndicate, Inc.
WOW!
HAPPY BEETHOVEN'S BIRTHDAY!
BIRD MUSIC? NO, BEETHOVEN NEVER WROTE ANY BIRD MUSIC..
SCHULZ

HOW COME THEY'RE NOT PLAYING CHRISTMAS CAROLS ANYMORE?
CHRISTMAS IS OVER
THAT'S TOO BAD..
I MISS THAT STUPID DRUMMER BOY..
© 1996 United Feature Syndicate, Inc.
2-5
SCHULZ

AND WHEN PEOPLE HEAR YOU SINGING ON A SPRING MORNING, IT MAKES THEM HAPPY..
YOU PERFORM A REAL SERVICE..
THAT'S TRUE.. THEY SHOULD GIVE YOU A GOLD RECORD..
© 1996 United Feature Syndicate, Inc.
SCHULZ
3-9

PEANUTS by Schulz

THINK ABOUT THIS..

LET'S SAY YOU AND I WERE MARRIED..

AND LET'S SAY YOU ARE A FAMOUS CONCERT PIANIST..

BUT SUDDENLY YOUR CAREER BEGINS TO GO BAD..NO ONE WANTS YOU ANYMORE..

INSTEAD OF PLAYING IN BEAUTIFUL CONCERT HALLS, YOU'RE FORCED TO PLAY IN SLEAZY JOINTS..

© 1996 United Feature Syndicate, Inc.

AND I HAVE TO GIVE UP MY LUCRATIVE TEACHING CAREER AT THE UNIVERSITY, AND TAKE IN LAUNDRY TO SUPPORT US..

5-5

HOW DO YOU THINK THAT WOULD AFFECT OUR MARRIAGE? LET'S TALK ABOUT THIS..

BONK!

MUSICIANS NEVER WANT TO DISCUSS ANYTHING..

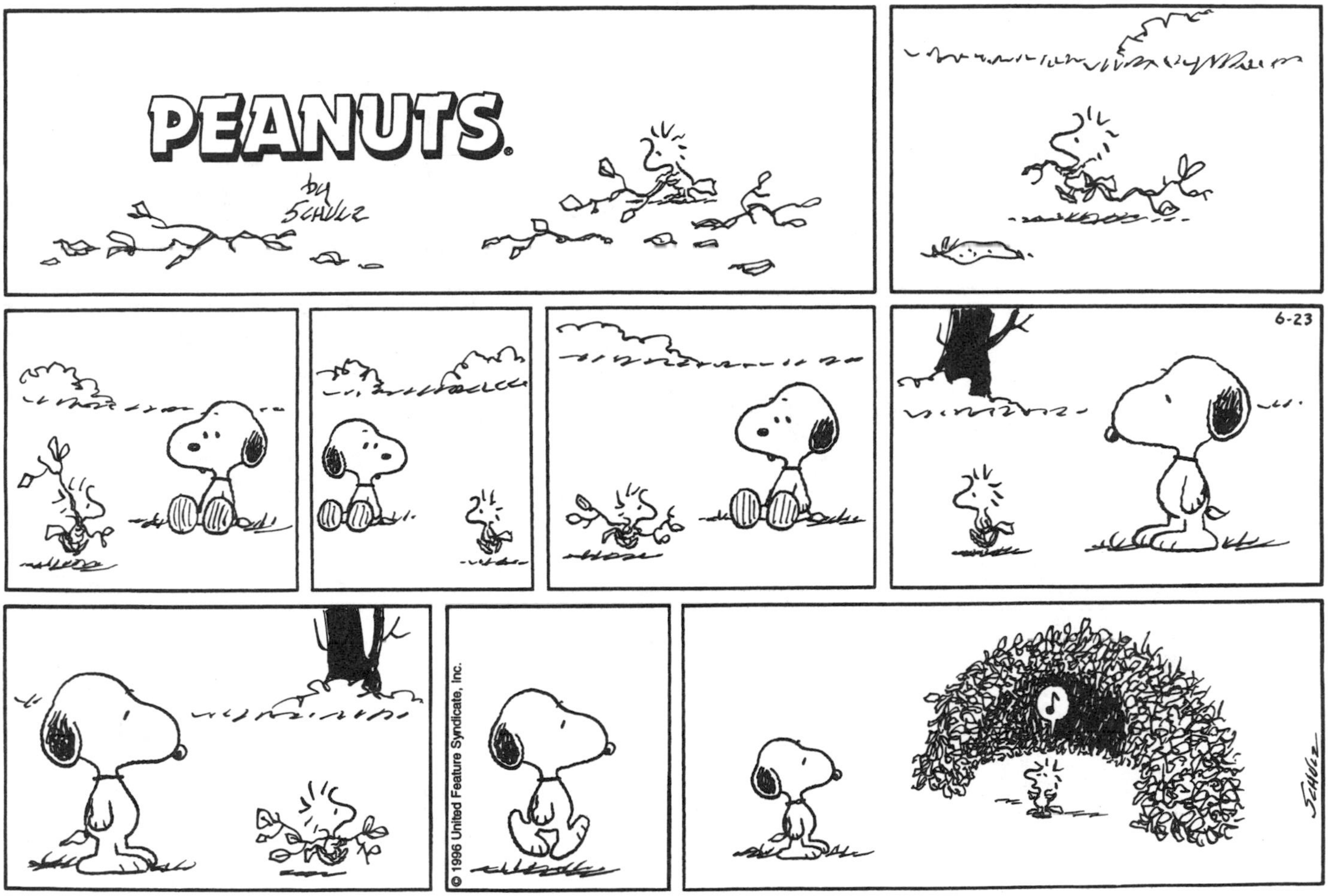
PEANUTS
by SCHULZ
6-23
© 1996 United Feature Syndicate, Inc.
SCHULZ

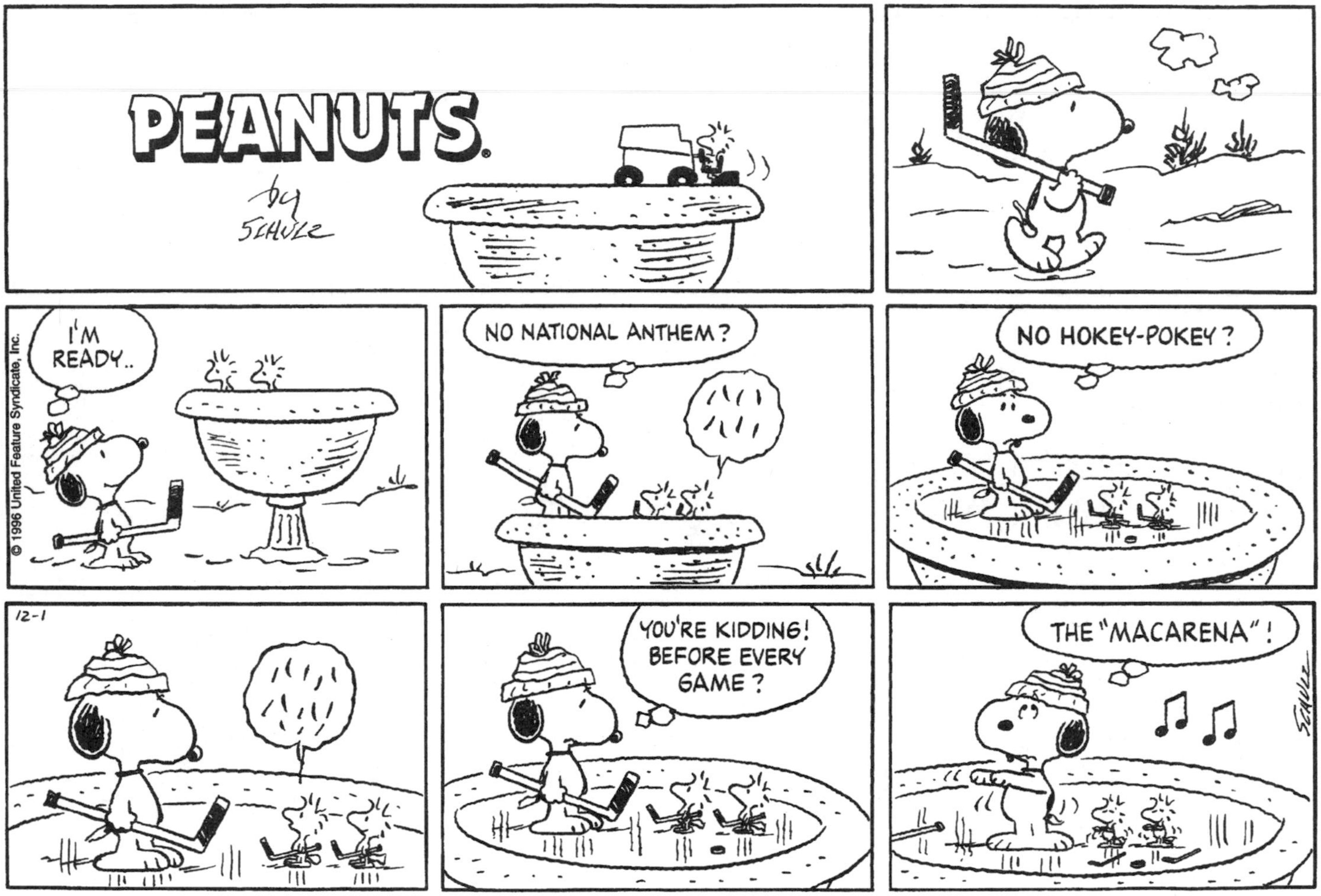
PEANUTS
by SCHULZ
© 1996 United Feature Syndicate, Inc.
I'M READY..
NO NATIONAL ANTHEM?
NO HOKEY-POKEY?
12-1
YOU'RE KIDDING! BEFORE EVERY GAME?
THE "MACARENA"!
SCHULZ

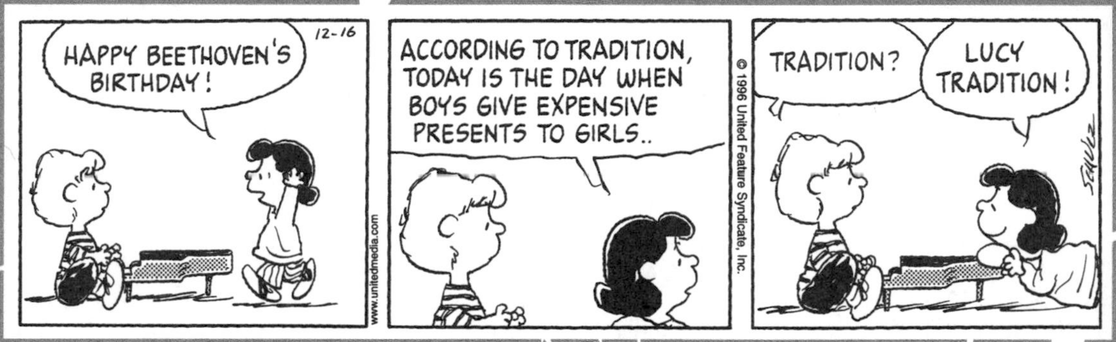
12-16
HAPPY BEETHOVEN'S BIRTHDAY!
www.unitedmedia.com
ACCORDING TO TRADITION, TODAY IS THE DAY WHEN BOYS GIVE EXPENSIVE PRESENTS TO GIRLS..
© 1996 United Feature Syndicate, Inc.
TRADITION?
LUCY TRADITION!
SCHULZ

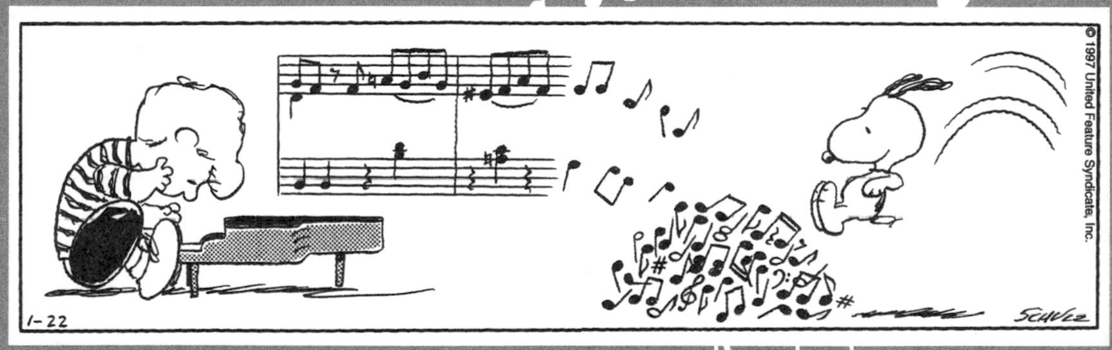
© 1997 United Feature Syndicate, Inc.
1-22
SCHULZ

AND I CONCLUDE MY REPORT BY OFFERING THIS SUGGESTION...
AS SOON AS A CHILD IS BORN, HE OR SHE SHOULD BE ISSUED A DOG AND A BANJO..
www.unitedmedia.com
1-29
MA'AM? THAT'S RIGHT.. A FAMILY OF EIGHT.. EIGHT DOGS AND EIGHT BANJOS..
© 1997 United Feature Syndicate, Inc.
YES, MA'AM.. WE'RE TALKING HAPPINESS HERE!

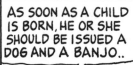

LET'S HEAR THIS AGAIN, CHARLIE BROWN..
YES, TELL US YOUR IDEA AGAIN
AS SOON AS A CHILD IS BORN, HE OR SHE IS ISSUED A DOG AND A BANJO..
WHAT GOOD WOULD THAT DO?
THE DOG COULD LEARN TO PLAY THE BANJO..
© 1997 United Feature Syndicate, Inc.
SCHULZ
1-31

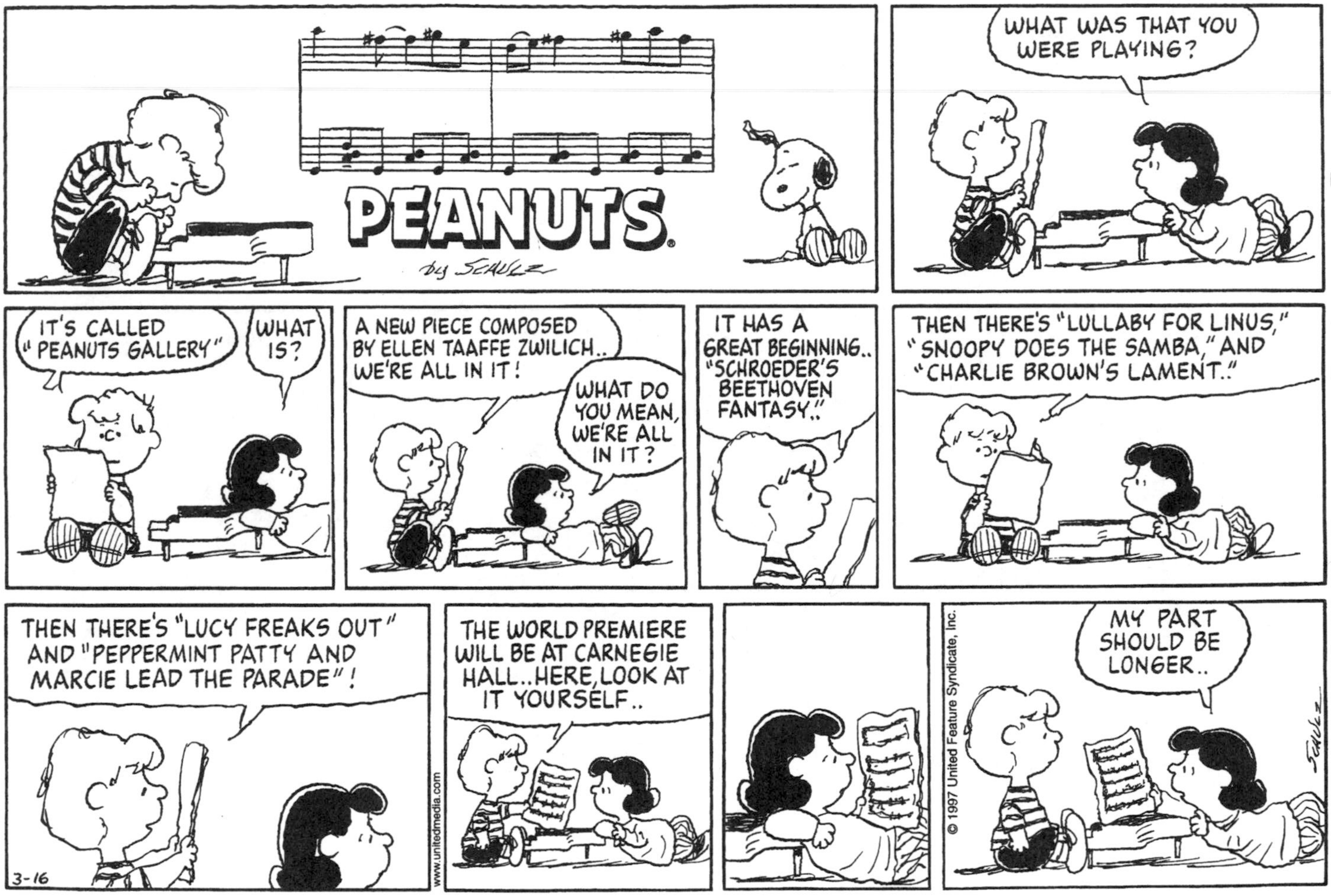
PEANUTS
by SCHULZ
WHAT WAS THAT YOU WERE PLAYING?
IT'S CALLED "PEANUTS GALLERY"
WHAT IS?
A NEW PIECE COMPOSED BY ELLEN TAAFFE ZWILICH.. WE'RE ALL IN IT!
WHAT DO YOU MEAN, WE'RE ALL IN IT?
IT HAS A GREAT BEGINNING.. "SCHROEDER'S BEETHOVEN FANTASY.."
THEN THERE'S "LULLABY FOR LINUS," "SNOOPY DOES THE SAMBA," AND "CHARLIE BROWN'S LAMENT.."
THEN THERE'S "LUCY FREAKS OUT" AND "PEPPERMINT PATTY AND MARCIE LEAD THE PARADE"!
3-16
www.unitedmedia.com
THE WORLD PREMIERE WILL BE AT CARNEGIE HALL..HERE, LOOK AT IT YOURSELF..
© 1997 United Feature Syndicate, Inc.
MY PART SHOULD BE LONGER..
SCHULZ

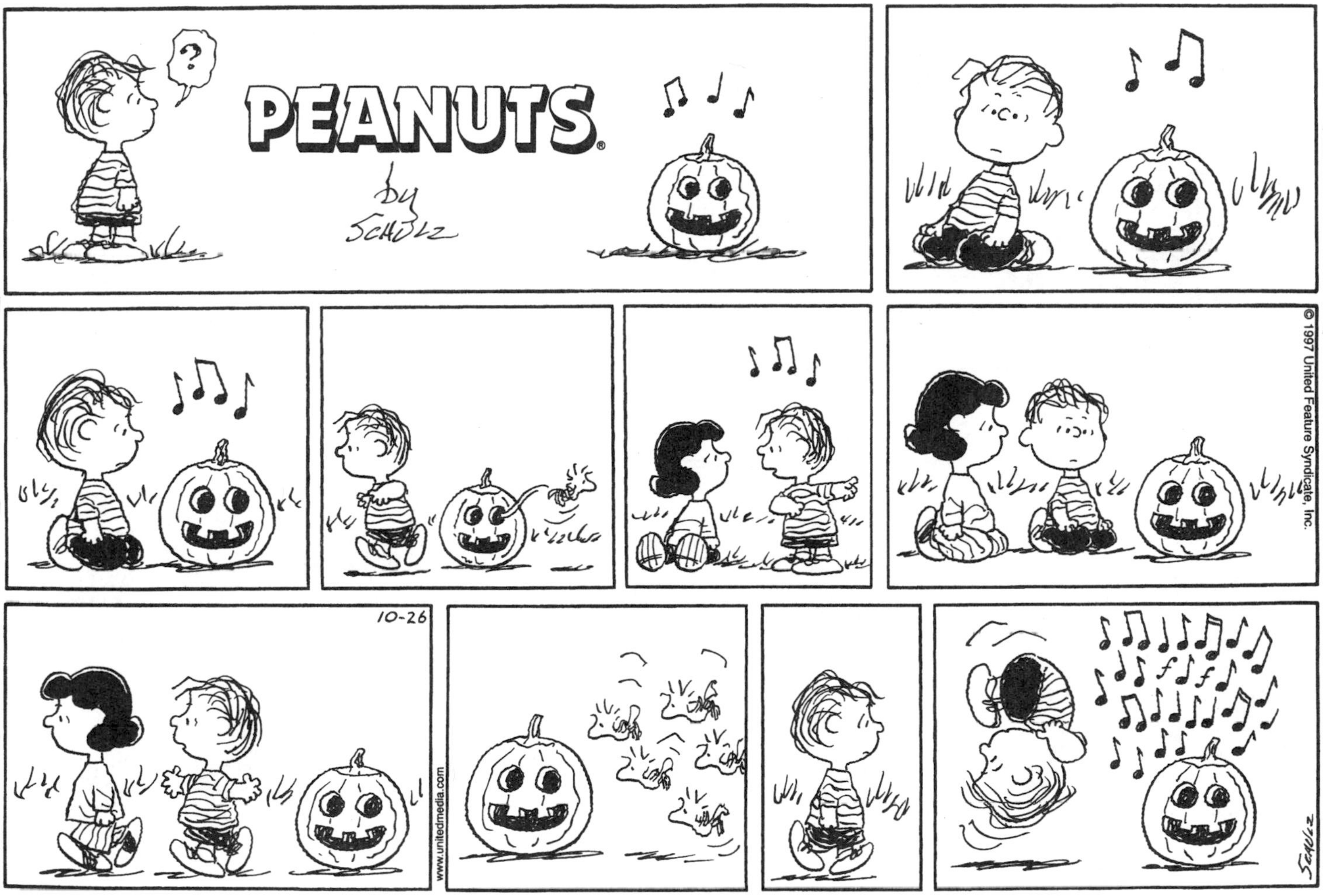
?
PEANUTS
by SCHULZ
© 1997 United Feature Syndicate, Inc.
10-26
www.unitedmedia.com
SCHULZ

© 1997 United Feature Syndicate, Inc.
OUCH! OO! OW! OUCH!
SCHULZ
11-20

DID BEETHOVEN EVER PLAY "JINGLE BELLS"?
12-16-97
HE PROBABLY THOUGHT HE WAS TOO GOOD TO PLAY "JINGLE BELLS"
© 1992 United Feature Syndicate, Inc.
BONK!
IF I HAD BEEN THERE, I WOULD HAVE SAID, "HEY, LUDWIG, PLAY 'JINGLE BELLS'!"
SCHULZ

IS BEETHOVEN IN THE BOWLING HALL OF FAME?
I DOUBT IT..
6-10
www.snoopy.com
PROBABLY BECAUSE HE DIDN'T WRITE BOWLING MUSIC..
KLUNK!
© 1998 United Feature Syndicate, Inc.
I'LL BET HE'D BE IN THE HALL OF FAME IF HE HAD WRITTEN BOWLING MUSIC..
SCHULZ

7-16
www.snoopy.com
© 1998 United Feature Syndicate, Inc.
SCHULZ

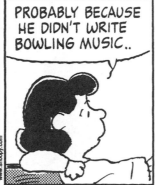

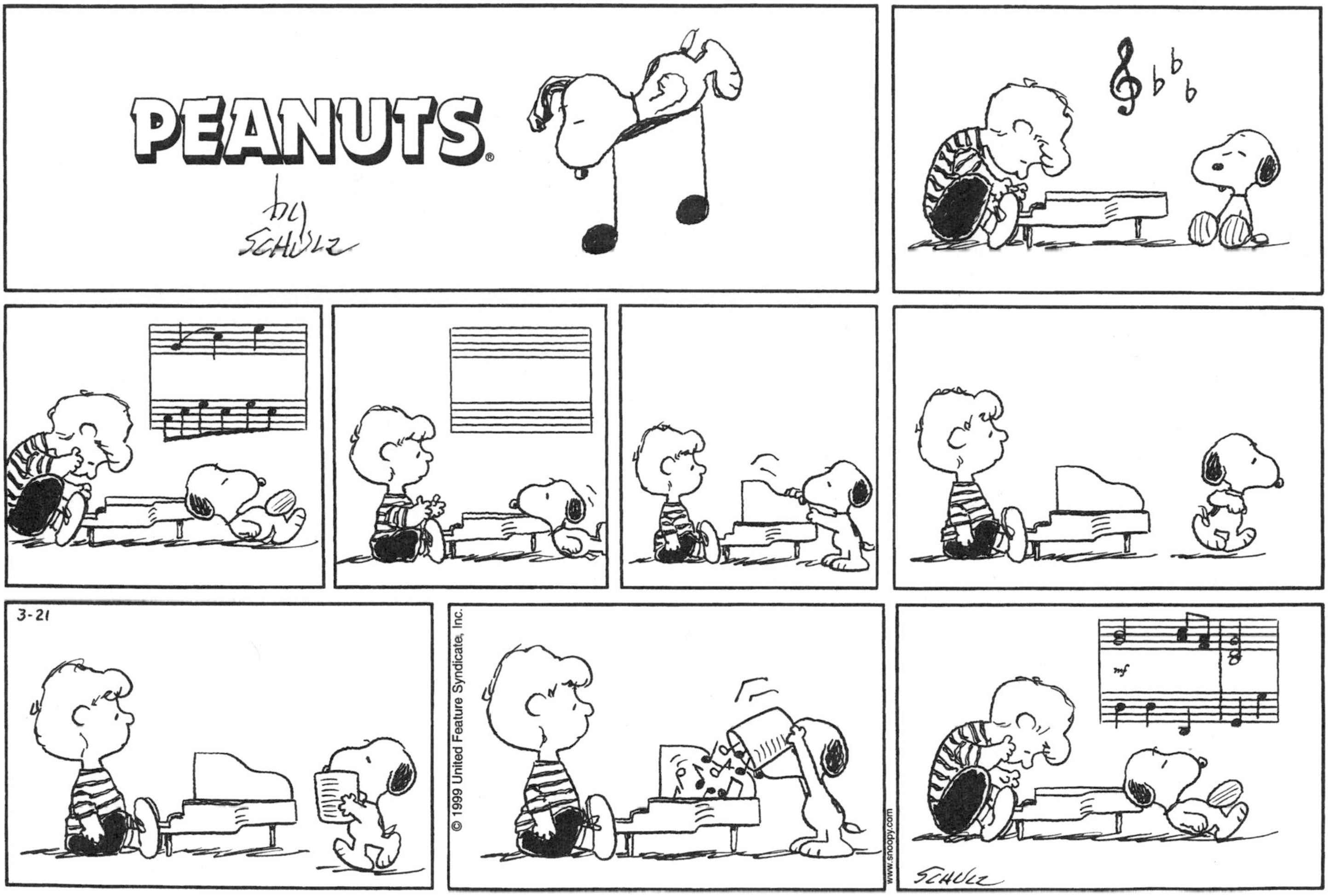
PEANUTS
by SCHULZ
3-21
© 1999 United Feature Syndicate, Inc.
www.snoopy.com
SCHULZ

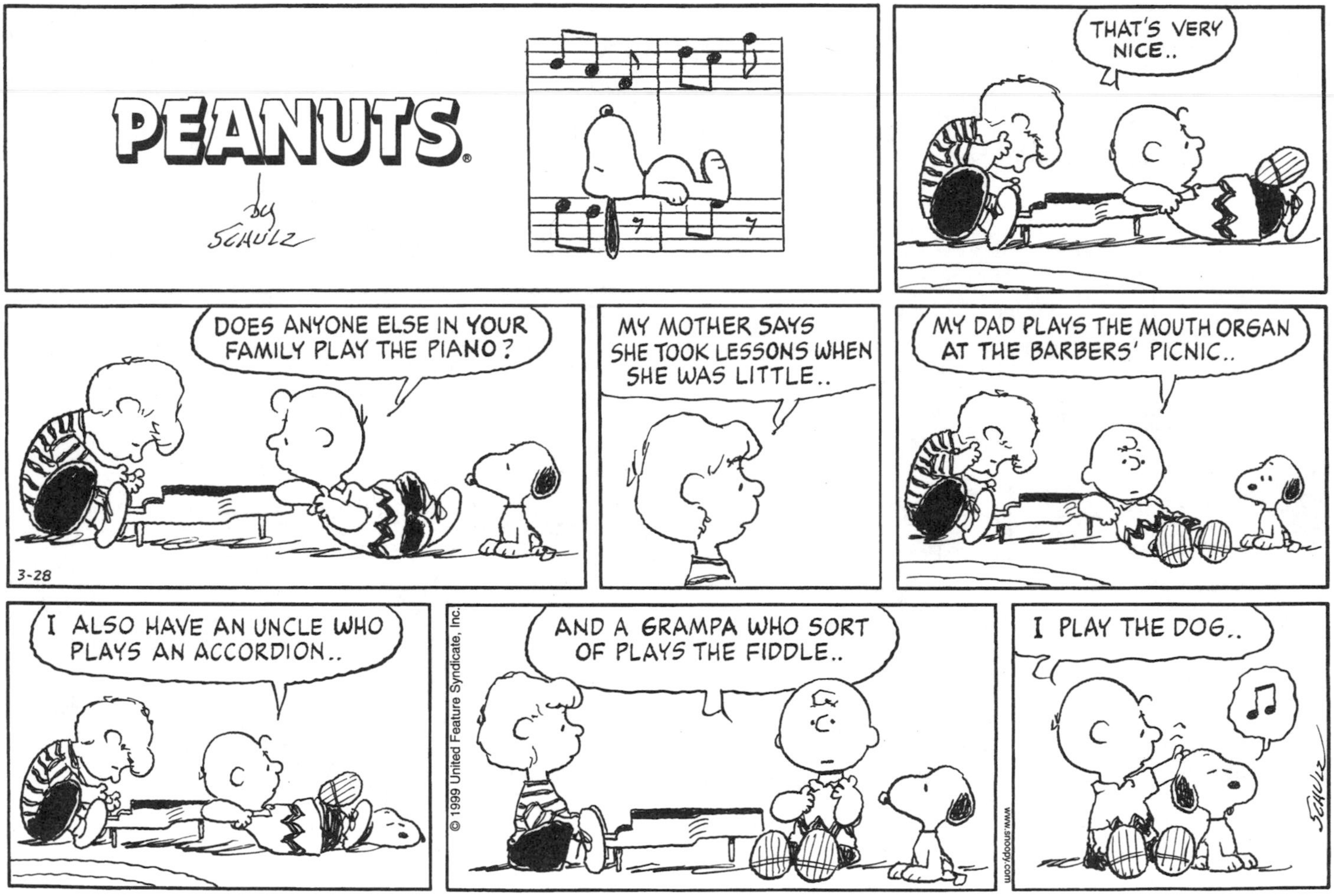
PEANUTS
by SCHULZ
THAT'S VERY NICE..
DOES ANYONE ELSE IN YOUR FAMILY PLAY THE PIANO?
3-28
MY MOTHER SAYS SHE TOOK LESSONS WHEN SHE WAS LITTLE..
MY DAD PLAYS THE MOUTH ORGAN AT THE BARBERS' PICNIC..
I ALSO HAVE AN UNCLE WHO PLAYS AN ACCORDION..
© 1999 United Feature Syndicate, Inc.
AND A GRAMPA WHO SORT OF PLAYS THE FIDDLE..
www.snoopy.com
I PLAY THE DOG..
SCHULZ

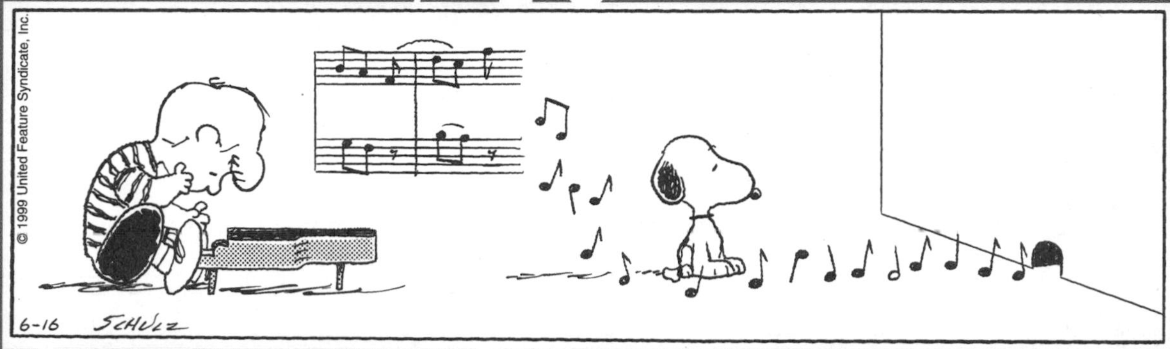
© 1999 United Feature Syndicate, Inc.
6-16
SCHULZ

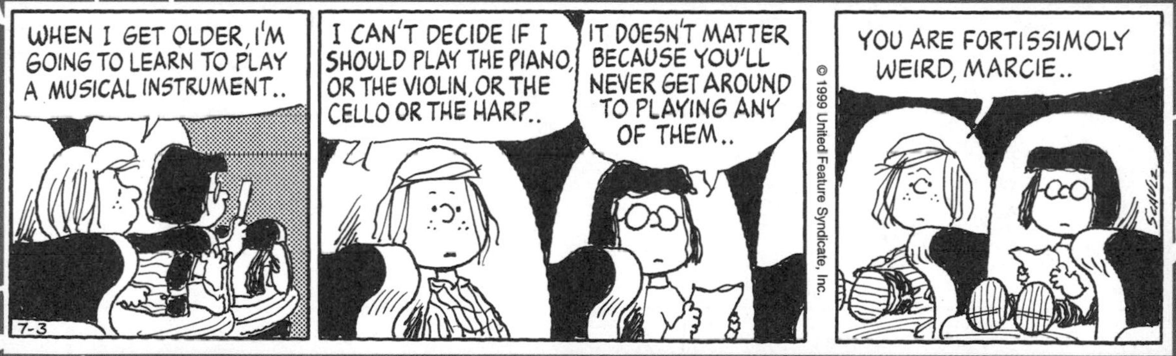
WHEN I GET OLDER, I'M GOING TO LEARN TO PLAY A MUSICAL INSTRUMENT..
I CAN'T DECIDE IF I SHOULD PLAY THE PIANO, OR THE VIOLIN, OR THE CELLO OR THE HARP..
IT DOESN'T MATTER BECAUSE YOU'LL NEVER GET AROUND TO PLAYING ANY OF THEM..
YOU ARE FORTISSIMOLY WEIRD, MARCIE..
7-3
© 1999 United Feature Syndicate, Inc.
SCHULZ

9-4
© 1999 United Feature Syndicate, Inc.
SCHULZ

© 1999 United Feature Syndicate, Inc.
12-15
SCHULZ